Pascal

ADVERSARY
AND
ADVOCATE

Pascal

---◆---

ADVERSARY
AND
ADVOCATE

BY

Robert J. Nelson

HARVARD UNIVERSITY PRESS
CAMBRIDGE, MASSACHUSETTS, AND LONDON, ENGLAND · 1981

Library of Congress Cataloging in Publication Data

Nelson, Robert James, 1925-

Pascal, adversary and advocate.

Bibliography: p.
Includes index.
1. Pascal, Blaise, 1623-1662.   I. Title.
B1903.N46   230'.2'0924 [B]   81-6330
ISBN .0-674-65615-6   AACR2

ACKNOWLEDGMENTS

I HAVE ACCUMULATED many debts in writing this book. It is with pleasure and gratitude that I acknowledge them here. My thanks go to many colleagues and associates at the University of Illinois, especially members of the University's Research Board, who provided aid by granting funds for research assistants in the years 1969–1974 and 1977–1978 and for preparation of the manuscript in 1978–1980; to the trustees of the University of Illinois for granting me a semester of sabbatical leave (fall, 1975) to pursue this project; to my research assistants in the periods noted: Claude Covo, Nancy Randa, Steven Farver, Jeri Guthrie; to colleagues in the Department of French and in the Program in Comparative Literature at the university, especially Yves Velan, Stanley Gray, and Bernard Benstock, who lent greatly of their learning, judgment, and capacity for listening during the years I worked on the book; to Philippe Sellier of the Sorbonne (Paris V) whose reminders of the Augustinian cast of Pascal's thought, during many happy hours of conversation about Pascal in Paris in the fall of 1975 and the summer of 1976, find their reflection in these pages; to my colleagues in the Department of French and Italian at Stanford University, whose interest and support during my service as visiting professor (spring, 1979) created the ideal conditions that enabled me to complete the manuscript; to Christina A. Heifner of the nonacademic staff of the Department of French at the University of Illinois, who assisted me "secretarially" and serenely with the extensive correspondence in both the research and the writing phases of this project; to Brenda Masters, who drew a definitive manuscript from a draft in which the combination of my own typing and handwriting posed more than a few challenges to her patience and ingenuity.

Some debts are of longer standing, predating the period in which I worked on this book, yet informing its pages, however implicitly, in a profound manner. I wish to thank my teachers at the schools, primary and secondary, of the Catholic Diocese of Brooklyn, New York, for preparing me at an early age to understand the central concern of Pascal: "How, then, shall we live?" I also wish to thank my teachers at Columbia College and Columbia University Graduate School—particularly the great seventeenth-century scholar, the late Nathan Edelman—for introducing me, in the years 1946–1955, to the "dreams of glory, dreams of repose" that shape so much of French literature and that give special shape to the writings of Pascal.

Certain debts of less direct thematic relevance are no less pertinent here. They are personal. I wish to thank the members of my family and friends "outside the field" for the patience and good humor they showed toward me while I was working on this book. I wish especially to express my gratitude to the person who most closely sustained me during that period by dedicating the book to her.

Urbana, Illinois
May 1981

CONTENTS

Pascal
ADVERSARY
AND
ADVOCATE

NOTE ON ANNOTATION

Within my text, reference to fragments of the *Thoughts* is given, after quotation or citation, by abbreviation of the editor's name—Br for Brunschvicg, Ch for Chevalier, L for Lafuma, S for Sellier—followed by the number of the fragment.

Quotation from or reference to other works by Pascal, his contemporaries, and others from the edition of Jean Mesnard, *Oeuvres complètes de Blaise Pascal,* is given, upon first citation or quotation, for the entire pagination in the appropriate volume, including, with rare exception, Mesnard's commentary and annotation. In certain instances, in order to acknowledge Mesnard's particular perspective, I have indicated his commentary in a note. In all annotations of Mesnard's edition I have given his name followed by the volume and page number.

I have also followed this procedure, with occasional exceptions, in the case of Lafuma's *Pascal: Oeuvres complètes,* Philippe Sellier's *Blaise Pascal: Pensées,* and H. F. Stewart's *Les Lettres provinciales de Blaise Pascal.*

See the bibliography for full bibliographical information on all of these works.

INTRODUCTION

BLAISE PASCAL (1623–1662) was an intense and paradoxical man. Indefatigable in his dedication to science, he disdained science in its ultimate meaning for human existence. Arrogant in his esteem of his own worth as a thinker, he was convinced of the worthlessness of the self. Selfish in wanting to keep his own part of the world's treasures, he was unworldly in his charity toward the poor and the suffering. Determined to demonstrate the utility of reason in matters of faith, he was persuaded of the primacy of faith over reason in the attainment of heaven. Disingenuous in his dealings with his fellow scientists, he was infuriated by what he considered the dishonesty of the Jesuits. Committed to the improvement of man's material lot, he was dismissive of the ways of the world. A relentless reader of philosophers, he derided philosophy as not worth an hour of one's time. Logical and orderly in his style out of respect for readers in his scientific writings, he was deliberately paradoxical and disorderly in his assault upon the readers of his most extended religious writings. Theologically convinced that all men would not be saved, he was anxiously concerned with the fate of man.

Above all he was concerned. From his earliest days as a public person, he could not understand those who were not concerned with ultimate questions in science and religion. His first conversion was his dedication to a stricter piety along with the other members of the Pascal household under the influence of the religiously conservative doctors who attended his father's leg injury in January 1646. It was surrounded by his invention of the first calculating machine (1644–45) and, in the fall of the year of the conversion, his earliest experiments

1

on the vacuum. His first public act as a religious thinker, his censure of
the rationalistic theologian Jacques Forton, abbé de Saint Ange, early
in 1647, is framed by his continuing researches on the vacuum. In the
midst of writing the intended *Apology for the Christian Religion* that we
know as his *Thoughts* in late 1656 and probably through the remainder
of his life, he was intensely engaged in mathematical and other scientific work, notably on the cycloid. While developing religious reasons
on the need to humilate the reason, according to some, he proudly and
deceitfully set up a competition for the solution of problems in this
area of mathematics for which he had already himself found solutions,
submitting them in full knowledge that he would win his own prize!

The last years of his life, dedicated to self-abnegation, Christian
charity, and the apparent abandonment of commitment to either scientific or religious controversies, are not unmarked by his double concern for fundamentals in the scientific as well as the religious sphere. In
his last letter to the great mathematician Fermat on August 10, 1661, a
little over a year before his death, Pascal seems to confirm a final abandonment of at least one of the two domains in which he had always
manifested a concern with ultimate questions.

> To speak frankly of geometry, I find it the highest exercise of the
> mind; but, at the same time, I know it to be so useless that I make lit-
> tle distinction between a man who is only a geometer and a skillful ar-
> tisan. Thus I call it the finest métier in the world; but, in the end, it is
> only a métier; and I have often said that it is fine for testing our
> capacities, but not for the regular employment of them: so that I
> would not take two steps for geometry, and I am sure you agree with
> me. But there is now this also in my case, that I am pursuing studies so
> distant from that frame of mind that I hardly remember what there is
> to it.[1]

The studies into which he had newly entered were religious. Yet
Pascal's distinction about a man who is *only* a geometer is much to the
point, for these new studies did not prevent him from pursuing an idea
he had first put forth in 1658 (a year of intense work on the *Apology*):
the development of an intraurban public transportation system for
Paris, the so-called five-penny bus. Having begun his scientific career
as a self-made engineer, applying himself to the construction of a
machine he had conceived as a theorist, he ended it as a social engineer
by seeing through the application of an idea that he had conceived in
what we nowadays call social science.

To some the pattern may seem less of paradox than of contradiction, showing Pascal divided between religion and science, the only unity being found in his passionate pride and fierce energy. It is as if, in keeping with one of the tenets of the Jansenist sect, to which he gave his allegiance, he alternately lost and regained his faith. If his first biographer, his sister Gilberte, is to be believed, this pattern is to be applied more in large than in small as we look at his life. For she claims that upon his so-called second conversion of November 23, 1654, movingly recorded by the convert in his celebrated *Memorial,* her brother renounced the world to dedicate himself first to the defense of his beleaguered coreligionists at Port Royal and finally to the salvation of his own soul. The continuing commitment to mathematical, scientific, and social-scientific enterprises that is a matter of record beyond that famous "night of fire" is ignored by her, except for the competition on the cycloid, which she explains away as a distraction for her brother to relieve him of the pain of a bad toothache. If Gilberte is wrong in the large about her brother's alternation between science and religion, does the pattern compel us to the alternative of seeing him at best as a pathetically indecisive man—distracted from the highest enterprises of the mind by the pettifoggery of religious doubts—and at worst as a proud, domineering spirit, opportunistically bent on having his own way in the things of the next world as much as in those of this world?

I think not, for that choice would belie the fundamental cast of Pascal's mind, the grounding conviction that unitary explanations for the whole of human experience that do not take account of God are neither possible nor desirable. The reader of his *Thoughts* will sense immediately that I am thinking here of Pascal's famous distinction between the three orders, the flesh, the mind, and the heart:

> All the splendor of greatness lacks luster for those engaged in the pursuits of the mind.
>
> The greatness of intellectual people is not visible to kings, rich men, captains, who are all great in a carnal sense.
>
> The greatness of wisdom, which is nothing if it does not come from God, is not visible to carnal or intellectual people. They are three orders differing in kind. (S 339)

The distinction about the autonomy of human orders had been adumbrated several years before by Pascal in one of his earliest scientific writings, the Preface to his *Treatise on the Vacuum* of 1651:

If it is a question of knowing who was the first of the French kings, in what place geographers place the first meridian, what words are defunct in a dead language, and all things of this nature, what other means than books can guide us? And who can add anything new to what they teach us, since we wish to know only what they contain?

It is authority alone that can illuminate us. But where authority has its principal force is in theology, because there it is inseparable from truth, and we know truth only through it such that, to provide complete certitude in matters totally incomprehensible to reason, it suffices to have them shown in sacred texts (just as to show the uncertainty of things most likely to be believed, it is necessary only to make it clear that they are not included therein), because the principles of certitude are above nature and reason and because, man's mind being too weak to attain it by his own efforts, he cannot attain these high perceptions unless he is borne to them by a force that is all-powerful and supernatural.

It is not the same thing in those matters that fall within the senses or reasoning: here, authority is useless; reason alone has the opportunity to know them. They have their separate rights: now one has all the advantage, here the other reigns in its turn. But as subjects of this kind are proportionate to the breadth of the mind, it finds complete freedom to extend itself here: its inexhaustible fecundity produces continuously, and its inventions can be, all at once, unending and uninterrupted.[2]

Obviously the grounding conviction of the autonomy of the orders of human existence, particularly the mind and the heart, informs as well the lines that I have already quoted from the last letter to Fermat written near the end of his life.

The great drama of that life, as I hope to show later, lay precisely in an anguish *before* and as a *function of* this grounding conviction when Pascal set about writing anything. Broadly speaking, his intellectual and spiritual career follows a tripartite pattern that I would summarize in theological terms as conservative–liberal–conservative. His projected *Apology,* unfinished as his *Thoughts,* falls within the middle, or liberal, period. How this Pascalian liberalism is defined and how it helps to illuminate his conception of the libertines for whom he purportedly envisioned the projected *Apology for the Christian Religion* is in part the subject of my pages on the *Thoughts.* That the *Thoughts* are liberal at least in their appeal to the spirit rather than the letter of the law provides the grounds for seeing Pascal's thought in a tripartite

A–B–A dialectical development. On one side of the liberal moment I would cite Pascal's conservative role in the "Affaire Saint Ange" as well as in certain theological positions emerging in his scientific writings. In the texts emerging from his second conversion in late 1654 we find a transition, in which the convert is pulled now forward, now backward, both theologically and psychologically. On the other side of his liberal phase, which includes, as I see it, the last two *Provincial Letters* as well as the projected *Apology*, I would cite the *Three Discourses on the Condition of the Great* (probably late 1660), which, though perhaps not actually composed by Pascal, are clearly Pascalian in theme, as well as Pascal's last known text, *The Writing on the Signing of the Formulary,* presumably of November 1661. Between these texts there are many others that I seek to situate in this essay on the now adversarial, now advocative dialogue that Pascal conducted throughout his life with others and with himself.

At a certain point in his ceaseless inner dialogue, Pascal took it upon himself to call upon the libertine in particular to think more clearly. That point was notably in the liberal phase of his thinking. Even here it is important to stress that his thought was not fundamentally at odds with the theological positions of the conservative phases of his thought, particularly in the matter of grace. Pascal does not share libertine skepticism about the mortality of the soul, the existence of God, the value of a virtuous life, and so on. (This strategy does betoken a more inclusive Christianity as executed particularly in the *Apology*.) Secure in his own faith through the grace of God, he knows that he cannot secure faith for others. The very logic of his faith precludes such presumption on his part, for God's action is unique and supreme in such matters. Confronting the disastrous consequences of libertine and atheistic positions in the life of both the individual and society, nevertheless, he adapts himself to the thinking of "the other" in order to provide new grounds of consent to a faith more inclusive and more generous than that which he defends in his conservative phases.

This adaptive stance is, according to his sister, characteristic of his relations with others:

> But he conceived of this art as consisting of certain dispositions that should exist between [on the one hand] the mind and heart of those to whom one speaks, and [on the other] the thoughts and expressions one uses, but that the proportions [here] are properly adjusted only by the turn one gives them. This is why he had studied the heart of man and

his mind: he knew all the springs perfectly well. When he thought something, he put himself in the place of those who were to hear it, and, looking to see if all the proportions were to be found, he then saw what turn had to be given them, and he was not happy until he saw clearly that this turn was made in such a way for the other—which is to say, he was concerned about the mind of the one who was expected to see—that, when all this would come to be joined together by the application one would have for it, it was impossible for the spirit of man not to give itself thereto with pleasure.[3]

Pascal becomes liberal, then, by dint of circumstance, in a call to reason in many of his theological writings. Content in his youthful pursuit of science, confident at the time in his conservative religious outlook, he is compelled to consider antireligious and liberal religious outlooks when his conservative coreligionists are attacked. He is driven to public considerations of such outlooks when the threat comes from those purportedly within the fold: from Jesuit and, to a lesser extent, Dominican purveyors of liberal religious notions. In turning his attention to them, he perforce turns his attention to nonbelievers and antibelievers. In sum, he considers the three sorts of people who must, as he sees it, make up the readership of any text that might (and, in matters of religion, for him *should*) fall beneath their eyes: believers, would-be believers, and the indifferent.

These three readers are then, at once, both virtual and historical readers. Virtually, they are the readers whom Pascal might have addressed in his own time or at any other time. Historically, they are the parties involved in the quarrels of Jansenism in the seventeenth century. It is primarily with the historical readers that I am concerned in my assaying of Pascal's writings. For each of Pascal's major religious writings (and to a lesser extent certain of his scientific writings), I put myself in the place of each of these readers—for example, Maître de Sacy—in order to assay the probable or, at least, possible impact of that writing on the historical reader's own philosophical or theological position. Could the conservative reader accept this or that Pascalian position? If such and such a position is acceptable to the libertine reader, what are the implications for the conservative reader of this acceptability? Are there positions acceptable to all three readers? Analysis from each perspective can enhance one's understanding of the complexities and tensions of Pascal's own thought more than traditional single-viewpoint readings. Pascal himself being one of his readers, it is often to the reading of Pascal by himself that I turn in considering the phases of his religious life.

When assaying Pascal's view of what was called by Montaigne "the human condition," one observes how great was the influence of that constant source. The impact of the author of the *Essays* on Pascal's thought is apparent, for example, in Pascal's *Conversation with M. de Sacy*, where the new and fervent convert overwhelmed the composed solitary of Port Royal with his critique of Montaigne and one of that thinker's spiritual guides, Epictetus. Pascal's assay of the human condition differs from Montaigne's in that the persona of Pascal's "I" is neither the confessional self-seeker of traditional views of Montaigne nor the detached literary self-maker of more recent views on the great essayist of the sixteenth century. The Pascal of the personal or self-regarding "I" is to be found unabashedly more in the scientific than in the religious writings, although even in the latter he wrestles with this imperious "I" almost to the end. There we find a proud and even vain Pascal. The "I" of the numerous treatises and letters in the eighteen-month controversy on the cycloid (mid-1658 to late 1659), an "I" that is defensively self-regarding and disdainfully disregarding of others, can already be heard beneath the formulaic sycophancy of the "Dedicatory Letter" the young inventor of the calculating machine wrote to Chancellor Séguier in 1645. Having explained the circumstances that had led him to the invention, including the doubts of more illustrious fellow mathematicians, Pascal wrote,

> But I willingly accept that they accuse me, and even condemn me, if they can justify that I have not strictly kept the promises I made; and I ask of them only the favor of examining what I have done, and not that of approving it without knowing it. Thus, My Lord, I can say to Your Excellency that I already have the satisfaction of seeing my small work not only authorized by the approval of certain of the principal authorities in this science, which, by a very particular preference, has the advantage of teaching nothing that it does not demonstrate, but still further, honored by their esteem and their recommendation; and that even he among them, whom the others admire every day and they welcome, has not judged it unworthy of himself to take the trouble, in the midst of other great preoccupations, to teach both its operation and use to those who might want to use it. Those, My Lord, are the real recompense for the time that I have spent on it, and for the expense that I have taken to put it in the form in which I present it to you. But allow me to flatter my vanity to the point of saying that these

recompenses would not completely satisfy me if I had not received an even more important one from Your Excellency. Indeed, My Lord, when I remind myself that your lips, which each day issue oracular judgments from the Throne of Justice, have deigned to speak in praise of this effort by a man of twenty, that you have adjudged it worthy once more to be the subject of your conversation, and to see it placed in your cabinet among so many other rare and precious things, I am at the peak of glory and I can find no words to show my gratitude to Your Excellency nor my joy to the whole world.[4]

And yet, as one of the most famous *Thoughts* puts it:

The self is hateful. You cover it up, Miton, but that does not mean that you take it away. So you are still hateful.

"Not so, because by being obliging to everyone as we are, we give them no more cause to hate us." True enough if the only hateful thing about the self were the unpleasantness it caused us.

But if I hate it because it is unjust that it should make itself the center of everything, I shall go on hating it.

In a word, the self has two characteristics. It is unjust in itself for making itself the center of everything; it is a nuisance to others in that it tries to subjugate them, for each self is the enemy of all the others and would like to tyrannize them. You take away the nuisance, but not the injustice.

And thus, you do not make it pleasing to those who hate it for being unjust; you only make it pleasing to unjust people, who no longer see it as their enemy. Thus you remain unjust, and can only please unjust people. (S 494)

The rhetoric of this fragment is a clue to the nature of the "I" in all the fragments of the *Thoughts*. It is a dialogue with Damien Miton, an adventurous financier and gambler, who, along with Pascal and the Chevalier de Méré, had presumably (some scholars doubt the journey took place) accompanied Pascal's coreligionist, the Duc de Roannez, in March 1651, on a journey to the duke's estate in Poitou. This fragment may be a recollection, if it is not a note made in the course of the journey or after a salon encounter with Miton. In the dialogue, the only interlocutor to use the first person singular pronoun as subject is Pascal himself and he does so to say that he hates the self (*moi*). The recorder of this dialogue does not say: "I hate myself," but "I hate it," with the object pronoun referring to the *moi*. The "I" who makes this judgment is one who has judged not only his own *moi* but the *moi* of all others; it is an "I" who speaks from the suprapersonel experience of having observed and read the operations of his and others' personal "I."

I ADOPT an unsentimental approach to Pascal because he perhaps more than most great men has suffered the fate of being remembered more as great than as men. This fate is ironic in the case of the man who, more than others, finds that an indispensable part of the significance of the man-God, Jesus Christ, lies in his very man-ness, that, through his humanity, to use a key term of Pascal's vocabulary, we seek (*chercher*) his divinity.

As Pascal attained Christ's divinity through His humanity, so I have sought to attain Pascal's greatness through his humanity. This seeking involves me in the application to his own life of those paradigms of human behavior that he overtly applied to the lives of all men: the concupiscence of the flesh (*libido sentiendi*), the concupiscence of the mind (*libido sciendi*), the concupiscence of the will (*libido dominandi*). Much of my seeking is, necessarily, to use another term of his vocabulary, of a probabilistic nature, closer, I trust, to his own strict mathematical and theological probabilism than to the latitudinarian probabilism of certain Jesuits that he excoriates in the *Provincial Letters*. I say "necessarily" of this aspect of my seeking for two reasons. First, little is known about Pascal's personal life, particularly about the life of the flesh. His own reticence on this matter, combined with the protective hagiography of many of his biographers, especially his sister Gilberte in her *Life of Pascal*, provides such scant evidence that one is obliged to an unusual amount of what is, in my case I hope, informed and fair speculation. Second, for all his genius, Pascal does not escape the human condition. I thus apply to his life paradigms of human behavior that, looking back to others (especially Saint Augustine and Montaigne) and anticipating still others (Freud and certain of his adepts), he uses in his own researches into the human condition.

As my avatars of Pascal here indicate, those paradigms are theological and psychological. I link the psychological to the theological because it is through Pascal's language and, even more, his conception of language and of systems of perception that I trace his own psychology in the more conventional sense of that term. In that sense I have adduced paradigms of the family drama associated with Freud and, to lesser extent in these pages, with Herbert Marcuse. How-

ever, in depending on father fixation and oedipal crisis and similar categories of "depth" psychology I am concerned to place them under the
etymological sense of *psychology* (*psyche* plus *logos*): the study of the
soul and, in a specifically Christian reference, the study of the symbi-
osis of soul or psyche and word or logos ("In the beginning was the
Word"). This understanding of psychology seems compelling not
only because of my subject's specific religious and linguistic concerns,
but more generally. As Noam Chomsky has said,

> One should not speak of a "relationship" between linguistics and psy-
> chology, because linguistics is *part* of psychology; I cannot conceive of
> it in any other way.
>   In general, the following distinction is often made: linguistics is the
> study of language, and psychology the study of the acquisition or utili-
> zation of language. This distinction does not seem to me to make
> much sense. No discipline can concern itself in a productive way with
> acquisition or utilization of a form of knowledge without being con-
> cerned with the nature of that system of knowledge.[5]

Pascal anticipates this view of the relation between psychology and
language. As the reader will see, however, what I call Pascalian linguistics is not what Chomsky calls Cartesian linguistics. Pascal's deep
structures are semantic rather than syntactic.

All his life, in scientific as well as religious contexts, Pascal was concerned with the nature of systems of knowledge. The first of his best
known works, the *Provincial Letters,* is an extended debate with various
adversaries on the use of words. The second and most famous of his
works, the *Thoughts,* extends this concern to a deeper probing of other
signs of knowledge, of what he calls *figures.* In light of the Pascalian
linguistics of those two works in particular, such concepts as father
fixation and oedipal crisis are figures of the system of man's knowing
himself in order to know God. I use such concepts, then, not in the
manner of some Freudian interpreters: to reduce Pascal to a sensually
or, in his terms, carnally immanentist and pessimistic psychology (of
Pascal and of humankind in general). I use them, rather, as instances in
his life of cathexes that he overcomes, thanks to a spiritually transcendent and optimistic psychology. Not the least of Pascal's paradoxes is
that through his linguistics he gets beyond a reality principle seeing
humankind as inextricably bound in the flesh and postulates a pleasure
principle that he derives from Saint Augustine, seeing humankind as
released to the spirit. For Pascal, as the psychoanalyst Charles Bau-

douin has shown in his scientific and humanistic study of the Pascal family drama (*Blaise Pascal ou l'ordre du coeur*), reductions of spirituality to carnality are themselves figures of corrupted nature. In and for Pascal, sublimation is not a psychological mechanism revealing humankind's deviation from or displacement of its fundamental animality; it is, rather, a striving for the sublime of which the deviation into animality after the Fall had deprived the soul.

Thus, I am concerned to link the young Pascal with the mature Pascal precisely in order to explain the relation between the figures of his youth and the figuralism of his maturity. That relation is complex. Pascal never fully achieves a personal resolution of the attractions of the various libidinal orders that he himself so brillantly elucidates. He is finally pulled back to the adversary posture in which he had begun, but after having known and shown us a long moment of advocacy that belies the widespread view of him as a quarrelsome and arrogant genius.

In tracing this dialectic I have moved through Pascal's and related texts, "in the order of time," a phrase he uses in his *Abridgment of the Life of Jesus Christ*. My method is that of the psychologist who lets the analysand speak and then pieces the statements together for a continuous interpretation of past and present. In order to interpret Pascal in the order of time, I have been most dependent on the editorial portion of Pascal scholarship—on Jean Mesnard, for his dating and editing of those writings by and on Pascal that makes up the first two (and, as yet, only) published volumes of his monumental edition of Pascal's work; Philippe Sellier for his edition of the *Thoughts*, which builds on and advances the work of the remarkable editorial scholarship in Pascal studies of this century; Jan Miel for his editorial commentary on Pascal's long-neglected *Writings on Grace*; Hugh M. Davidson and P. H. Dubé for their indispensable *A Concordance to Pascal's "Pensées."* I have also drawn on certain of the interpretive studies of these scholars; in particular, Mesnard's *Pascal*, Sellier's *Pascal et Saint Augustin*, Miel's *Pascal and Theology*, Davidson's *The Origins of Certainty—Means and Meanings in Pascal's "Pensées."* As these *Pascalisants* will see, I have also at times drawn away from them in both editorial and interpretive matters. The distance at these points between myself and my mentors constitues a Pascalian abyss into which they did not lead me but which I could not have probed without their indispensable establishment of its borders.

I have sought throughout to show both my dependence and my independence from these scholars in as noncontentious a fashion as possible. Too frequently literary scholarship moves away centrifugally from its purported subject, the consideration of the text or writer under study, toward a consideration of the views of other scholars on the text under study. This book might easily have become a study not of Pascal but of Pascal criticism. As much as possible I have tried to avoid this shift of emphasis, particularly with respect to other studies with which, as knowledgeable Pascalians will note, I disagree both specifically and generally. Pascal is himself sufficiently controversial that no further controversy is needed about that controversiality. Thus specialists will note that I have referred only sparingly to the provocative recent study of Louis Marin, *La Critique du discours: sur la "Logique de Port Royal" et les "Pensées" de Pascal* (1975). Nevertheless, though the knowledgeable reader will sense throughout the fundamental differences between myself and Marin both generally and specifically, I think it just at this point, to both Marin and those of my readers familiar with his provocative book (whether or not they share his basic view of Pascal as a harbinger of the semiological problematic), to indicate the broad lines of my disagreement with him.

That Pascal should be assimilated into the present-day view, especially widely held in French literary studies, of language as essentially self-referential and of every text as the site of its own potential deconstruction is not surprising. The situation is not without some irony, I would hasten to add. It is not surprising that a writer as preoccupied with language, both theoretically and practically, as Pascal — consultant to the Port Royal grammarians, inventor of a method for teaching children to read, critic of the language and style of both adversaries and cohorts, creator of a style that is thought by many to have founded modern French prose — not surprising, indeed, that such a writer should draw the attention of the deconstructionist current of semiotic inquiry in literary studies. It is ironic, however, that this implosive current should attempt to assimilate Pascal into its own problematic, for it is precisely against notions like the self-referential and the intracursive that Pascal's work strives, bluntly and passionately in its early phase (through the first sixteen *Provincial Letters*), subtly but no less passionately in the *Thoughts*. It is precisely this irony that Marin fails to appreciate as he, like so many Pascal scholars before him, views the *Thoughts* as emblematic or as a *terminus ad quem* of the entire Pascalian canon.

To be sure, with its emphasis on the nonapodictic notion of figure and its composition in fragments, this most famous work of Pascal does seem to lend itself to a theory of language skeptical of verbal mimesis, to a catachresis suggesting, at least to Marin, that Pascal views all language as aporetic, disjoined from the things, either objects or immutable ideas, that a mimological view of language posits as the referents or signifieds of words or signifiers. It is Pascal's stress on the paradoxical that lies at the heart of the disjuncture between, on the one hand, Pascal's notion of language (at least in the *Thoughts*) and use of language (again: at least in the *Thoughts*) and, on the other hand, the notions and recommended use of language of the Port Royal grammarians. The linguistics propounded at Port Royal is far too Cartesian for Pascal in its internality, potentially too skeptical of the reality of the signified, of the referent as object-bound. More perceptive than his coreligionists at Port Royal in linguistics as well as in theology, Pascal senses that Cartesian linguistics is more appropriately the ontological ground of his adversaries, the Jesuits (as well as, ironically, that of his coreligionists). It is the Jesuits who were the harbinger of present-day views of language as an internal system of reference, and it is precisely with that internality that he charges them bluntly in his early work and then, perceiving the generality of their view of language, more subtly in his later work. However skeptical of verbal mimesis Pascal may be in the *Thoughts*, he attains to this skepticism only after a long period in which he himself is apodictic (and, at times, apoplectic) before the too easy catachresis of others: Saint Ange in the mid-1640s, the Jesuits in the mid-1650s, and others. It is to trace this shift, in fact, that I treat the *Provincial Letters* so extensively and so closely, extending my commentary on them to a degree somewhat unusual in general studies of the Pascal canon.

My reservations about Marin's view of the *Thoughts* as aporetic, moreover, are relative not only to their expression as a different phase in Pascal's complex development. I also believe that the skepticism about language that Marin finds radical (at the root of Pascal's thought) is relative in another sense, not radical, not absolute, not fundamental within that thought, but, rather, framed within and, theologically speaking, against a precedent reality that is not in doubt, that cannot, to be sure, be fully *apprehended* exclusively through language (or any other purely human means), but that can be approached through language, imperfect as it may be, for it is the best of our purely human means for such an approaching. That reality is, of course, the supreme reality of God. In the *Thoughts* Pascal is relatively unapodictic, far less concerned with linking a host of individual signifiers (particularly, catechetical injunctions on specific mortal and venial sins) to signified conduct than he was in the *Provincial Letters*. Instead, in the *Thoughts,* he is more concerned with paradoxically signifying through fragmentary, indirect, subtle, elliptical, and seemingly endlessly variable signifiers the summary referent of these signifiers, the supreme "sign" (in Saussurian terms, that which equals signifier plus signified): the sign of the Cross. Where the Pascal of the Father-centered *Provincial Letters* may be said to emphasize the vertical / ascendant / divine bar of that universal symbol of Christianity, the Pascal of the *Thoughts* (a filicentric work to be called *Apology for the Christian Religion*) may be said to emphasize the horizontal / earthbound / human bar of that symbol. Marin tends to read that horizontality as a bar to a Pascalian belief in the reality, the existence of an object or referent beyond what Marin calls the "zero degree of proper names, the first and last but still a figure": the name of Jesus Christ.[6] Yet, however aware Pascal may be that the name of Jesus Christ is only a figure, the very architecture of the fragments raises them to a telling figure. Thus, in the very process of fragmentary composition, Pascal makes literal sense of the life of the man-God, that life through which we human beings can, mimetically, aided by divine grace, live our lives and thus hope to be saved. Great as the emphasis on the horizontal bar of the Cross may be in the *Thoughts,* Pascal does not forget nor does he let his reader forget that the horizontal intersects with the vertical, the human with the divine, and that, linguistically, the aporetic fuses into the apodictic to point to the Supreme Signified toward whom all language tends.

SINCE MANY of my readers may be exclusively English speakers, I have used English translations (my own) of passages quoted from other languages. Quotation from the early Pascal is rather extensive. I hope thereby to extend the Pascalian patrimony beyond the two masterpieces by which he is known in translation to the reader who does not know French: the *Provincial Letters* and, especially, the *Thoughts.* However substantial both quantitatively and qualitatively, these famous works are only a part of his canon. I hope that in my juxtaposition of other works with the well-known masterpieces the reader will have the opportunity to sense the constant complexity and richness of Pascal's thought. I trust that the reader will also see in the dialectic that I trace between the well-known and the relatively unknown works more than the esthetic significance that a concentration on the masterpieces has so often fostered. Pascal was a great writer, but an almost exclusively esthetic appreciation has isolated him for too many readers as a superior example of what he would have called diversion from the fundamental question that he asked throughout his life in a variety of ways and with a tormented awareness that existence *forces* the question upon us: How, then, shall we live?

PART I

The
Adversary

· 1 ·

ADVERSARIAL
BELIEVER,
ADVERSARIAL
MAN OF
SCIENCE

BLAISE PASCAL would twice undergo a profound conversion, a private *agon* of faith-renewed whose public expression would be at once an exemplary advocacy and a turbulent *antagon*.

The first conversion occurred through the agency of two boneset-ters, the Deschamps brothers, who had been called in by the Pascal family to treat the father, Etienne, for a leg broken when he slipped on the ice on a wintry day early in 1646. The occasion must not have been without its symbolic overtones for the young Pascal: the Deschamps had been renowned swordsmen before being converted to a strict Jansenist piety by an adept of the spiritual mentor of the Jansenist movement in the 1630s and early 1640s, Jean Duvergier de Hauranne, abbé de Saint Cyran. In keeping with his duties as an officer of the crown at Rouen, Etienne had his accident while walking briskly to a field of honor where two gentlemen were to have a duel in spite of the Crown's (Richelieu's) injunction against dueling. The bonesetters stayed in the Pascal household some three months, in the course of which they communicated to the members of the family, principally through Blaise, it appears, their faith renewed à la Saint Cyran. Pascal himself left us no record of this *agon*, but his sister Gilberte, if elliptical on the facts of the "providential" occasion, raises it to the level of a conversion that later commentators have seen truer of the so-called second conversion recorded by Pascal himself in his famous *Memorial* of 1654. Gilberte writes in the *Life of Pascal:*

> God's Providence having given birth to an occasion that obliged him to read works of piety, God enlightened him in such a way by these holy readings that he understood perfectly that the Christian religion

19

obliges us to live for God alone and to have no other object but him; and this truth seemed to him so evident, so necessary, and so useful that it ended all his researches—so that from this time on he renounced all other forms of knowledge in order to apply himself to the unique thing that Jesus Christ calls necessary.

Gilberte's chronology is false: she sets this occasion before her brother's famous experiments on the vacuum, when in fact they occurred *afterward*. Moreover, she is also obliged to pass rapidly over several years of her brother's life, covering the period in five pages of which four deal with the Affaire Saint Ange, her brother's exemplary ministry within the family itself, his own modeling of his religious life on that of their sister Jacqueline, who had decided to enter holy orders. Of her brother's contest over Jacqueline's worldly goods now that the younger sister had "withdrawn from the world" Gilberte says nothing, as she says nothing of his continuing work on the vacuum nor of his other scientific and mathematical work in this period. This period, to be known to later scholarship as Pascal's worldly period, is summarized in a short paragraph by his sister-biographer that begins "There he is then in the world" and that would have us believe, as it races to its end, that he was more a student of than an actor in this world.

The contradiction might have seemed less evident to Pascal himself. For him the separation of the two worlds was pro forma. The *agon* of the first conversion would only have solidified a conception of two ways or, in terms that he was later to use, two "orders": the order of the mind and the order of the heart. Like Montaigne, he believed in this separation. Unlike Montaigne, however, he committed himself with equal intensity to each of these two realms. As for the third order, that of the flesh, Gilberte reports he had always, "thanks to divine mercy, been preserved from vice." But, one must insist, the orders were for him distinct, and, as can be seen from the passage already quoted from the Preface to the *Treatise on the Vacuum*, would remain so at least through the early 1650s. The Pascal of the early period lived the separation of the orders in good conscience. One of the chief expressions of this conscience is his irritation before those who mix the realms: theologians who might proceed in science as they do in theology, invoking authority where they should invoke only reason; or, contrariwise, theologians who proceed in theology as one ought in science, invoking reason where they should invoke only authority.

Such a theologian was Jacques Forton, abbé de Saint Ange, with whom Pascal the religious thinker first enters the stage of history.[1] A former Capuchin who by the time of his encounter with Pascal early in 1647 had become a secular priest, Saint Ange was a prolific author of theological works with a curiously rationalistic and pre-Leibnizian cast of mind. His reputation as a somewhat liberal theologian had preceded his arrival in Rouen, putting on their theological guard three fervent young Rouennais who were at once of a scientific and theological bent: Raoul Halle de Monflaines, Adrien Auzout, and Blaise Pascal. Friends in matters of science as well as of religion, the three young men felt compelled to challenge the itinerant theologian on a number of his positions, chiefly his contention that man could, through reason unaided by the Divine, understand the mystery of the Trinity. They thus summoned him to an "interview" that was more in the nature of an inquisition in mid-winter 1646–47. The interview occurred on two occasions in which the three, apparently with great ridicule, drew from the abbé a number of propositions whose excessive rationalism they found scandalous. Hoping for a censure of the abbé, the three interviewers submitted over their signatures a *récit* of their conversations to the archbishop of Rouen, François de Harlay (who passed the affair for adjudication on to his coadjutor, Jean-Pierre Camus, bishop of Belley, himself a prolific author of, among other works, pietistic novels in a Salesian vein).

It is difficult to discern the specific positions of Pascal in this document. He arrived somewhat late during the first conversation, at a point, as the *récit* puts it, when his two friends were "disputing with some heat" Saint Ange's contention that, apart from the necessity of faith to know that God was man's supernatural end, reason sufficed without faith to know the other mysteries of religion for powerful thinkers (*esprits puissants*), while only for those whose powers of reasoning were less vigorous was faith necessary as a supplement. To the objection, based on Saint Paul and "all the other fathers," by Halle de Monflaines and Auzout, that faith was beyond reason and concerned those things that man could not conceive without revelation, Saint Ange replied that Paul and the other Church Fathers intended their position to apply only to those things that fell under the faculty of imagination. Pascal was rapidly brought up to date, and, apparently

with him in the lead, the three lay theologians advanced a number of
their own propositions in a seemingly rhetorical way.

There is a rhetorical cast to the document recalling the procedure
Pascal was later to use in the *Provincial Letters*, especially the early ones,
suggesting that, although Pascal was absent at the start of the first
conversation, he may have been the most present of the document reporting the entire interview. (As Jean Mesnard has demonstrated in his
edition, contrary to earlier scholarly assumptions, a considerable time
undoubtedly elapsed between the interviews themselves and the
writing of the *récit*.) In any case, the author begins with a seeming
objectivity, identifying the participants and setting a tone of courtly
civility among these distinguished conversationalists, positing even a
certain friendliness as he reports that "after introductory civilities, the
aforementioned *sieurs* du Mesnil (Halle de Monflaines, *fils*) and Auzout
stated to *sieur* Saint Ange the desire they had to get to know him
because of the great esteem that they had heard expressed for him,
[and] there was a certain amount of indifferent discussion." The voluble Saint Ange seems to have been caught in this trap of flattering
civility as readily as the voluble Jesuits whom the "I" of the *Provincial
Letters* visits in a seemingly disinterested desire to know what the
argument between Jansenists and Jesuits is all about. Like the author
of those letters, the three young men seem mere "honest men"
(*honnêtes hommes*) exercising their amateur concern with science and
religion. Yet the way in which the actors are presented is linked to
their purpose in sending this document to the highest ecclesiastical
authorities. The way in which Pascal himself is identified upon his late
arrival is not irrelevant here.

> There was heated dispute on this, and while we were dealing with the
> matter, *le sieur* Pascal arrived—son of Monsieur Pascal, counsellor to
> the king in his state councils and, in private, commissioner deputized
> by His Majesty in upper Normandy for the setting and collection of
> taxes, and for the subsistance and garrison of troops, and other matters
> in the service of His Majesty, who came to see *le sieur* du Mesnil. After
> the [usual] civilities, he was told in brief something of what *le sieur* de
> Saint Ange had advanced.

Such worldly pride in the future author of some of the most searing attacks in any language of the "hateful self"! Yet such a view seems to
miss the rhetorical point of this extended indentification by title and

rank. As with Pascal *fils*, so with Halle de Monflaines *fils* at the very outset of the *récit.*

> On Friday, the first day of February 1647, *le sieur de* Saint Ange, accompanied by a gentleman friend of his, came to the house of *Monsieur* de Monflaines, counsellor to the king in his councils of state and in private, appointed master of requests of the king's household, to see *le sieur* du Mesnil, his son, who had expressed the desire to see him, and who was at the time with *le sieur* Auzout.

The authors of the *récit* (Pascal alone perhaps) are appealing to the authority of their station in order for the archbishop and, as necessary, civil (perhaps even royal) authorities to know that the opposition to Saint Ange is not without political influence. By implication the king himself is implicated on the side of the three inquisitors; the parallelism of title between Monflaines *père* and Pascal *père* is striking in this respect.

The participants themselves are not without some weight: each is a *sieur,* a term difficult to translate into English but with considerably more than the force of "Mister," coming closer, especially for the period, to "Sir" and perhaps, somewhat pretentiously, "Lord." All this is, of course, camouflaged through the civil, casual and even friendly premises of the encounter: Saint Ange is with a gentleman friend (*gentilhomme de ses amis*); Auzout seems just to happen to have been at his friend du Mesnil's house and Pascal seems just to have come to see du Mesnil with the same casualness. As we know from Gilberte, however, the occasion was more causal than casual: "He [Blaise] was, at the time, in Rouen, where my father was employed in the service of the king, and where there was at the same time a man who taught a new philosophy that was attracting all of the curious. My brother having been pressed by two young men who were his friends, he was with them." Obviously, the curiosity of the three young men, their salonlike approach to the itinerant philosopher, was not the curiosity of those whom the philosopher was attracting. It was precisely because of Saint Ange's purposes at Rouen that the young men felt obliged to denounce him with the highest seriousness of purpose matched to the most artful curiosity of approach: the ex-Capuchin was seeking an appointment as a curate, a post from which his inquisitors feared in particular his influence on the children who would be in his charge.

If there is any irony in Pascal's reliance, in his individual or joint authorship of the *récit,* on the use of the worldly power of paternal and royal authority, it lies in his rhetorical posture in the affair. He is, to a certain extent, mixing the lowest order ("the grandeur . . . of kings, the rich, captains of the earth . . . the grandees of the flesh" S 339) with the highest order of the heart precisely in order to establish the latter's authority in its own domain. The political inconsistency that might give rise to the irony dissolves into the psychological consistency of his position: the appeal to authority in each of the two realms in question, flesh and heart. In this respect, the debate between Saint Ange and inquisitors is a chapter in the "Quarrel between the Ancients and the Moderns" that figures chiefly as a purely literary quarrel throughout the century, from Malherbe to Boileau and beyond. Pascal and his associates here consistently defend *ancient* authority, the fathers of the Church, against Saint Ange with his constant recourse to the *new* "doctors in theology," including, of course, himself.

The *récit* is replete with this stark difference of position. It maintains only in its first few pages the courteous civility of a casual inquiry:

Position of Pascal, Auzout, and du Mesnil	Position of Saint Ange
We [*On*] asked him by what means he knew the Trinity.	He replied that he demonstrated it by reason.
We asked him if God were bound to act according to these conventions, because it would follow that God could do only what he has done.	He answered that, if one considered God's power in itself, God was able to do an infinity of other things that he had not done, but that if one considered it in connection with His wisdom, He could do only what He has done because He always did what was the most appropriate.
We told him that by this means he therefore knew all the [divine] mysteries by reasoning, and thus those of the Incarnation and the Eucharist, and so on, since they were the consequence of some convention.	He replied that he knew them.

We offered some doubts on that, among others that if all that were so, one would not need faith to know the aforementioned mysteries, and that therefore without faith one could be saved.

He answered in these terms: "And if I said so?"

At which we having said to him that that was contrary to the Scriptures: *Without faith it is impossible to please God.*

He said that we needed faith to know one thing, that is: to know that God is our supernatural end, not being able to attain this knowledge unless we are aided by a higher light, because of the difficulties that come to us from the infinite distance between God and us; but, for the other mysteries, a powerful mind could attain them by reasoning and that faith was but a supplement for minds whose reasoning was not vigorous enough and who did not have enough light to conceive said mysteries.

We countered that faith was above natural reason and things that we could not conceive without revelation, from which it comes that Saint Paul calls it *argumentum non apparentium* [argument without appearance]; that all the Church Fathers said the same thing.

He said that that was to be understood of things that fell under the imagination.

Foreshadowed are the conversations between the "I" of the *Provincial Letters* and the windy Jesuits. Like the Jesuits, Saint Ange has only the names of the new doctors on the edge of his tongue, names that sound like tin against the names of Paul and the fathers that his interlocuters utter. Saint Ange is a probabilist as Pascal will characterize his Jesuit adversaries in the *Provincial Letters*: as in his disputes with the doctors of theology at Paris, Saint Ange finds justification for his doctrines in the opinions of the many rather than of the Scriptures and the Church fathers.

Pascal arrived at just that moment in the discussion when the position of the young amateurs in theology shifted from asking to countering. The text subsequently falls, from the point of view of the three young men, into a rhetorical and theological field of derision and opposition:

> Someone being astonished, we opposed him; we did not understand this term; this proposition pleased no one, someone countering him, after having first evinced his astonishment; although this discourse managed to surprise each of us, we were nevertheless not so astonished, turned [thereby] to ridicule; nevertheless we laughed among ourselves at that; this comparison seemed amusing—we really wanted to know what passage of Saint Augustine he could apply to his opinion [*sentiment*]; we brought up Saint Paul against him—upon which we were greatly astonished with an explanation so far into the thought of that father; we proposed difficulties that we wished to have clarified; we could not keep from laughing at all these strange discourses, we disputed heatedly against this explanation . . .

The *récit* of the two conversations closes on this note of opposition: "no more did he respond to the passage of Saint Paul that we brought up against him: *Only one is the mediator*." The language of inquiry is still sounded by the author(s) of the *récit*, but within this overwhelming context of derision and opposition even the asking of questions or statement of positions reads like synonyms of the adversary formulations I have just listed.

The form is not all, of course. The form, the rhetorical frame, is the surface structure of the deep structure of doctrinal positions that these performatives introduce. The mysterious humanity of Jesus Christ is a constant of Pascal's thought, from this, his first public debate on faith and reason, to his last, the question of whether the religious of Port Royal should sign the formulary subscribing to Jansen's purported heresy not merely because it is a mystery of the Church taught by Scripture and expounded by the Church fathers, but also because it responds to the deep-felt sense of human suffering and human alienation from the divine ground of being that Pascal would express so movingly in his *Abridgment of the Life of Jesus Christ* and especially *The Mystery of Jesus*. One can thus understand the shock (as the text of the *récit* puts it) of Pascal and his coreligionists at this alienation of Jesus Christ from man himself, at Saint Ange's assertion that Jesus was not "animal," meaning, as they go on to explain their adversary, not "a feeling, living being."

Saint Ange's shocking liberalism is manifest in all of the doctrines on which his interlocutors led him to comment. As with Christ, so with the Virgin Mary: she, too, was of a different species than other human beings (though not, it would seem, of the same species as Jesus); that the grace of salvation was given equally unto all men and that this grace was to be distinguished on the basis of Augustine himself from the grace of the minister, which was the only one that was distributed unequally, and so on. For the three young men these and his other doctrines were far removed from the "common sentiment of Catholics."

Their understanding of that common sentiment may have been a Jansenist one. Some commentators on the Affaire Saint Ange seem unduly concerned with separating Pascal on this occasion from the Jansenist controversy. Yet that controversy had begun to erupt soon after the publication of Jansen's *Augustinus* (1640). Arnauld's defense of that book had been published three years before the interview, and his defense of Jansen's lifelong friend, Saint Cyran, had been published only two years before. Nor is the awareness of the controversy absent in the encounter between Saint Ange and the three young men of Rouen, among them the Pascal who, as his sister tells us in her biography, had been the most influenced by the Saint Cyranian Deschamps brothers only the year before this encounter. Alert to the currents of controversy surrounding Jansen, then, it would be surprising if the three young amateur theologians did not raise the matter with Saint Ange. They do so, asking him to comment in a manner that, once again, suggests the rhetorical link with the *Provincial Letters*: "And as each would have liked to know what were his lights on the matter of grace, we asked which opinion he considered in greatest conformity with truth, that of Jansen or that of the Jesuits, and whether he thought that Jansen had understood Saint Augustine." Saint Ange's response is equivocal; he finds a measure of truth on both sides, going on to elaborate the general framework of a series of books he was projecting in which *he* would explain the truth more fully. That Saint Ange also claims that Jansen did correctly *appropriate* (not *understand*, as in the question posed him) the thought of Augustine seems irrelevant to his questioners. They find his projected work ridiculous, particularly in his far-fetched comparisons with the myth of Orpheus, the Menades, and the Bacchantes; they come back to Augustine as their own ground for truth, as if to say to Saint Ange that he has not yet answered their question. This persistent reliance on Augustine suggests a greater sympathy for, if not outright alliance with, Jansen on the part of Saint Ange's adversaries, especially in light of the itinerant abbé's Jesuit-like manipulation of the ancient authorities and Jesuit-like predilection for new doctrines and probabilism. Remembering the influence of Saint Cyran on the Deschamps brothers and their influence on Pascal, the Pascal of the Affaire Saint Ange might be less ready than the Pascal of the *Provincial Letters* to say, "I am not of Port Royal." At least, in this moment, he is of the Port Royal that had been directed by Saint Cyran.

It is clear that Pascal and his fellow interlocutors are at least Saint Cyranian and Augustinian in their reproach to Saint Ange in mixing the order of mind with the order of the heart. His confusion for them is part of the general confusion of his spirit, including his mind when it functions in that faculty's proper domain. The *récit* mocks Saint Ange not only on his theological positions but on his scientific positions as well. He puts forth an elaborate theory of the quantifiability of matter according to which the number of men who will ever live can be predicted; he posits notions on the continuity, imperishability, and transformation of matter; he comments on Pascal's experiments on the vacuum. That certain of these positions will in later periods find some adumbratory validity is interesting and might suggest to some that, even in the scientist Pascal, the heart hears reasons to which reason will not listen. Pascal's head may have been the dupe of his heart: his theological animadaversion may have prevented him even from entertaining the scientific hypotheses put forth by Saint Ange. I think a more compelling explanation lies in the comment made in the *récit* at this point however: "We began [to expect] no longer to be astonished to hear extraordinary things contrary to all appearances and without any [foundation in] reason or experience." It is the future author of the *Preface* to the *Treatise on the Vacuum* who is repelled. Saint Ange as a scientist proceeds as falsely in that domain for Pascal as Saint Ange the theologian in the domain of theology. As he fails to respect authority in theology, so he fails to rely on reason and experimentation in science.

We come full circle. The Pascal of the Affaire Saint Ange is at once within a world in Christ and within a world without Christ, within the order of the heart and within the order of the mind. An *orderly* thinker, he is upset by the disorder of Saint Ange's thought in both worlds. Pascal's temperament seems to have been as paradoxical as his thought: at once reflective and spontaneous, compassionate and combative, submissive and impetuous. As Gilberte portrays him in society, so was he in theological and scientific controversy: "the extreme vivacity of his spirit made him so impatient that at times it was difficult to satisfy him." In theological controversy, in particular, this impatience was the agent of that tenderness of charity that he distinguished for Gilberte from tenderness of sensitivity. Like the Flaubert of *Bouvard and Pécuchet* before the stupidities of the nineteenth century, so Pascal, before the stupidities of the seventeenth century, was "objectively angry," moved by a principle of charity transcending kindness and tolerance between men. As Gilberte writes,

> "A heart is hard," he said, "when it knows the interests of one's neighbor and it resists the obligation pressing it to be concerned; and, on the contrary, a heart is tender when all the interests of one's neighbor enter into it easily, by, so to speak, all the feelings that reason would have us have one for the other in such situations; rejoicing when it is necessary to rejoice, reproaching oneself when it is necessary to reproach oneself." But he added that tenderness can be perfect only when reason is illuminated by faith and it makes us act according to the rules of charity. This is why he did not make much of a distinction between tenderness and charity, no more than between charity and friendship.

The charity in question is Saint Cyranian, Augustinian, Jansenist: the love the creature owes God without bargaining for God's love in return. This is the essence of the Pascal's early faith and, his reason illuminated by it in the Affaire Saint Ange, he is impelled to counterattack its derogation, Saint Ange's notion of faith as, at best, a supplementary illumination of sovereign reason. Safe in his separation of the orders at this time, secure in his own submission through faith in the order of charity, Pascal's head had to be "turned," as he puts it in a famous fragment of the *Thoughts* (S 670), to the scandal of Saint Ange's thought: du Mesnil and Auzout, we remember from Gilberte, "pressed" her brother into joining them in opposition to Saint Ange. But, as he had taken the lead in the conversion of the household in light of the religious instructions of the Deschamps brothers a year earlier, so he takes the lead among the three. From the reactive he moves to the initiative. The pattern will repeat itself throughout the adversary phase of his religious development.

FOR ALL the separateness of the orders of mind and heart in which Pascal lived during the Affaire Saint Ange, there is a certain unity of outlook as he addressed himself now to this order, now to that. In theology as in science, he proceeded on the basis of his own observation, his own *experience*, of the order in question. In science, during the years on either side of the Affaire, he tested ancient and authoritarian assumptions, being especially infuriated by speculations in defiance of observable phenomena. Some of this scientific outlook characterizes his exchange with Saint Ange himself in the latter's scientific as well as theological speculations. In theology, during these years, in light of the experience of his first conversion, he tested modern and antiauthoritarian assumptions, being especially infuriated by speculations in defiance of the received phenomena of grace. Ever reactive and concrete, the Pascal of this period addresses himself adversarially and often antagonistically to the data of experience as inhabitant of either order, mind or heart.

His adversarial attitude persists well beyond the moment of his celebrated second conversion during the night of fire of November 23, 1654. In the very months of January and February 1647 during which Pascal began his "pursuit" of Saint Ange for the latter's ill-founded speculations in theology, he was pursuing his inquiries into the void on the basis of carefully conducted experiments that were to bring him to the attention of such notable scientists and philosophers as Guiffart, Roberval, Gassendi, Descartes, and the latter's Jesuit mentors, on this occasion in the person of the Jesuit, Father Noël, Descartes' mentor when the future philosopher had studied at La Flèche. The young scientist's relations with his scientific confrères in the long series of reports, exchanges, and reflections on his experiments manifest with friend and foe alike the same fierce rectitude and pride, often spilling over into arrogance, he had shown toward Saint Ange. Both in professional exchanges with his fellow scientists and philosophers and in family matters the young scientist-theologian shows this pride bordering on arrogance.

The experiments on the vacuum that he had conducted in the first few months of 1647 brought him to the attention of the scientific and philosophic community with an even greater force than his earlier work in mathematics, particularly on the calculating machine. Guiffart, Roberval, Gassendi, Descartes, and others followed Pascal's work with interest and approval, many of them modifying their own theses on the vacuum. But not all followed that work with approval. The young scientist had undoubtedly not laid a particularly collegial ground for discussion with his fellow scientists, especially for those whose dubiety he seemed eager to appease. Preoccupied first by the Affaire Saint Ange well into April 1647 and then by a debilitating illness in the late spring, Pascal was not to return to scientific matters until the fall. He had moved to Paris in the summer; his early stay there is marked by two meetings with Descartes, in late September. The older philosopher-scientist advises the younger not only on his health but also, according to his correspondence with Mersenne a few months later, on the value of experiments with the vacuum in an elevated situation. Descartes' attitude in each of these counsels seems characteristic of the charity and self-effacement that marks so much of the writing of this philosopher concerned with improving man's lot in this world, an attitude that contrasts sharply with the self-aggrandizement and worldliness that one finds in the younger philosopher historically so closely associated with the imperatives of the other world. Some two and one-half years later, in two letters to Carcavy, Descartes himself manifested what might be considered a certain egocentrism as he reminded his correspondent that it was he who had recommended to Pascal this particular experiment.

The young savant manifested a tremendous preoccupation with self-distinction, particularly in relation to those who concerned themselves with issues that interested him. This self-concern was manifested even in the generally objective text in which Pascal had first reported his experiments on the vacuum, *New Experiments on the Vacuum,* published October 8, 1647, only two weeks after his meetings with Descartes. The report of experiments is itself rigorously clear and objective, but in its preface addressed to the reader the author evinces an almost frantic concern not only lest his own work be misinterpreted but lest it, if properly interpreted, not be attributed to him. He acknowledges that he offers here an abridgment (*abrégé*) rather than the more extensive treatise on which he has been working "because having conducted these experiments at great expense of money, energy, and time, I feared that someone else who would not have spent the money, energy, and time, anticipating me, would give to the public things that he would not have seen, and which therefore he could not report with exactitude and the order necessary to deduce them as required: there being no one with pipes and siphons as long as mine, and few who would give themselves the necessary difficulty to obtain."[2] Were he to stop here, we might find Pascal at worst guilty of the experimenter's pride in the scientific accuracy of the report of work that he had conducted. However, he goes on:

> And since polite people combine, with the general inclination that all men have to maintain themselves in their just possessions, an inclination to refuse honor to him to whom it is due, you will undoubtedly approve that I protect myself as well both from those who would deprive me of some of the experiments that I present here and that I promise to give you in the full treatise, since they are my inventions; and from those who would attribute the experiment in Italy of which I have spoken, since it is not among my own. For, although I have conducted that one in more ways than any other one, and with pipes of twelve and even fifteen feet in length, nevertheless I shall not speak uniquely thereof in these writings, because I am not the inventor, having the intention to give only those that are particular to me and of my own genius.

We should remember, of course, that Pascal uses the term "genius" in a sense close to its Latin root meaning of "individual spirit" or "individual nature." Nevertheless, the text gives sufficient warrant to believe that he considers his individual spirit to be not only unique but also superior. At the close of his Preface as at its outset, in acknowledging Torricelli's precedence in refuting the long-held theory of nature's abhorrence of a vacuum, he seems more concerned with highlighting his own experimentation than in crediting the Italian's originality in the matter.

One senses the fire (*fougue*) that his sister-biographer reports as having characterized all of his encounters in society, the fire of pride and self-esteem that may have communicated itself to Descartes. The latter responded to it with a reserved insistence on the facts as he knew them, an insistence that we may see at worst as subtly ironic toward the self-aggrandizing young man and at best as an exemplary respect for the truth. Others would be less reserved, particularly Descartes' old mentor, Father Noël. The Jesuit's irony is anything but gentle as he writes to Pascal near the end of October that he has read Pascal's report and finds it "quite beautiful and ingenious, but I do not understand this 'apparent vacuum' that appears in the tube after the descent, either of water or of mercury." He proceeds to respond to the questions that Pascal had, in his Preface, himself ironically and even derisively, left to more "knowledgeable and curious people" as to just what went on in this vacuum he had discovered.[3] For Noël the vacuum is indeed only apparent: it is really a body. Pascal replies with alacrity (October 29, 1647), neither frantic nor impatient, but with pride that shows through as complacency toward the older man; as Jean Mesnard has pointed out, it is in the spirit of an understanding teacher to a misguided pupil.[4] The "teacher" begins by positing a "universal rule" that he, unlike those who do science "in the schools," applies in all specific matters concerned with the truth: one must never affirm or deny the truth of a proposition unless what one affirms or denies satisfies one of two conditions: either that it appear so clearly and so distinctly of itself to the senses or to reason, as appropriate to one or the other, that the spirit (mind) has no way of doubting its certitude, these bases of certitude being called principles or axioms, or that it be deducible by infallible and necessary consequences of these principles or axioms. Having established this universal rule (which should have echoed, Pascal may have ironically hoped, Descartes' insistence on "clear and distinct ideas" in the *Discourse on Method* of 1637), Pascal then proceeds to a point-by-point refutation of Noël's objections to his own recent experiments on the vacuum.

The letter is not all condescension and ill-concealed contempt felt by the young scientific rebel for the masters of the desuetudinous school. It is also the occasion for scientific reflections on the nature of the vacuum that will bear on the religious debates that Pascal will have with still other Jesuits on the nature of another kind of void: the void that the polemicist of the *Provincial Letters* and the apologist of the *Thoughts* will discuss under the rubric of the hidden God (*le dieu caché*). Pascal does not, of course, make the analogy. In characteristic fashion, he raises the question of divine truth in this debate over scientific truth only to remove it from the discussion: "And we reserve for the mysteries of faith, that the Holy Spirit has itself revealed, this submission of the spirit [mind] that carries our belief in mysteries hidden to the senses and to reason." The posture is nonetheless scientific in the Pascalian view: this submission to mystery is based on the *revelations* that are the *experimental observations* appropriate to that domain or, as he will later call it, order. Characteristically, Father Noël does not respect this distinction in his considerations of the scientific issue before them. Elaborating his assertion that "every body is a space" and "every space is a body," he writes,

If you tell me that the species of the Holy Sacrament have parts one outside the other and nevertheless are not bodies, I answer, first, that, by the composite of parts one outside the other, one understands what we ordinarily call long, wide, and deep; second, that one can very easily explain the doctrine of the Roman and Catholic Church concerning the species of the Holy Sacrament, saying that the small bodies that remain in the species are not the substance of the bread. That is why the Council of Trent never uses the word "accident," speaking of the Holy Sacrament, although in effect these small bodies are truly accidents of the bread, according to the definition of "accident" accepted by everyone, which does not destroy the subject, either present or absent; third, that without miracle, every composite of parts one outside the other is a body, and I believe that, to settle the matter of the vacuum, there is no need to have recourse to miracles, given that we presuppose that all of your experiments have nothing beyond the powers of nature.

Not even in the Holy Sacrament does Father Noël see the mystery that Pascal would see there, for the Jesuit reflects the immanentism informing both the science and the theology that he defends. The "small bodies" are "in effect," as he says, "truly accidents of the bread," the bread that is the occasion of the sacrament in question. The Jesuit can no more conceive of the transformation of the species from bread to body of Christ (it is both bread and body of Christ) than he can of the vacuum as, in Pascal's terms, "holding the middle between matter and nothingness." Like man for the Pascal of the *Thoughts,* the vacuum is "neither angel nor beast."

The exchange with Noël was not to rest here. The Jesuit would publish a further reply to Pascal in the form of a book that, in a willfully and foolishly paradoxical way, he entitled: *The Fullness of the Vacuum.* He thus unwisely reopened a quarrel that, for the Pascal who had decided not to reply to the Jesuit's first reply, had seemed best closed. Noël's book in effect insists on the fatuity of Pascal's belief in (for Pascal: demonstration of) the existence of the vacuum, a vacuum that, given the present state of knowledge, as he insists, is empty. Pascal replies to Noël in the form of a letter to his friend, Le Pailleur, which Jean Mesnard believes may well have been concerted between the friends in view of the well-known mutterings against the young savant by the embarrassed Jesuits.[5] As he replies at once to the Jesuit's second letter as well as to the new book, Pascal demonstrates the easy scientific rigor and confidence of his formal reply to the Jesuit. This time, however, the tone mounts: the earlier hauteur gives way to a scolding sternness, the initial patience with the bumbling pupil to a scathing denunciation of the careless methodologist in Noël. The sternness is particularly severe as Pascal refutes the Jesuit's objection that Pascal's "empty space" is neither God nor creature. Reiterating his separation of the matters of faith and the matters of science, Pascal tells the Jesuit: "The mysteries that concern the divine are too holy to be profaned by our disputes. We should make of them the object of our adoration and not the subject of our conversations: so much so that, without discoursing on them in any way, I submit myself entirely to what will be decided by those who have the right to do so." The position is consistent with the one he had taken in the Affaire Saint Ange, a separation of Church and state, so to speak. In his letter to Le Pailleur again his position on the scientific validity of those who do not rely on experimentation and observation is no less consistent; when they persist in their error, they deserve only scorn:

> What is strange is that after proposing doubts to support his position, he [Father Noël] confirms it by false experiments. He proposes them nonetheless with a boldness such that they would be accepted as truth by all those who had not seen the contrary; for he says that the eyes make him see; that all this cannot be denied; that one sees it with the eye, although the eyes make us see the opposite. Thus it is clear that he has seen none of the experiments of which he speaks; and it is strange that he should have spoken with such assurance of things about which he knows nothing and on which he has been given reports of such little fidelity.

And when, in the course of writing to Le Pailleur, Pascal receives another text from the "learned" Jesuit takng back much of the *The Fullness of the Vacuum,* he mocks his adversary in a tone and in terms that anticipate those of his future theological debates with the Jesuits in the *Provincial Letters*:

> I find it rather difficult to refute the notions of this father (*ce Père*), since he is much more prompt about changing them than one can be in answering them; and I am beginning to see that his way of acting is quite different from my own, for he produces his opinions in relation to his conception of them; but their contradictoriness alone suffices to demonstrate their lack of solidity, since the power with which he disposes of this matter of the content of the vacuum testifies enough

that he is the author of it, and yet that it exists only in his imagination.

Noting the contradictoriness not only of Noël's hypotheses among themselves but of the various hypotheses of others objecting to his own, Pascal raises in this scientific debate the specter of the illegitimate confusion of orders—here of flesh (*chair*), the order of the "captains of the earth," and mind (*esprit*), the order of earthly knowledge or science)—that will preoccupy him both in the *Provincial Letters* and the *Thoughts:* "Thus, we have found some who, not daring to involve the immensity of God in this affair, have chosen among men a person sufficiently illustrious in his person and his rank to involve his opinion [*esprit*] and to have answer for [*remplir*] everything." Pascal reminds his reader that Noël had dedicated his foolish book to the Prince de Conti. In the young savant's scorn for this particular Jesuit's effort to invoke the power of the state for the resolution of an intellectual dispute one gets a glimmer of the righteous disdain of the combatant of the later theological quarrels who finds himself at odds with the ominous alliance of the Society of Jesus and the official powers, whose criminality and sinfulness the society will exculpate through its worldly morality of intentionalism and probabilism.

The indignation of young Blaise Pascal is shared by the older Etienne Pascal. In April 1648, the young scientist's father also attacks Noël's manner of conducting himself in the disputes over Blaise's experiments and hypotheses on the vacuum.[6] The father's approach is not essentially that of the physical scientist, though, given his own learning, he could well have treated the question in this way. Rather, it is that of what we would nowadays call the linguistic scientist, or, in a term consistent with the terms of his letter to Father Noël, the grammarian. He reviews the various exchanges in the quarrel up to this point, concluding this long "preamble" (one third of the letter) to his "review" of Noël's book with the observation that the real basis of his son's complaint against the Jesuit is that the latter has unjustly used invective and derision both in the title of his book and in the dedicatory letter to Conti. The older Pascal is especially indignant about the letter's charges of falsification and imposture in his son's handling of data. The difference between the Jesuit and the young scientist stands out for the father in the very contrast between the titles of the two principal texts in the dispute. "Here," Etienne Pascal writes, "is the title of your book":

The Fullness of the Vacuum
or
the body with which the apparent vacuum of the new
experiments is filled, proven [found] by other
experiments, confirmed by the same, and demonstrated
by physical reasons.

Let us begin, if you please, by examining your title: *The Fullness of the Vacuum.*

The small book of my son, against which you write, is entitled thus: *New Experiments of the Vacuum, performed in pipes, syringes, tubes, and siphons of several lengths and shapes, etc.*

To this simple, naive, ingenuous title — without artifice and very natural — you oppose this other title: *The Fullness of the Vacuum,* subtle, artful [*artificieux,* pejoration of *artificial*], ornate or, rather, made up of a figure that is called *antithesis,* if I remember correctly.

In good conscience, good Father, how could you make a better debut in [wanting to make] a derisive *abrégé?* It is easy to see that such is your purpose, without your taking much care about the terms of this antithesis, which can truly be passed off in the School, where it is not only permitted, but also necessary (the nature of man is so imperfect) to begin by doing harm; but certainly in the world, where one excuses nothing, it cannot be passed off, because in itself it does not have a perfect sense; and I do not doubt that you recognized it yourself and that this is perhaps why you have added a commentary, without which, although French in origin and dress, it could have been passed off in all of France for *incognita* and as mysterious as the Pythagorean numbers, which a modern author says are full of mysteries so hidden that till now none has been able to discover the secret of them.

Like son, like father. The father is even more like the son of the later theological debates with the Jesuits in setting a seemingly private matter in its properly public context: of language, which is the property of everyone and which is as subject to rules of evidence and experience (that is, testimony and testability) as the data of physical science. The father would reverse the roles of prosecutor and persecuted, beleaguerer and beleaguered, enfabulator and truthsayer, and like the son later appealing to the conscience yet ever aware of the inroads of evil in the ways of this world, would invoke good faith over bad faith. Like the son in his irony toward the *recherché* and mystifying erudition of the Jesuit moralists, the father would ironically dismiss the elaborate and the subtle in order to appeal to the general public with its simple taste for the simple truth simply said.

For Etienne Pascal the scientific errors of Noël, the prosecutor, enfabulator, and master of subtlety, can be pinpointed in his errors of grammar:

> If I dare, good Father, take the liberty of speaking here of grammar and establish a few principles for antithesis, I would say to you, first of all, that an antithesis should first of all contain in itself a completed meaning, as when we say that *to serve God is to reign*; that *human prudence is but folly*; that *death is the beginning of real life* and a thousand others of this kind. The reason for this is that an antithesis, to have true grace, must, by the very enunciation of these terms, uncover not only the meaning that it contains, but also its point and its subtlety. That if an antithesis is of such a kind that, however much its meaning be perfect, it is nevertheless not universally intelligible, it is necessary, in this instance, to have it preceded by a discourse that gives this [ground of] intelligibility to everyone, so that at the same time that one hears it uttered, one perceives the meaning and the force of it.

That the Jesuit's title is not preceded by such an explanatory preface is the first weakness of the antithetical title for Etienne Pascal. The antithesis of the title is rhetorically impossible, he claims, for it is composed of two adjectives, one in the nominative (*Le Plein,* in French, the adjective rendered a substantive) and the other in the genitive case (*du vide*) and, like all such formulations — the older Pascal cites *le faible du fort* 'the weak of the strong', *le petit du grand* 'the small of the big', *le riche du pauvre* 'the rich of the poor' — Noël's antithesis does not have a completed meaning because there is neither subject nor attribute. The father would seem to be denying the possibility of metaphor. He will not allow the Jesuit to escape reproach for his title on the grounds that it is only a metaphor, for the Jesuit obviously does not know the rules of this linguistic process either. The older Pascal invites the Jesuit to reflect on these rules:

> You will note at least the principal one, capable all by itself to relieve you of that fine notion that you have gotten based on the one on which you based this allegory, and you will realize that the metaphoric term must be like a figure, or an image of the real and true subject that one wishes to have represented in the metaphor, which means that the

metaphoric term cannot be adapted to the subject that is directly opposed to the first: thus we speak, metaphorically, of a serpent's tongue
when we speak of a bad mouth, because the venom of the tongue of
the serpent is like the image and the symbol of the evil and harm that
the bad mouth brings to the honor and reputation of the one whom it
vilifies; which means that the same metaphoric term of serpent's
tongue cannot be adapted to the opposite subject, that is, to the
tongue that sings the praises of another: it is thus that the Church is
called, in a holy metaphor, the bride of Christ, and it is on this
metaphor that the *Song of Songs* turns; it is thus that the Virgin says
that in her the Lord has made *the power of his arm* appear; and the Scripture is filled with them, because the divine mysteries being so unknown to us that we do not know their true names, we are obliged to
use metaphoric terms to express them.

Obviously, for Etienne Pascal, it is not only metaphor but language
itself that is a poor last resort. In this connection, the grounds of the
debate between him and the Jesuit are quite modern. The older Pascal
senses in the Jesuit's terms the notion of language as a self-sufficient
construct, an antimimesis, whereas for him language is a tool, a
signifier of a reality existing outside language itself and to which language only points. Etienne's crossing of the boundary between things
divine and things human in this scientific debate is two-edged. The indignant father-defender implicitly reminds his adversary that the latter
has offended not only human justice but divine justice in his pejora-
tions of Blaise. But in the very process of crossing this line the older
Pascal also surrenders in the attack on the divine implicit in the Jesuit's
conception of language: the implication that divine truth, like human
truth, is only a matter of language, that it does not exist apart from
man's talking and writing about it.

As Jean Mesnard has shrewdly noted, the significance of the father's
intervention on behalf of his son in this scientific quarrel is paramount.
Blaise will not have to await the influence of Nicole and his other
Jansenist mentors in the preparation of the *Provincial Letters*. Scotching
the imputation that Blaise himself may have written or at least largely
collaborated on this letter, Mesnard observes, "this is not to say that
the ideas developed therein are foreign to him. We believe that, on the
contrary, certain aspects of his personality, perhaps cultivated by his
father, are illuminated by this text. The concern for scientific rigor is
rounded out, in fact, in the literary domain, by a classic taste for a

natural and direct style, by the refusal of overwrought turns of phrase and the proliferation of baroque images." Yet, the questions of linguistic philosophy go beyond the question of style, to the very philosophy of language: the question of its relation to truth in any order of being. The influence of the father is contextual: he provides an example of the preoccupations that must have informed his relations with his children and especially his son at least from the moment of the family's conversion in the winter of 1646. This is not to say that Blaise Pascal fully shares his father's adamantly mimetic conception of language. Already, as I have noted, on the very occasion of this scientific debate, the son and the father differ on the appropriateness of involving questions of divine truth in the debate. If the father's classical style does reflect the son's own classical style — or, more exactly, *one* of the son's styles — the son here shows himself even more classical than the father in his Boileau-like exclusion of the religious from the secular.

The Jesuit involved in this quarrel on the vacuum may be said to have heeded the older Pascal's cease and desist order. In the summer of 1648 Noël published another text on the vacuum, *Gravitas Comparata,* in which, though all the while insisting on nature's abhorrence of the vacuum, the author bases his conclusions on the experiments of Pascal. Although, in this sense the Jesuit Noël relates more politely (and, for Etienne Pascal, ethically) to his former adversary, the antagonism between that adversary and the Jesuits becomes more exacerbated.

The debate is kindled in science as well as religion. In mid-November 1647, two weeks after his reply to Noël, Pascal wrote to his brother-in-law, Périer, at Clermont, asking him to implement the experiments on the vacuum at different altitudes as a way of further and more conclusively establishing the refutation of the theory of nature's supposed abhorrence of a vacuum. That the experiments were carried out as requested is confirmed in Périer's reply of September 22, 1648. This was some ten months later, to be sure; the lapse of time has led many historians of science, notably Félix Mathieu, to accuse Pascal of having antedated his letter to Périer in order to attribute to himself scientific independence if not priority in both the execution and the conception of these and related experiments. (His old friend and co-combatant in the Affaire Saint Ange, Auzout, had conducted such related experiments on the "vacuum within the vacuum" in the spring and summer of 1648.) As Mesnard has shown in his careful review of

Périer's activities in this long interval as well as of the character of scientific correspondence in this period, however, Pascal can be reasonably exculpated of the charge of forgery leveled at him by Mathieu and others.[7]

In this connection, the relations with Descartes are the most controversial. In his letters to Carcavy, Descartes' formulation of the question leaves much room to suppose that the idea for the experiment at different altitudes may as well have been his own as Pascal's.[8] Having asked Carcavy for a report on the experiment, Descartes goes on to say,

> I have the right to expect that from him rather than you, because it is I who recommended, two years ago, that he conduct this experiment, and assured him that, although I would not do it, I had no doubts about its success. But, because he is a friend of R [Roberval], who professes not to be mine, and because I have seen that he has tried to attack my subtle matter in a certain text of two or three pages, I have cause to believe that he is following the passions of his friend.

> I had a certain interest in knowing of it [the experiment], since it is I who had asked him two years ago to do it, and I had assured him of its success as being entirely in keeping with my Principles, without which he would not have had any reason to think about it, because he was of the opposite opinion. And because he has before this sent me a short text, in which he described his first experiments on the vacuum and promised to refute my subtle matter, if you see him, I would be put at my ease if he were to know that I am still waiting for this refutation, and that I will take it in good spirit, as I always have taken objections made to me without calumny.

The redundancy of this second letter to the same correspondent suggests that the usually urbane Descartes is himself feeling some of the pique that one associates with Pascal.

Descartes' pique seems more related to Pascal's refutation of his *Principles* than to the experiment as such. With no record of the occasion on which the two scientists first discussed the experiment, it is impossible to determine which of the two proposed the experiment. Given Pascal's knowledge of the mountainous region around Clermont, it is not hard to conceive that he may well have suggested to the older scientist that he was thinking of a further experiment, one testing the vacuum at different altitudes, and that the older scientist saw in this proposal the possibility of proving his own principle of the subtle matter contained in the apparent vacuum. Somewhat tenuously linked with the experiment itself in Descartes' first letter, his preoccupation with this principle becomes necessarily linked with the experiment in his second: "and I had assured him of its success as being entirely in keeping with my Principles." This restrictive participial phrase shows where the argument between the two scientists lay, and it is on this linkage of Cartesian principle and Pascalian experiment that the younger scientist was of an "opposite opinion." It is this reading of the relation between principle and experiment that explains the antecedents of the "which" and the "it" in the seemingly parenthetical clause: "without which he would not have had any reason to think about it." The "which" refers to the *assurance* of the connection between principle and experiment; the "it" refers to the *connection* itself. As Mesnard notes, neither Descartes nor any other reputable scientist of the day denied Pascal's priority in the conception of the experiment. Pascal himself does not contest Descartes' advice on conducting the experiment. This does not necessarily mean, however, that he acknowledges Descartes' priority in the conception of the experiment. Pascal would not have seen that priority in Descartes' claim; rather, he would have understood that Descartes was clinging to his claim that the experiment would validate his own theory of the subtle matter. Pascal does not reply to this claim either. Perhaps the death of Descartes in early February of the following year explains this lacuna. Even had Pascal known of Descartes' reflections soon after the letter of August 1649 to Carcavy, a lapse of six months for either a direct or indirect reply to Descartes would not have been exceptional in this kind of exchange in the period. Had he learned of it after Descartes' death, his silence on the matter might be expected as a gesture of simple decency. On the other hand, it is as likely that, in Pascal's view, he had sufficiently replied to all those (including Descartes) who would have filled the vacuum whose existence he had demonstrated with their own matter, subtle or otherwise.

One might consider his reply in the matter to still another Jesuit in July 1651 as his ultimate reply to Descartes. The reply is itself somewhat indirect. In late June of that year, the Jesuit in question, Father Médaille, had presented a thesis on the vacuum in which, without naming him directly, he had attacked Pascal even more fundamentally than his first Jesuit adversary, Father Noël: he claimed that Pascal had claimed for himself Torricelli's original experiment and results on the vacuum. The offended scientist decided to reply to M. Ribeyre, an official of the court at Clermont, to whom the thesis had been dedicated. Pascal's tone is peremptory and barely civil as he defends his procedure of writing to the dedicatee rather than the author:

> I do not conceal from you, Sir, that I was marvelously surprised to learn that this father, whom I do not have the honor of knowing, whose name I do not know, whom I have no recollection of ever having even seen, with whom I have nothing at all in common, neither directly nor indirectly, nine or ten months after leaving the province, while I am at a hundred leagues distant, and when I think of nothing less, should have chosen me for the subject of his discourse.
>
> I know that these kinds of contentions are of so little importance that they do not merit serious reflexion, and yet, Sir, if you take the trouble to consider all the circumstances of this procedure, of which I do not explain the detail, you will undoubtedly judge that it is capable of arousing some resentment. For I presume that it is difficult for those who were present at this act [the public defense of the thesis] to have refused to believe a matter of fact, enunciated publicly, composed by a Jesuit father whom one cannot suspect of animosity toward me. All these particulars render this supposition quite believable. But inasmuch as I would be very displeased if you, Sir, whom I particularly honor, had this thought of me, I address myself to you rather than to any other, in order to clarify the truth, for two reasons:
>
> The first for the very respect that I bear you; the other, because you have been the protector of this act in that it has been dedicated to you, and that therein it is up to you, Sir, to suppress the purpose of those who have undertaken to do harm to the truth.[9]

The dedicatee bears the brunt of Pascal's scorn. Nor does the touchy young savant spare the author himself totally from scorn. Reviewing at some length his earlier published attribution of the initial experiment to Torricelli, Pascal derisively notes Father Médaille's ignorance of this attribution: "I believe this good father from Montferrand is the only one among the curious of all Europe who had no knowledge of it. I do not know by what misfortune, unless it be that he flees from the commerce and communication of scientists, for reasons that I do not penetrate." But the good Jesuit is curiously secondary to Pascal's purpose of self-justification here, a purpose that, as many scholars have noted, leads him into the most serious errors of truth on the related experiments of Magni in Poland and on the role of Pascal's friend and fellow scientist, Roberval, in relation to Magni's experiments. Pascal's explanations to Ribeyre notwithstanding, Magni had conducted his experiments without knowing of Pascal's; Roberval had *not* mentioned Pascal's work in his exchanges with Magni; Magni had replied to Roberval's letter, the very one in which Pascal erroneously claims that his own work had been mentioned. In the very act of accusing Médaille and his supporters of bad scholarship Pascal does some bad scholarship of his own. Mesnard sympathetically observes that, without fully excusing Pascal, one should understand the circumstances that led him into this error: Pascal's illness at the time, which prevented him from keeping up with scientific publications; delays in the publication of his own works, which would explain why Magni would not have known of them as Pascal presumes he did and should have; and so on.

Yet, in reading Pascal's stinging prose one understands more than the historical circumstances that led him into error. One understands as well the intense self-regard that blinded him to the need for scholarly withdrawal. One also suspects that the Jesuits began to loom in his mind as the particular exponents of the authoritarianism he had so lucidly denounced as unsientific in the Preface to the *Treatise on the Vacuum* he had published the year before (1651). Nor are these two motives unrelated: as he concludes this first letter to Ribeyre, one wonders if his self-regard has not become so wedded to his animadversion toward the Jesuits that he himself illustrates the invasion of the intelligence by the "corrupted will" that he would explicate years later in his treatise on the "art of persuasion." As we know, only a year earlier in the Preface to the *Treatise on the Vacuum,* he had reiterated the position he had taken in his debate with Noël on the same subject: the need to separate matters of scientific truth from matters of divine truth.

Now, however, as he concludes his letter to Ribeyre, he calls on this public official to find out from the Jesuit who has spread false impressions of him the grounds of his accusations, for

> it is indubitable, either that it is the effect of the report of certain persons he believed worthy of belief, or it is the work of his own mind.
>
> If it is the first, I implore you, Sir, to have the goodness toward this good father to redemonstrate to him the importance of the lightness of his belief in others.

And if it is the second, I pray God from this moment to forgive him this offense, and I pray Him in the same sincerity that I forgive him it myself; and I implore all those who witnessed it, and yourself, Sir, to forgive him it equally.

Like his father in the latter's justification of the son's scientific work, so the son here crosses the boundary between the scientific and the religious. Pascal implies that Father Médaille has *lied* about him and thus committed an offense against both morality and divine justice. In this respect, Pascal takes the same stand as his father in justifying his son before Noël's accusations of falsification by Pascal. What is most striking is the alacrity with which Pascal shifts from one order to the other, from the order of mind to the order of heart. The shift is unwarranted by the very terms not only of Pascal's Preface of a year earlier but, by the terms of the alternative motives he attributes to the Jesuit author. Had the Jesuit learned these false impressions from others, Pascal sees him guilty of credulity and naïveté, faults of the order of mind. Had he learned them from himself, as Pascal alternately suggests, one wonders why Pascal would not at most have accused him of weakness of mind, a bad reading or an insufficient reading by the Jesuit of the evidence available to him as a scholar. Pascal speaks of praying to God to forgive the presumably ill-willed accuser, adding his own prayer that he be able to forgive him as well, that all those involved be capable of the same forgiveness. Pascal seems not only to patronize the Jesuit and (in Pascal's eyes) Ribeyre and the other cohorts but to patronize God himself. It is God who is on my side, he seems to say—not: I am on God's side. This slippage between the orders in Pascal's self-defense was implicit in the very act of writing to Ribeyre rather than to the Jesuit.

If, in this near final moment of his letter, Pascal slips from the order of mind to the order of the heart, in the very act of writing to a public official on a scientific matter Pascal shifts from the order of mind to the order of the flesh. Ribeyre is, to use a term from the famous *pensée* on the three orders, a "captain of the earth." True, the Jesuit himself had executed this shift in his very dedication of a scientific writing to a public official. Thus, it might be argued, Pascal takes the same ground only to protest the procedure. In doing so, however, he does not protest the procedure, the confusion of realms. Instead, he enjoins the public official to act on *his* behalf in the relation between the separate realms of discourse and being.

The confusion is indeed understandable: it is his own wounded heart that leads him to this confusion of the orders, his own *moi* that he has not yet found sufficiently hateful to move him beyond the concern with precedence and achievement in his relations with others. His invocation of the Divine, which might well have served both rhetorically and sincerely as his final word in this letter of self-defense, is not his last word. He goes on to establish his priority not only over Auzout and others who had worked on the vacuum in the mid-1640s, but over Torricelli himself! Not in the conception, to be sure, but in the execution of the conception and in the important new knowledge that emerged therefrom. The great Italian's conception, he tells Ribeyre, "was but a simple conjecture" that had to be tested as he, Pascal, had tested it and thus: "It is true, Sir, and I say it to you boldly, that this experiment is my invention; and moreover, I can say that the new knowledge that it has revealed to us is entirely from me." Having promised to outline the "very beautiful and very useful consequences" in a forthcoming treatise on the subject, he continues:

> And in this detail, one will find exactly and separately what is of Galileo's invention, what is of the great Torricelli, and what is of my own. And finally it will appear by what degrees one has arrived at the knowledge we now have on this subject, and that this last experiment on the Puy du Dôme constitutes the last of these degrees.
>
> And as I am sure that Galileo and Torricelli would have been delighted to learn in their time that one had gone beyond the knowledge that they had, I protest to you, Sir, that I will never have greater joy than in seeing that some one goes beyond that which I have given.

That the some one in question has not yet arrived only underscores the imperative of superiority over Galileo and Torricelli that Pascal manifests here. The antagonist takes on not only his contemporary scientific adversaries (Noël, Magni, Médaille, perhaps Descartes in this passage) and their public cohorts (Ribeyre), he also takes on his scientific forebears.

The fierce pride of Pascal shows through even in his reply to Ribeyre's embarrassed answer to his first letter. Ribeyre assures Pascal of the innocence of Médaille's actions, based as these were on a certain ineptitude and ignorance. As for his own role in the matter, his explanations are somewhat flimsy and border on self-contradiction. On the one hand, in the thesis itself, he sees the thinly veiled allusion to Pascal (the experimenter of Normandy and Auvergne who wanted to take credit for Torricelli's work) as containing nothing offensive, to be attributed only to "an emulation excusable among scientists."[10] On the other hand, he claims that, in the preamble, he did not observe that Médaille accused Pascal of dubious novelty or of wishing to take credit for the inventions of others. Moreover, at the defense of the thesis itself, neither he nor other witnesses, with whom he had since checked, could see Médaille as personally attacking Pascal. Surrounded by frequent and obsequious protestations of his own respect for Pascal's genius, Ribeyre's explanations were sufficiently satisfactory for Pascal to express his regret at the embarrassment his own public discussion of the affair had caused Ribeyre. Nevertheless, he does not relent even on this occasion to reiterate the lesson in morality he had given Ribeyre in his first letter. Interestingly, he reminds Ribeyre that the need to give such lessons is itself a lesson—a "duty"—he had learned from his father.

> On this basis, I urge you, Sir, to consider, as far as it concerns me, that among all those who practice the profession of letters, it is no less a crime to attribute to oneself a foreign invention than in civil society to usurp the possessions of another; and although no one is obliged to be learned any more than to be rich, no one is dispensed from being sincere: so that the reproach of ignorance, no more than that of indigence, is in no way injurious except to the one who proffers it; but the reproach of larceny is of such a kind that a man of honor must not suffer the accusation without exposing himself to the peril that his silence serve as grounds for conviction.[11]

His anger calmed to a certain extent, Pascal no longer confuses the orders of mind and heart, of reason and faith. His comparisons still suggest some crossing over between the orders of flesh (the possessions of others) and of mind (the inventions of the researcher), but the larceny in both cases is left at the level of human rather than divine morality. Pascal draws back from the temptation, born of wounded pride and a need to prevail, to shape the world "in God"—God the Father.

As the occasion of this exchange brings out, the figure of the father is crucial to Pascal. His involvement of his own father in this scientific quarrel as in the quarrel with Noël is paramount. It is an involvement at once theological and psychological. We remember that the first conversion of the Pascal family began with the conversion of the father after his accident in the winter of 1646, a conversion that returned the members of the family to a faith nurtured in the fathers of the Church, particularly Augustine. As many scholars have noted, Pascal's separation of the sacred and profane in his various scientific writings up to this time (notably, the Preface to the *Treatise on the Vacuum*, 1651), is anchored in Augustinian doctrines. These doctrines undoubtedly informed the "example and instruction," as he puts it to Ribeyre in his second letter, which he had gotten from his father as the grounds for his dutiful defense of his own scientific inventions. In some respects, the son was more rigorous than the father in the application of these doctrines. Thus, it was he who enjoined Noël not to mix the religious with the scientific, whereas the father raised the question of scientific ethics to the level of religious ethics. The son is *plus royaliste que le roi,* more paternal or patristic than the father. The pattern is a familiar one in the period: one thinks of Corneille's Rodrigue and Chimène implementing the code of the fathers more rigorously than all father figures of *Le Cid,* including the king. Even as Pascal rejoins his father, invoking his lessons in morality for Ribeyre, one notes how the son, his anger calmed, does not go so far as his father might have by anchoring the duty in divine example or ordinance.

Pascal's deference to authority in the religious domain as in all those where reason did not prevail reflects the strong influence of the dominant father figure, Etienne Pascal. One of these domains is the personal and the familial. In the Pascal household the father was the central figure. From the death of their mother in 1626, the father had raised the three small children (Gilberte six, Blaise three, Jacqueline an infant at the time). His education of his son in particular is legendary. One can imagine the interior drama of the brilliant child's early years: formed by his father in the "things of the mind" where the father himself excelled, the extraordinarily gifted and, as Gilberte indicates, temperamental boy may have been torn by, on the one hand, his love and respect for his father and, on the other, his awareness of his own superiority. This is even more likely because one of the lessons the father gave the emerging young scientist was the lesson in the independence of science from authority. Growing up in the close presence of this unusually powerful father, the young man may have constantly felt the need to establish his own identity, to assert the distinguishing marks of his own contributions. This is perhaps the root of his frequent insistence, in both scientific and theological matters, on the advancement he has made over others: "And in this detail, one will find exactly and separately what is of Galileo's invention, what is of the great Torricelli, and what is of my own" (first letter to Ribeyre). Yet, even as he asserts his own identity, he does so additively, for he cannot totally reject the father (or fathers) whom he loves, even when they are surrogates, as in the case of his scientific forebears: Galileo, Torricelli, and, in his role as fellow scientist, Pascal's real father, Etienne Pascal. The tension will not be resolved even partially until his later engagements with the Jesuit fathers and their adversaries, in Pascal's eyes, the Church fathers, in the religious controversies following his second conversion.

2

THE
ADVERSARIAL
BELIEVER
AND HIS
FAMILY

DURING PASCAL'S EARLY YEARS, except for the Affaire Saint Ange, religion was essentially a private matter and, still more essentially, a family matter. If the closeness of the Pascal family can be felt in the father's guidance and, at times, intervention in the formation and progress of his son's scientific career, it can be felt even more strongly in the formation and progress of the religious "career" of all of his children. The efficient cause of the first conversion of his children, Etienne Pascal was, until his death in September 1651, the *continuing* cause of their faith, particularly in the case of his son. From the son's first reflections on the family's religious convictions in a letter to Gilberte of January 26, 1648, composed on behalf of himself and Jacqueline, to his last on the subject in a letter to Gilberte of October 17, 1651, also composed on behalf of himself and Jacqueline, one senses the dependency of the son on the father's spiritual guidance.

Yet, as in science, so in religion: the filial dependency leaves much room for self-assertion and self-distinction. Thus, writing to Gilberte in late January 1648 to rejoice with her in her renewal of faith (she too we might say had a second conversion) Pascal would add to what both the Heavenly Father and the earthly father had taught him.

> I beg you to believe that although I have not written to you, there has not been an hour in which you have not been with me, and when I have not made a wish for the continuation of the great plan that God has inspired in you. I felt a new joy at receiving all your letters testifying to it, and I have been delighted to see its continuation without your having had any news from us. That made me acknowledge that it had a more than human support, since it did not have need of human

supports to be maintained. I would wish nevertheless to contribute something to it, but I have none of the things necessary to this end. My [physical] weakness is so great that, if I undertook it, I would be acting out of temerity rather than charity, and I would have cause to fear for the two of us the misfortune whereby one blind person leads another.[1]

"I would wish nevertheless to contribute something to it," that is, to the plan that God had inspired in his sister to lead a more saintly life. He would make this addition to God's plan even though he has just acknowledged that the plan had no need of human support to be maintained. Here again, this time in the religious domain, is the tension between authority and self that characterizes Pascal's relations with his confrères in the scientific domain. The authority in question on this occasion is ultimately God, of course. That authority is not without a mediate expression with whom the tension becomes overt. If the occasion of the letter is Gilberte's renewal of faith, the real subject of the letter, as he tells her in the eighth line of the printed text, is his encounter with Antoine de Rebours at Port Royal, where Rebours served as director of the women religious.

The encounter shook him. Indeed, as he returns to the subject after the remarks on her faith just quoted, it becomes clear that even more than his illness this encounter provides the reasons for which he feels his inability to add something to God's plan for his sister. From the encounter, he tells her, he brought back only feelings of confusion and trouble for himself, feelings "that only God can calm and on which I shall work." As he adds this human effort to what appears to be God's effort ("only God"), we might sense the familiar pattern of self-assertion once more. As he repeats and explains the phrase, however, we understand that he means he must get away from the occasions that only increase rather than dissipate his confusion. Even this crisis with its lesson of the utter surrender of self shows Pascal clinging to a human reliance on self and family that compromises the surrender of self in and to God.

Thus, as he tells Gilberte, he will write to her a bit about the matter of his meeting with Rebours. A strict adept of Saint Cyran, Rebours seems to have anticipated for Pascal on this occasion the role to be played by his interlocutor in a more famous encounter at Port Royal, Isaac de Sacy. Like him, Rebours seems to have sensed in this fiery partisan of the beleagured partisans of Jansen a too great readiness to oppose their adversaries with the very weapon considered by Jansenists the root of all evil, human reason. Pascal reports that he had told Rebours "with my usual frankness and naïveté" that he had read the books of both sides and that this was sufficient for Rebours to understand that "we were of their opinion." *We:* possibly the pronoun is editorial, but given the familial context of the letter, it probably refers to himself and Jacqueline and more probably the entire Pascal family. *Their:* Rebours and the Jansenists, which produced joy in Rebours, Pascal notes. But then, providing the grounds for the difficulties he had on the occasion, Pascal reports that he said he "thought that one could, following the very principles of common sense, show many of the things that the adversaries say are contrary to it, and that reasoning, well conducted, led to believing them, although they must be believed without the help of reasoning."

This passage is crucial for an understanding of the theological position of Pascal as the adversary who would write the first sixteen *Provincial Letters.* The passage shows the same pairing of two orders, mind and heart, in a relation suggesting their fusion while only concessively and secondarily asserting their separateness ("although they must be believed without the help of reasoning"). Moreover, in this particular formulation, the emphasis with respect to mind and heart or, in psychological terms, authority and self, has shifted. In the beginning of the letter, as he rejoiced with Gilberte on her renewal of faith, he placed in primary position the order of the heart, God's action on his sister that had no need of human support. There, his own desire to "contribute something to the plan" was supplemental: "I would wish nevertheless to contribute." With Rebours he stresses the order of mind and adds, with the concessive clause at the end ("although . . ."), the order of heart as if it were supplemental to the workings of human reasoning.

Rebours, Pascal reports to his sister, found or seemed to have found in Pascal's discourse a "principle of vanity and of confidence in reasoning." I say "found or seemed to have found" because Pascal formulates this possible explanation of his own position in general terms: "But, as you know that all actions can proceed from two sources, and that this discourse could have proceeded from a principle of . . . ." For Rebours, the troubled correspondent tells his sister, "this suspicion, which was augmented by the knowledge he had of my study of geometry, sufficed for him to find this discourse strange, and he indicated so by a response so full of humility and modesty that it would have undoubtedly confounded the pride he wished to refute." It would appear that the "suspicion" is more explicit on Pascal's part than on his interlocutor's. On the occasion, as in reporting it, Pascal shows himself to have been very perceptive of human psychology. He senses in Rebours' response that his interlocutor would show the vanity of pride and reason by refusing to engage Pascal in reasoning. Yet, he also shows that Rebours was as astute a judge of human psychology and perhaps even more astute in matters of theology. "I nevertheless tried," Pascal continues, "to make him see my motive, but my justification increased his doubt and he took my excuses for obstinacy. I admit that his discourse was so beautiful that, if I had believed myself to be in the state he imagined, it would have withdrawn me from it; but as I did not think myself in that sickness, I opposed the remedy he offered me. He fortified it all the more that I seemed to flee it, because he took my refusal for a hardening on my part, and the more he strove to continue, the more my thanks testified that I did not consider it necessary." Pascal did not sense during the conversation, any more than he does in his report of it to his sister, that he may have been protesting too much, just as he was to continue to protest in all of the other conversations that followed. The "misunderstanding," he writes, failed to be cleared up. With characteristic stubbornness Pascal sought to prevail in his personal exchanges with Rebours. The *libido dominandi* he was later to condemn in the *Thoughts* had its hold on him.

His sister Jacqueline has provided the occasion for him to pursue his compulsion to distinguish himself beyond what others have contributed. For all the "trouble and confusion" that the encounter with Rebours created for him, as the year wore on he may even have formally sought to justify himself at least in his own eyes in writing the first two of those rarely read Pascalian texts known as the *Writings on Grace*. Four in number, these texts have usually been assigned to the two-year period after his second conversion in late November 1654 and usually after the first few *Provincial Letters* (early 1656). As Jan Miel has suggested, however, this assignment, based on the largely scholarly character of extensive references to the parties of the disputes in the letters, resists certain circumstantial and internal evidence of the *Writings on Grace*.[2] Like so many others, these texts came to light long after Pascal's death, but, beyond their tone and style, their authenticity is guaranteed by Pascal's frequent "executor" in such matters, his nephew Louis Périer, who deposited the original manuscripts at the Library of Saint Germain des Prés as works by his uncle.

As Miel says, the differences in form among the four basic texts, plus certain internal allusions and our knowledge of Pascal's activities and preoccupations even since his first conversion argue for an earlier dating of some of these texts. Noting, for example, that the *Second Writing* is a simple exposé of the Augustinian doctrine, with the adepts of the liberal Spanish Jesuit, Louis Molina (1535–1600) identified, in a formulation used in Jansen's *Augustinus,* as "the rest of the Pelagians," Miel would place it as early as 1647. A not very sophisticated exposition of the theological differences among Calvinists, Molinists, and Augustinians, the text might have been intended, Miel says, for someone not well acquainted with but concerned about theological disputes, perhaps Jacqueline or Gilberte. Similarly, the first portion of the *First Writing*—matter of fact, direct, and not too theologically ambitious in its continuation of the same tripartite subject—would be written at the same time or perhaps slightly later. The more ambitious second portion, a capsule history of the doctrine of grace from the early Church fathers to the seventeenth century, would belong later, perhaps 1656–1658. The *Third Writing* is obviously a letter, replying to an as yet unidentified correspondent, concerning a matter very much to the fore in the battle of the *Provincial Letters:* the meaning of the Council of Trent's article that "The commandments are not impossible to the just." The great Pascal editor, Jean Mesnard, has suggested that, given the subject and the timing and knowing of Pascal's assumption of the "spiritual direction" of his noble patron, the Duc de Roannez, the letter is probably written to the penitent patron after the battle of the *Provincial Letters* had begun. Miel suggests that the letter might have then shown the same awareness of that battle apparent in Pascal's letters of the time to the other Roannez in his life, Charlotte. Therefore the *Third Writing* and the epistolary portion of the *Fourth Writing* that so obviously belongs to it in form and content might well be in 1655, before the *Provincial Letters.* The *Fourth Writing,* except for the epistolary portion, Miel would put in 1655, given its linguistic approach to the disputes on grace, an approach that, as Mesnard has noted, most likely took place in that year.

Miel's earlier dating of the *Second Writing* seems to me as cogent as that of the *First Writing.* I would support Miel by developing one of his clues. In discussing the first portion of the *First Writing,* Miel suggests that its "method . . . could suggest a rapprochement with the 'raisonnement bien conduit' [well-conducted reasoning] that Pascal mentioned to M. Rebours as applying to these questions in 1648, or to a similar attitude as expressed to Nicole, presumably around 1656–58." The phrase from Pascal's letter to Gilberte of January 26, 1648, falls in a final clause to an earlier one that is apposite: "one could, following the very principles of *common sense,* show many of the things that the adversaries say are contrary to it" (my italics). The textual closeness to the *second* portion of the *First Writing on Grace* is striking. Having reviewed the three "proponents," Pascal writes,

> And although it is not necessary to adduce other proofs of the truth and the falsity of these opinions, we shall not fail to respond to the passages of the Scriptures that the one and the other errants explain according to their sense, and which seem to favor them. And, although common sense must not enter into competition with a matter of faith, we shall not fail to answer the objections of the one and the other. And finally we shall show how this doctrine is in conformity with common sense itself.

Certain tonal homologies with the letter of January 26, 1648, are equally striking: in spite of objections, Pascal will not "fail to answer the objections." Indeed, twice the phrase "we shall not fail to" comes up in this short passage and the English "fail to" itself fails to render the defensive tone of the French: "nous ne laisserons pas" (literally, in English: "we shall not leave from," which, however awkwardly, renders the "nevertheless" implied in the French formulation).

In the context of the *First Writing,* the first use of this formulation is obviously a defensive parrying at the Molinists and Calvinists. But I suggest that the second is written with Rebours in mind. As in the letter of January 26, Pascal concedes that faith has no need of common sense and well-conducted reason. The strength of the second formulation, however, suggests that Pascal is demonstrating what Rebours would not heed. Moreover, the more scholarly character of the second portion of the *First Writing* suggests that Pascal wants to enunciate the fact (noted generally to Rebours and to Gilberte in reporting the conversation) that he had read the books of both sides. Miel has pertinently noted that, so far, none of the references in all four of the *Writings on Grace* has been found to be later than 1649. Further in this connection, one of the references that Pascal makes in the second portion of the *First Writing* is to Florent Conrius "in his book published fairly recently entitled *Peregrinus Hiericontinus.*" Pascal is obviously referring to the edition of that work published in 1641. I suggest that "fairly recently" supports Miel's close connection in time of composition between not only the *Second Writing* and the first portion of the *First Writing* but of both *Writings* in their entirety. Pascal might have approached the meetings with Rebours confident of his ground precisely for having developed his rationalistic yet, in his eyes, pious views in the short treatises of the *Second Writing* and the first portion of the *First.* These may well have been undertaken, as Miel suggests, for one of his sisters.

If Miel is right, I would say for Jacqueline, because in Pascal's letter of January 26, 1648, to his other sister he makes no mention of her knowledge of his rationalistic approach to the matter. He reports it in all its freshness for her. He may have intended it for Gilberte but not yet sent these texts to her, but then one would expect him to have mentioned them or even drawn on them to some extent in defense of himself. But this line of conjecture would affect even the choice of Jacqueline as the intended reader of his texts, had they been written prior to the encounter with Rebours. It is not difficult to imagine Pascal instructing his younger sister-secretary in his way of looking at matters of faith. (After his conversion and his "submission" to his spiritual director, M. de Sacy, Gilberte would write to him, wondering how the director was taking to his lively new directee.) But then, even if they were written down for Jacqueline, she, too, may not yet have read the intended lessons by her brother. In this case, though, he should have mentioned the supposed composition for the very Jacqueline whom he accompanied to the fatal encounter with Rebours or at least mentioned the similar lessons he would have given her orally. In the face of these circumstances and in light of the internal evidence, I tentatively suggest that not only the second portion of the *First Writing* but perhaps the entire *First* and *Second Writings* may have been written after the encounter with Rebours. They were the fruit of the "work" on the questions he had promised to do in his letter to Gilberte in January 1648.[3]

The *First* and *Second Writings on Grace* are important for the light they shed both on the fundamental consistency of Pascal's theological views throughout his life and on the personal tensions linked to that theology throughout that life. As the passage on common sense shows,

Pascal sees his theological position here as centrist, occupying the ground, as he says later, in which the truth is ordinarily to be found. Following Augustine, he situates himself between, on the one hand, the Molinists (*First Writing*) and Pelagians (*Second Writing*) and, on the other, Calvinists (both *Writings*). He raises several thorny theological problems, all of them centering around the relation between God's foreordaining will and man's "free will" as it bears on the salvation of the individual soul:

> It is a question of knowing if God, submitting to himself the wills of men, had an absolute will to save some and to damn others; and if, as a consequence of this decree, he inclines to the good the wills of the elect, and to evil those of the reproved, to make them conform thus one and the other to the absolute will that he has to save them or to condemn them.
>
> Or if, submitting to the free will of men the use of his graces, he has foreseen in what way the one and the other would make use thereof, and, following their wills he has formed that will of their salvation or their condemnation.[4]

He then briefly outlines the Calvinist position as a radical divine foreordination, at the creation, of some men to eternal salvation and some to eternal damnation, with God not only making but permitting Adam and all men through him to sin, sending Jesus Christ to redeem only those whom God had already designated for salvation, and abandoning and depriving of charity those whom he had already designated for damnation. Pascal characterizes this opinion as "frightening . . . injurious to God and insupportable to men." He outlines the opposite position of the Molinists as a conditional divine foreordination to save generally all men, with Christ being incarnated to redeem all men without exception and, his grace being given to all, with their will to make good or bad use of those graces being independent of God's will such that God, having foreseen from all eternity the good or bad use men would make thereof through free will, without the aid of a discerning grace, saves those who make good use and damns those who make bad use of these graces inasmuch as he had no absolute will to save nor to damn any man. Refraining from criticism of this opinion, he simply notes that its effect is the opposite of the Calvinist one: it flatters the common sense that the other wounds by rendering it master of its salvation or damnation, depriving God of absolute will.

He then (also briefly, but still at more than twice the length for each of the others) gives the position of the "disciples of Saint Augustine" as a divine foreordination that takes into account the two "states of human nature": the first "in Adam" of man coming from the hands of God healthy, without stain (of sin, obviously), just and righteous; the second in which man's nature has been "reduced by the sin and revolt of the first man, and by which it has become soiled, abominable, and detestable in the eyes of God." Acknowledging these two states, the disciples of Augustine form two different sentiments concerning the will of God in relation to the salvation of men. For the state of innocence, God has a general and conditional will to save all men provided they wished it through the free will aided by the sufficient graces he gave them for their salvation, but which did not infallibly determine them to persevere in the good. For the state of sin and revolt, the disciples of Saint Augustine maintain that God willed absolutely, out of a mercy at once pure and gratuitous, that he wished to save a part of the mass of men, all of whom had merited damnation through Adam's sin, and condemn the rest. To this end God sent Jesus Christ to save absolutely and by very efficacious means those he had chosen and predestined from this mass, but nevertheless some of those who are not predestined do not fail to be called for the good of the elect and thus to participate in the Redemption of Jesus Christ, that it is the fault of these people if they do not persevere, as they could if they wished, but, because they are not numbered among the elect, God does not give them the graces that are efficacious and without which they would never so wish in effect; that all the men in the world are obliged to believe, but with a belief mingled with fear and not accompanied by certitude that they are among the small number of elect whom Jesus Christ wants to save and that they are obliged never to judge whether any man on the earth, however wicked or impious he be, for so long as he has a moment of life, is or is not one of the predestined, leaving in the impenetrable secret of God the discernment of the elect among the reproved.

I have compressed all three positions as outlined by Pascal, but have rendered more fully and as literally as possible the text on the disciples of Augustine. I have done so to indicate that there is hardly a motif of Pascal's religious and moral thought, particularly in relation to the *Provincial Letters* and the projected *Apology for the Christian Religion,* not already implicit when not explicit in the remarkable overview of that position he sketches here with brilliant, if tendentious, concision. The remainder of these two *Writings on Grace* (particularly the *First*, but with important sections of the *Second*) like so many of his later writings, develops with an ever greater honing the motifs he posits here.

As he counsels against the danger and the theological fault of judging even the most impious of men as condemned to eternal damnation, Pascal is laying the grounds for later attacks on the Calvinists' and others' emphasis on good works as the sign of salvation. He is also laying the grounds for the wager itself: the bettor will have to make his bet precisely on the awareness that his "impious life" is irrelevant in the game of chance that Pascal proposes to him, and it is so precisely because God is secret or, in the term he will later use, hidden. God is nonetheless desirable because of that concealment; the key terms of the motif of the "eternity of life of happiness" that could be the bettor's gain, against the "foul pleasures" of this life, his stake if he bets, are also anticipated in these connected first two *Writings on Grace*. In the *Second*, as he turns to the question of the two states of human nature — the one before, the other after the fall of Adam — he writes,

> This sin having passed from Adam to all his posterity, which was corrupted in him like a fruit coming from a bad seed, all men coming from Adam are born in ignorance, in concupiscence, guilty of the sin of Adam and worthy of eternal death.
>
> Free will has remained flexible to good and evil; but with this difference, that whereas in Adam it had no tickling movement toward evil, and it sufficed for him to know that good to be able to bring himself to it, now it has such a powerful suavity and a delectation in evil through concupiscence that infallibly it brings itself as to its [highest] good, and it chooses it voluntarily and very freely and with joy as the object where it feels beatitude.[5]

Thus,

> To save his elect God sent Jesus Christ to satisfy his justice, and to merit by his mercy the grace of Redemption, medicinal grace, the grace of Jesus Christ, which is nothing more than a suavity and a delectation in the law of God, spread in the heart by the Holy Spirit, which, not only equaling, but, more, surpassing the concupiscence of the flesh, fills the will with a greater delectation in the good than concupiscence offers it in evil, and thus, the free will, charmed by the sweetnesses and the pleasures that the Holy Spirit inspires in it, more

than by the attractions of sin, infallibly chooses itself the law of God for this sole reason that it finds therein more satisfaction and that it feels there its beatitude and felicity.

This is the lesson of the second half of the projected *Apology*: man's felicity in God. Pascal expresses the philosophical oneness with Augustine that many recent critics have stressed (particularly Sellier and Miel). Against a long tradition, expressed most fully in Duns Scotus in the Middle Ages but with its antecedents in Gnosticism and other Hellenized movements of the early Church, Pascal rejects the idea of a self-sufficient free will, of a will operating in a vacuum, as it were. For Pascal, man's will abhors a vacuum and it does so both before and after the Fall. In both states, free will is flexible, capable of choosing either good or evil, but in each state it chooses that which is its logical and natural goal (that is, the goal appropriate to the state). In this Augustinian/Pascalian conception pleasure is a principle rather than an effect, a function rather than an object, a process rather than a result. God is not a pleasure any more than the delights of the flesh are a pleasure; each is, rather, the effect, the object, the result appropriate in the separate (and separated) states Pascal describes. He would develop this notion more fully in the *Third* and *Fourth Writings*. The later development of this motif is consistent with the premises of its presentation here: both before the Fall and after, man has a will that chooses—choice is its function by definition—an object other than itself to express itself; before the Fall, God; after the Fall, the flesh. Man is concupiscent in both states, a slave in both as Pascal will later say. The concupiscence of the fallen state may be described as a kind of negative grace; its seemingly invincible magnetism can be overcome only by the more powerful magnetism of the special grace that God sends to some men in the fallen state.

In the notion *some* men too, in the *First* and *Second Writing on Grace* of the late 1640s is the motif of election that will be the very battleground of the *Provincial Letters* and the problem demanding of Pascal all his ingenuity in the projected *Apology*. The occasion of these texts, Pascal's defense of the disciples of Saint Augustine against Pelagians, Molinists, and Calvinists, could not fail to raise this motif. Pascal treats it differently, however, and as he discusses the problem of perseverance in prayer (*First Writing*), already states the division of mankind into three basic types that he will restate in the *Thoughts*.

Both doctrinally and tonally, he does so less generously, though, less inclusively, and, ironically, less logically. He summarizes several "sentiments' of "the disciples of Saint Augustine" to counter the "contrary errors" of Molinists and Calvinists, noting that Augustine's disciples say "that, as to the state of innocence, God has had a general and unconditional will to save all men, provided they wish it by free will aided by sufficient graces that he gave them for their salvation, but which [graces] did not determine them infallibly to persevere in the good." These disciples, Pascal writes, further say that

> nevertheless some of those who are not predestined are nonetheless called for the good of the elect, and thus to participate in the Redemption of Jesus Christ. That is the fault of those [other] persons that they do not persevere; that they would be able to, if they wished, but because they are not of the number of the elect, God does not give them the efficacious graces without which they do not in effect wish it. And thus there are three sorts of men: the ones who never come to the faith; the others who come to it and who, not persevering in it, die in mortal sin; and the last who come to the faith and persevere in charity unto death. Jesus Christ did not have absolute will that the first receive any grace by his death, since they have not in effect received any.
>
> He has willed to redeem the second, he has given them graces that would have led them to salvation if they had used them well, but he did will to give them this singular grace of perseverance without which one never uses [the others] well.
>
> But for the last, Jesus Christ has willed their salvation absolutely, and he leads them to it by certain and infallible means.

Just as later in the *Apology,* the experimental tendency of Pascal's mind seems of crucial importance if we are not to be repulsed by the frightening rigor of this position. He is closer to predestinarianism here than he will ever be: God damns some to whom he has given initial graces, but *to whom he then refuses the special grace of perseverance.* These people also seem to "participate in the Redemption" for the "good of the elect." Cruel as the tenet on initial grace without further grace of perseverance may be, it does highlight the concrete, experimental, and historical cast of Pascal's mind. Unlike many of the "schoolmen" with whom he does battle in theology (even as he does in science at this time), Pascal is not concerned with the pure theoretical and logical consistency of his position; he is concerned with the interplay of position and historical, experiential situation.

The experimental cast of Pascal's rationalism comes to the fore in religion, then, as well as in science. If the tone and structure of his arguments with Saint Ange were anything like that of the first *Writings on Grace,* particularly the *First,* that hapless theologian must have felt he had come into a very fire of reason. If there is intellectual brilliance here, there is also anger. The anger at the Calvinists is vituperative, and it leads him to that excess of well-conducted reasoning and common sense that will lead many to admire the *Thoughts* for their intelligence and penetration but regret their harshness and pity and to belabor their author for not seeing the inappropriateness of such fragments as the wager. I have already noted that, having summarized the positions of his two opponents, Pascal makes no subjective commentary on the Molinists but describes the Calvinists as "frightening . . . injurious to God and insupportable to men." When he returns to the separate adversaries after his summary of the opinion of the disciples of Saint Augustine, he makes a subjective comment on each: "If the error of the Molinists affects [the Church], their submission consoles her, but the error the Calvinists, joined to their rebellion, makes her cry out to God: I have nourished children and they have scorned me." He goes on to speak favorably of the Molinists as people who can be reconciled to the Church (through the popes and the councils), who hold the tradition of the Church in veneration, who do not try to twist the words of the Scriptures and who follow the interpretations given by the crowd and series of the Church's holy doctors, popes, and councils. "As for the Calvinists," he continues, "their rebellion renders her inconsolable. She must act with them, equal to equal, and, in putting aside her authority, must use reason. She calls them all to her nevertheless, and she prepares herself to convince them each according to his own principles." The last sentence seems to embrace both Molinists and Calvinists, although it may be addressed to Calvinists alone. In either case, the "nevertheless" is interesting. If applied to both, it could mean that the Church will use both authority and reason, as appropriate to each: authority for the Molinists, reason for the Calvinists. If applied only to the Calvinists, the "nevertheless" may be read rather as "nonetheless" in the sense that reason is nonetheless effective as authority. In this case, Pascal would be the spokesman of reason for the Church.

Whatever the meaning of "nevertheless," what is striking is that this call to reason is framed with an emotionally charged series of

63 - womb b̄

(sometimes I contort
the psychology - 132

CURRENT ADDITIONAL BENEFIT

As a member of Bankard Club you can stop worrying about the safety of your credit cards by registering in the Credit Card Protection service. Using the handy registration form, you give the Club a list of all credit cards and account numbers–then you can relax. If your cards are ever lost or stolen, the Bankard Club will notify all the companies and new cards will be issued at once. You just call one toll-free number.

This valuable benefit alone normally costs $6.00 to $18.00 per year. You can get it as part of the Club by returning your application within 30 days.

words: the earlier *frightening, injurious, insupportable* and, here, *rebellion* (twice in a dozen lines), *cried out, nourished, scorned, inconsolable*. The treatment of Molinists is so gentle by comparison that Pascal might well have given them the honorific form of address that he reserves for those we might have expected him, by grammatical analogy, to call "the Augustinians"—the "disciples of Molina." The very intention of that honorific precludes such an appellation: *disciple* connotes the submissiveness and dependency that should characterize those whom he carefully denigrates by naming them after men who are not *saints*. Still, the Molinists do come off rather well here—they are not called "heretics" like the Calvinists—a rather ironic fact when one thinks of the vituperation the Pascal of the *Provincial Letters* would later visit upon these Jesuit worthies. It is clearly the Calvinists who receive the full lash of his reason.

He is not only angry but hurt and the motif of consolation is also central. The Calvinists are attacked principally for the unconsolable pain they bring the Church by their rebellion against authority. We have by now ample reason to understand Pascal's tension in this connection. The dutiful son of a father so dutiful to the Church is scandalized by the rebellion of the Calvinist children against the holy doctors and the popes and the councils. What is striking is that Pascal emphasizes this patritropic rebellion as part of an overarching rebellion against a mother figure: the Church.

The metaphor "mother Church" is a banal one in Catholic tradition, but it and other maternal or, for that matter, womanly metaphors are rare in Pascal. The *Thoughts*, largely a project of Christian apologetics, does not contain a single use of the term *mother Church*. (It does contain the scathing use of "mistress" [*maitresse*], of course, but not surprisingly that is a negative use of female gender.) Pascal not only uses the banal metaphor but he prolongs it at some length:

> Now, although it is a very sensitive displeasure to the Church to see herself torn by contrary errors that combat the holiest truths, and although she has cause to complain of both Molinists and Calvinists, she nevertheless recognizes that she receives fewer injuries from those who, wandering around in their errors, remain within her womb than from those who have separated themselves in order to raise altar against altar, without having either tenderness for her maternal voice, which calls to them, nor deference for her decisions, which condemn them.

The unusual development of this metaphor of the mother, the rarity of such metaphors and of mother figures in Pascal's work (the Mother of God is mentioned rather little), the fearful preoccupation with loss and conslation here—all this reminds us of the absence of a mother in most of Pascal's life.

His mother died when he was three years old. Marguerite Périer tells of the intense reactions of the small boy, during the brief time his mother was with him in this life, upon his seeing her close to his father. Jealous of his mother's love, like many another child whose parent dies, he may have felt betrayed—("abandoned" in the religious vocabulary he would cultivate) by his mother in her death. The love of the mother might then have become resentment and the other members of the family the recipients of this strong love/hate: the father the beneficiary of more positively expressed love; both sisters of an avatar of the love/hate felt for the mother who had abandoned him, because they were both women and thus reminders of the mother, but also of a resentment that they might deprive the boy of the love of the father on whom he now poured much of the love he had felt for the mother. The feelings toward Jacqueline may have been especially complex: resentment at her as the probable cause of his mother's death (the consequences of the birth of Jacqueline in the year before Antoinette Begon Pascal's death) and, later, jealousy of her for their father's attention to her. At the same time, as the last child of his beloved mother, Jacqueline may also have become for him a love object in the most sensual sense, and this would create a severe oedipal conflict with the father around the time of Jacqueline's desire to become a nun.

Here, the relevance of these considerations on Pascal's mother seems to me to be in the possible insight it gives us into the special zeal with which, all his life, he clung to authority, particularly parental authority. But he was not without some fascination with rebellion. It is interesting to underscore the irony concerning the Molinists. Later he would condemn the Jesuits precisely for thier reliance on Molina, a reliance that destroyed the authority of God to exalt that of man. He excoriates the Calvinists precisely for dissolving the Church, while he finds the Molinists' utter independence of God not too horrible because they do submit to the visible authority of the Church. Those who do not submit to visible authority, proclaiming in fact a God hidden in the abomination of the theory of radical predestination, he excoriates. What calls forth this particular wrath for one of the extremes? I suggest that the wrath is due to Pascal's fascination with the rebellion, with the rebels. His own rebellions have all thus far been quelled by himself. This self-immolation is made not out of a pious respect for authority as such but out of his fear that in rebelling he also risked the frustration of his deeper need for the stability, certitude, security, and constancy of the parental love whose fragility his mother's early death had so dramatically impressed upon him.

If this need comes out implicitly in the *First* and *Second Writings on Grace*, it comes out more clearly in the final frame of the letter of January 26, 1648, to Gilberte, which reports the crisis to which the *Writings on Grace* offer a conscious defense.[6] The main portion of the letter may show the same aggressive rationalism one finds in the *Writings*, but in its frames it shows a new side, a murmur of self-doubt. In the first frame, we have heard him speak of the confusion and trouble that the encounter had brought him. As he goes on in that frame to add that he had behaved with his "usual frankness and naïveté," we sense that the self-effacement is only apparent and that, beneath, there is a pride wounded by the fact that Rebours had not accepted him in this light. This observation on his innocence of approach is on a rhetorical and psychological par with the invocation of his father at the very outset of the report itself: "The first time that I saw M. de Rebours, I made myself known to him and I was received with all the civilities that one could wish for; they all belonged to my father, since I received them in his regard." (The formulation might suggest that he addresses the clause on his father to his correspondent rather than to Rebours, but the French indicates that he made the same remarks to his interlocutor). As with Ribeyre on the question of Médaille's attack on his scientific integrity, the tutelary image of the father is invoked as if to give warranty, perhaps even more than his own "frankness and naïveté," to the line of defense the son is about to undertake. Yet, again as on earlier occasions of the kind, the son strikes out on his own.

He does so perhaps to distinguish himself from the father on this religious occasion even as he would later on scientific occasions. It is difficult to say, for we have so little direct testimony by Etienne Pascal on his own religious views. From Etienne's letter to Noël later in the spring of the same year we may infer that, in replying to Rebours, Blaise is applying the kind of linkage between reason and religion that the father would undertake with Noël. The father demonstrates for the foolish Jesuit the scientific invalidity of his scientific language, and he paradoxically emphasizes his points by demonstrating the "scientific" validity of scriptural language. Nevertheless, the father's invocation of religious language in this rational demonstration is not without its morally ironic edge for the Jesuit. Even so, moreover, Etienne does not fail to insist on the fundamental inadequacy of language (metaphor in this case) to render the divine mysteries. In his exchanges with Rebours, the son reverses the emphases, underplaying the mystery in order to insist on the rationality. In sum, the same ambivalence toward the father seems to be manifest in this religious invocation of his name as in scientific invocations of his name: the son surpasses him and, in doing so, perhaps falsifies his thought.

The encounter with Rebours was understandably troubling to the son. Rebours' links with his father cast Rebours in the familiar surrogate role that Pascal was to assign to all such figures, from Augustine to Arnauld. The exception, once again ironically, would be those who had come to be known as "the fathers", the Jesuits. One can imagine Pascal's irritation at having to address the despicable adversaries by that name. They had long been the adversaries of himself and his own father, Etienne, so little wonder that they should prove to be the enemies of his spiritual father, Saint Augustine, and, thereby, of his Father in Heaven, God himself. Given his need for the constancy of love of all his true fathers and their kind, we can well understand that, in the confusion Pascal reported to his sister Gilberte after the encounter with the "father" he had alienated in Rebours, he would fall back on his deep need for family support. In the final frame of his letter on the encounter to Gilberte, he writes, "But I beg you above all to draw no consequences from all that I ask of you, because it could happen that I do not say things with enough precision; and that could give rise in you to a suspicion perhaps as disadvantageous as unjust." The disadvantage would be to himself as both brother and believer. In religious matters far more than in scientific, an adversary is uneasy. Dependency on authority learned at the father's knee and in the texts of the Church fathers clashes with his pride and ambition. The troubled Blaise would not wish to be cut off from either his God or his family. Beneath the appeal to his older sister in these lines one senses an appeal to the father in the two guises that counted so much for Pascal before his second conversion: the divine and the earthly.

If the relation between Blaise and Gilberte was one of dependency by brother on older sister, the relation between Blaise and Jacqueline was one of dependency of younger sister on older brother. As we have seen, from the first family letter written by Pascal, the older brother was writing on behalf of the younger sister. When for reasons of ill health he could not write, Jacqueline was the hand of her brother. She was also perhaps an influence as significant if not more so for the spiritual development of her brother than their older sister or their father.

The relationship was not without ambivalences of the kind we have noted in the son's relationship to the father. From her earliest years Jacqueline had shone in the arts even as her brother had in the sciences. She had been initially recalcitrant to learn to read, but she decided to do so at seven in order to be able to read poetry. As much a prodigy in the arts as her brother in the sciences, she had composed verses even before learning to read. Her verse made her publicly recognized before her brother's scientific efforts brought him such recognition: a collection of her poems was published in an anthology in 1639. The event only increased the attention she had gained from the public and especially the court from her writing and acting. Early in 1638, when she was twelve years old, she and some young friends had composed and acted a five-act drama that won much acclaim. She had composed verses on the queen's pregnancy that had won her an invitation to the court, where she improvised still other impressive verses to please Mademoiselle de Montpensier. She later (1640) composed verses on the Immaculate Conception that won a first prize conferred by the leading dramatist of the period, Pierre Corneille.

Even before that her fame served the Pascal family well: it was instrumental in restoring to the three children their father, who had had to abandon them for fear of being arrested by the agents of the prime minister, Cardinal de Richelieu. Early in 1638, the government having fallen behind in interest payments on bonds held by the family, Etienne joined with a number of other bondholders in leading a protest before the chancellor of the treasury. The action frightened the government, and Cardinal de Richelieu ordered the arrest of Etienne Pascal and two alleged coconspirators. The latter were captured and imprisoned in the Bastille, but the elder Pascal escaped. For several months he remained in hiding, managing nonetheless not only to take care of his younger daughter after she had been struck by smallpox but also to attend to the publication of her poems. Jacqueline's illness left

her seriously marked physically—a blow that she later believed she had
received as part of the will of God that encouraged her later spirituality. It did not discourage her artistic activities: not only were her
verses prepared for publication, but, more importantly, she was in-
vited to take part in a play by Georges de Scudéry, one of the important dramatists of the period, to be performed before the Cardinal de
Richelieu in February 1639. She took advantage of the occasion to
plead with the cardinal, who had very much enjoyed her performance,
to pardon her father so that he might once again lend his well-known
scientific and administrative talents to the government. The cardinal
granted the pardon and called upon Etienne to serve as a tax commis-
sioner in Upper Normandy.

On the occasion of the performance of Scudéry's play, not only Jacqueline but her fifteen-year-old brother were presented to the cardinal,
he for his outstanding mathematical and scientific abilities. But the
presentation was clearly on account of and in the shadow of the presentation of Jacqueline. Early in the following year he would emerge
from that shadow with his own first publication, the *Essay on Conics*,
and through the 1640s he would gain more renown than his talented
sister through his work on mathematics and physics. The poetic talent
of his sister may have been a goad to the fiercely proud and ambitious
young man. There is sufficient ground to believe that a short poem (in
a collection made by Tallemant des Réaux) and another known in
manuscript by "M. Pascal" may be not by the father, as long believed,
but by the son. If the conventional lover's complaints are by Blaise and
are to be assigned, as Mesnard suggests, to the year 1645, we may speculate that the brother would have wanted to equal if not excel the
sister in that order of the spirit that had been hers alone.

Other and more serious grounds of tension arose between the two
younger Pascal children. Jacqueline outshone her brother not only in
poetic but in other graces as well, personal, social, and religious. Her
successful appeal to Richelieu is to the point, though it is but one
manifestation of the charm in society that stands in such contrast to the
brusqueness that, as Gilberte notes in her biography, marked their
brother in such settings. Jacqueline's physical suffering, the devastat-
ing effect of the pox on her pretty face, became for her an occasion of a
deepened faith in God. She thanked him for it in a poem in which she
regarded her pockmarks as the "sacred witnesses" that she was not
among those whom God loved least. During the 1640s however, even

beyond the first conversion of 1646, her brother was to cite his own frequent illnesses chiefly as reasons for his failure to have performed this or that scientific or religious task (for example, in the letter to Gilberte of January 26, 1648). Not until much later would he achieve an understanding of the Christian "witness" of suffering in his beautiful *Prayer for the Good Use of Illness,* written two years before his death. It is undoubtedly this joining with Jacqueline toward the end of their lives (she preceded him in death by a little less than a year) that Gilberte has in mind when she writes, "He could not have loved anyone more than he loved my sister, and he was right. He saw her often, he spoke to her of everything without reserve, he received from her satisfaction in all things without exception; for there was such a correspondence in their feelings that they agreed in all things . . ."

But they were not so close in the early and middle years of their lives, especially not in those years when Jacqueline tried to implement her decision to enter religious orders. She took this decision in 1648, which had begun with her brother's report of the troubling encounter with M. de Rebours at Port Royal. If the brother had left the abbey confused by its leaders' hostility to his kind of commitment to its values, the sister apparently left with a more serene commitment to those values. Even before her letter of June 19 of that year, seeking her father's approval to make a retreat at Port Royal (linked to her decision to become a religious there), she and her brother had written to their older sister on April 1 in a religious vein very different from that of the letter of January 26. The second letter is as remarkable for its theological range and depth as it is for its greater serenity of tone. Although it is in the hand of Jacqueline, this letter, like the first, is composed by the brother. One of the proofs, as Mesnard observes, lies in the grammatical agreement between the pronoun subject, "I" (*je*) and the past participle.[7] This technical proof of the authorship is reenforced by the allusion, in the first sentence using the first person, to the "rebuffs" that prevented the "I" from writing and that "you [Gilberte] know of." From the first letter, we remember that it was only Blaise who seems to have been "rebuffed" by Rebours. This seems to be a forgotten matter now, all the more so as the writer seems reassured in the matter that most concerned him at the end of the first letter: Gilberte's confidence in his religious and familial integrity.

What lies at the root of the more confident, reassured tone is in good part the text that serves as pretext for the writing of this letter:

Saint Cyran's letter on *Vocation,* which Jacqueline and Blaise have just
read and whose reading they now urge on Gilberte and their father.
The union of the brother and sisters in God through their father is a
constant motif of the letter: "for you know that my father has anticipated and, so to speak, conceived us in this plan." Their earthly father
becomes for Pascal the inspiration for one of the earliest formulations
of an idea, rooted in Augustine, that he will elaborate majestically in
the *Provincial Letters* and the *Thoughts*: "It is this [their father's anticipation and conception of them in God's design] in which we must
admire that God has given us both the figure and the reality of this
alliance; for, as we have said among ourselves often, corporal things
are only the image of spiritual things, and God has represented invisi-
ble things in the visible." This figuralism is, in theological terms,
sacramental in concept — a point that should make us leery of the
tendency to see in Pascal's religious conceptions a marked tendency
toward a pure transcendentalism. As he elaborates this notion
throughout the letter we sense that Pascal (dictating to Jacqueline) is
far from the rationalistic premises of his exchanges with Rebours. His
references to the family discussions on the matter indicate that he has
returned to the notions of the *mystery* of faith upon which his father
had insisted in his own reproaches to Noël and upon which he must
have insisted in his discussions of religion with his children. But even
as Pascal reiterates that there is little point in going over this familiar
ground, he cannot prevent himself from doing so to a great extent:

> For, as our sins hold us enveloped in corporal and terrestrial things,
> and they are not only the pain of our sins but also the occasion to com-
> mit new ones and the cause of the first, it is necessary that we use the
> very site into which we have fallen to raise ourselves up from our fall.
> This is why we must manage and use well the advantage that the
> goodness of God gives us to leave always before our eyes an image of
> the goods we have lost, and to surround us, in the very captivity
> where his justice has reduced us, with so many objects that continu-
> ously serve us as a lesson ever present.

Obviously, Pascal's figuralism is not the easy sacramentalism of the
reigning Catholic orthodoxy of the period as represented in the Jesuit
theology so opposed to the principles of Saint Cyran and Port Royal.
As he discourses here on the world and human beings as criminals in
the prison of the world (an image anticipating one of the most magni-

ficent of the *Thoughts*), Pascal is closer to the solitaries of Port Royal than he is to the easy moralists of the school. His sacramental view of the material world, of images, is informed with a keen awareness of the besetting temptation of the sacramental view: that it fall into an idolatry of the object for its own sake.

> [God alone] must be the only end as he alone is the true principle. For, whatever resemblance nature have with its Creator, and though the least things and the smallest and vilest parts of the world represent at least by their unity the perfect unity that is found only in God, one cannot legitimately bear them sovereign respect, because there is nothing so abominable in the eyes of God and of men as idolatry, because therein one renders to the creature the honor that is due only to the Creator. The Scriptures are full of the vengeances that God has wrought on those who have been thus guilty, and the first commandment of the Decalogue, which includes all the others, forbids above all to adore images. But as he is much more jealous of our affections than of our respect, it is visible that there is no crime more injurious to him, nor more detestable, than to love sovereignly creatures, whatever they represent.

To take the figure for the reality is to remain in a "blindness" that is "carnal and Judaic." Having sketched this notion, which will figure so centrally in the *Apology* he will later prepare, Pascal closes with a reminder of Christ's injunction in Matthew 5:48, to "be perfect as your Heavenly Father is perfect." A religion of the Father, but one coming closer to the notion later so crucial for Pascal: of the Son as the intermediary with the Father.

The notion of Father's Child as intermediary reminds us of Etienne's youngest child's role as intermediary for her brother's more confident, more serene expression of faith. If Jacqueline copied what her brother dictated, it is not unreasonable to conjecture that her well-known suavity of spirit had an effect on the tone and perhaps the very point of view of this remarkable letter. For once, in these early years, in the presence of his sister "in Christ," Pascal relents in the antagonism in things of faith as in things of science that has marked his encounters with others.

The mood was not an enduring one. The spring of 1648 saw the eruption of the quarrel with Noël. True, after his letter of February to his friend Le Pailleur on the views of the Jesuit scientist, Pascal left the quarrel to his father. But he himself reentered the lists in the fall of that year with the publication of the account of his brother-in-law's experiment on the Puy de Dôme. In that account, the exactitude with which he notes in his address to the reader the date of his letter to Périer asking him to perform the experiment reflects the familiar preoccupation with self-distinction that the scientist has manifested since his early years. Moreover, the address, if without the rancor of other public statements, is characterized by an authoritativeness couched in a peremptory and didactic tone.

The same tone characterizes a letter on religious matters that he and Jacqueline wrote to Gilberte on November 5, 1648.[8] The intent of the letter was to emphasize that a quarrel that had developed between the three Pascal children and their father, particularly between Gilberte and the older Pascal, is at an end and was so even before Gilberte wrote about it once again in a letter to which Blaise and Jacqueline here reply. Yet even in affectionately reassuring Gilberte, Blaise does not refrain from chiding his sister: "You know how much these disputes trouble the peace of the household, exterior and interior, and how much one needs in these situations forewarnings, which you have given us too late." He then haughtily tells Gilberte that "we have some [forewarnings] to give you on the subject of your own." These are three in number: first, that she has incorrectly stated that they had told her what she has only just told them in her letter (presumably on the matter of the quarrel with the father); second, that she has incorrectly stated that it is unnecessary to repeat things (presumably views he expresses under the first forewarning concerning the need to pay special attention to instructors like fathers, bishops, and spiritual directors); third that she—and, for once, correctly—writes only to assure them that she has the same sentiments about persevering in certain family values, especially religious ones, as do Blaise and Jacqueline.

The brunt of the brother's haughty instruction to his older sister lies especially in the second reproach he makes, on the need to repeat certain moral lessons. Her failure to understand this leads them, he writes, to fear

> that you do not make sufficient distinction between the things you speak of and those of which the world speaks, for undoubtedly it suffices to have learned once the latter and to have retained them without having further need to be instructed in them, whereas it does not suffice to have once understood those of the other kind, and to have known them in the right way (that is, by the interior motion of God)

in order to retain the memory of them in the same way, even though one may well retain the recollection of them. It is not that one cannot remember them and that one retain as easily an epistle of Saint Paul as a book of Virgil, but the knowledge that we acquire in this fashion as well as its continuation is but an effect of memory, whereas to hear this language that is secret and foreign to those who are so in relation to heaven, one must have the same grace, which alone can give the first understanding, continue that understanding, and render it always present in retracing it incessantly in the heart of the faithful in order to make it always live, as in the truly happy God continuously renews their beatitude, which is an effect and a follow-up of grace, and as likewise the Church holds that the Father continuously produces the Son and maintains the eternity of his essence by an effusion of his substance that is without interruption as well as without end.

The concept of the figural (and, implicitly, the sacramental) that was so central in the letter to Gilberte of April 1648 has yielded almost completely to the reality signified by the figure: the presence of God in the soul. In Pascal's concept of grace the figural and the real fuse: "Thus the continuation of the justice of the faithful is nothing more than the continuation of the infusion of grace, and not a single grace that subsists always; and it is this that teaches us perfectly the perpetual dependence where we are in relation to the mercy of God, since, were he to interrupt its flow ever so slightly, dryness would necessarily ensue." It is as if the secret language were not a language at all—that is, a code in which signifier and signified are separate. Not that Pascal fuses God and grace, for, from God's point of view, grace is a gift of God, in linguistic terms a signifier that is not wholly or even partially identical with the sign-giver who is God himself. In receiving grace man is "with God"; he is not God but only, indeed, a signifier of God's presence.

The insistence on the role of God, through his grace, in the "justice of the faithful" is a positive formulation of the premises more negatively stated in the letter of April on the criminality of man, including the faithful, in his prison of sin. The positive note anticipates even more the shift from an adversary to an advocacy temperament that characterized the earlier letter. The shift may be further noted in the capacity that Pascal assigns to man even as he insists on man's eternal dependence on the mercy of God: "Thus we must incessantly attend to purifying the interior, which soils itself always with new stains while retaining the old ones, for without this assiduous renewal one is not capable of receiving this new wine that will not be put in old vessels."

For all the anticipatory notes of Pascal the advocate, the letter only hints at the tone and theme of that advocacy and does so in the adversary framework of the reproach to his older sister. The younger sister, to whom he dictates this letter, seems to have less of an effect on her brother than in the letter of April that she also penned for him. Perhaps she was too preoccupied with the concern her decision to enter orders had created. It is very likely that it is to this decision that she alludes in the postscript: "I hope to write to you on my own of my business on which I will send you details: however, pray to God for its realization." Without her influence we may conjecture that Blaise's imperious temperament had prevailed during the composition of this letter of November and that now in religion, as in science, he became a peremptory and didactic authority. We may conjecture that Jacqueline merely copied down all the while reflecting on the matter she would raise in the postscript—the matter of her religious vocation, to which she knew not only father but brother would be opposed. Given the closeness of father and son and what she knew to be the son's conscious tendency to follow the father especially in religious and family affairs, perhaps the brother's opposition or concern can be glimpsed in the postscript which he himself adds—in his own hand: "If you know some good soul, have him or her pray to God for me also." *Pray for me also*: and also on the same matter? That he may sort out the difficulty caused by his desire, on the one hand, to encourage his sister in her vocation and, on the other, not to upset the father?

It had been an upsetting year for the father, including the exchange with Noël concerning his son's veracity, and the difference with Gilberte that occasioned this very letter, as well as Jacqueline's desire to enter orders. The latter had ill effects not only on the would-be postulant but on her brother as well, for it was he who had conveyed his sister's intention to Etienne Pascal in May. Although the father did not immediately reply, his firm refusal was apparently not long in coming, for in mid-June we find Jacqueline writing to him for at least the permission to make a retreat at Port Royal. In the meantime he had shown his distemper with his two younger children by having an old family servant, Louise Delfault, look closely at their activities. One suspects that it was especially his son whom he wished to place under this watchful eye. As Gilberte reports in her account of her sister's life, "he complained even about my brother, that he had fomented this plan without knowing whether it would be agreeable to him, and this reflection hardened him so against my brother and sister that he no longer trusted them." The surveillance by the servant who had helped the widower raise his children was designed to contain this revolt within the limits the father had set. In his revolt the son in particular challenged the father's direction of the daughter. Of her father's opposition to his daughter's vocation Gilberte writes that "he was strangely divided: for, on the one hand, as he was committed to the maxims of the purity of Christianity, he was easily content to see his children in the same sentiment; but, on the other, the tender affection he had for my sister attached him so strongly to her that he could not resolve himself to be separated from her forever." Later, when Jacqueline was at last to realize her vocation, after the death of the father, the same grounds of tender affection and fear of loss informed the opposition to Jacqueline's vocation—by *the brother*!

Like father, like son. The son was so much like the father that, in the initial "fomenting" of Jacqueline's vocation, we might see in the son's motives not merely the revolt against the father that his father saw but a complex of rebellions by the son and brother: desire to remove the worldly sister from the social and especially familial limelight; jealous desire to displace the sister in the father's affection; desire to place at Port Royal an adept whose religious views, formed (he would presume) under his tutelage, would vindicate him in the quarrels he had had with Rebours earlier in the same year. More positively but still expressing the son's ambivalent relationship with his father, we may conjecture that Blaise miscalculated in his assessment of the effect of Jacqueline's vocation on their father and of the effect of his own encouragement. Knowing his father's commitment to Christianity, he may have assumed that both his and Jacqueline's actions could only have pleased Etienne Pascal. Indeed, imbued with this fatherly piety, he may not have calculated one way or the other.

Whatever the assumptions or calculations, it is clear from Jacqueline's letter of June 19, 1648, that the daughter, if not the son, was fully aware of the father's anger at their actions. She begins by insisting on her filial obedience and submissiveness: she reminds him that she has obeyed him absolutely on the thing that touches her the most in this world—her wish to become a religious. She then elaborately explains why she is writing him now on another matter of so little consequence that she might well have done it without telling him beforehand. However, she would not do so lest that action itself be construed as an "image of disobedience." The matter in question is the retreat at Port Royal, and, having sought his permission in the matter, she supports its validity by noting that she has nothing to do in the house, "for since your departure, I have not written a single word for my brother, which is the thing he would need [me] most for; but he can get along by using someone else." On the surface, Jacqueline is telling her father that her brother does not need her services as his secretary; below the surface, she is reassuring her father that she is not listening to her brother. This was an act of rebellion and of courage at one and the same time: rebellion against the brother and against the father for seeing her (especially in her religious vocation) as her brother's creature, a dependent soul to be "fomented" by her brother and not to be capable of an autonomous relation with her own father; courage in separating herself from both brother and father in the independent action she is taking here.

Her courage and independence seem all the greater when one penetrates to the real subject of her letter. If its stated purpose is the request for permission to make the retreat, one has only to note its frequent, seemingly parenthetical appeals to her father on a related matter to understand that its real purpose is to move her father to change his mind on that thing that touches her most in all the world.

So I see nothing where I could be the least useful until your departure for Rouen, principally if one compares this usefulness with the necessity that there is for me to make this retreat, especially in that place; for, since God gives me day by day the grace to augment the effect of the vocation it pleased him to give me (and that you have permitted me to conserve), which is the desire to realize it as soon as he will have made his will known to me by yours, since, I say, this desire increases in me day by day, and I see nothing on this earth that could prevent me to realize it if you had permitted it to me, this retreat will serve me as a test to know if it is in that place that God wants me. There I will be able to listen to him alone, one to the other, and perhaps thereby I shall learn that I was not born for those kinds of places; and, if it is so, I will ask you frankly no longer to think nor to prepare yourself for what I have told you; or, again, if God gives me to understand that I am appropriate to them, I promise you that I will take every care to await without anxiety the hour you wish to choose for his glory; for I believe that you seek only that; such that I now live in a continual desire of a thing that I do not know will succeed even if you welcome it, so much so that I am in a trouble of spirit that cannot be expressed; but after this test, I will be able almost with certitude to assure you of one and the other, and wait with patience the time you will order me to take.

The conviction and the pertinacity of Jacqueline are remarkable: she separates herself from her father with an ingenious yet ingenuous emphasis not on her own but on *his* religious commitment. In this she recalls Agnès, the heroine of Molière's *School for Wives*, writing to her suitor, Horace, who, she fears, seeks only to exploit her, as do all young men with young women according to her guardian, the prurient Arnolphe. But the young Horace yields to his beleagured correspondent as old Etienne does not: he did not grant her the permission to make the retreat and, as Gilberte tells us, her sister was thereafter obliged to go to the abbey of Port Royal "in secret" and to see M. Singlin, the spiritual director of the abbey, "by astuteness and inventiveness."

Astuteness, inventiveness, ingenuity—Jacqueline's wit, her excellence in the "order of the mind" were as marked as her brother's. However, in this year of 1648, the year of what we might call *her* second conversion, these mental gifts were placed at the service of her conversion. Her brother's gifts, as we have seen in both the scientific exchanges with Noël and the religious exchanges with Rebours, were still at the service of his *moi*, the self whose sufficiency he strove to assert particularly in relation to the domineering image of his father, Etienne Pascal. After the disturbing vocational quarrel with the father, neither son nor daughter irritated him in the three years of life that were to remain to him. Gilberte tells us that, without forgetting the religious vows she so yearned to take, Jacqueline renewed, so to speak, her vow of obedience to her father, in particular agreeing, in May 1649, dutifully and apparently lovingly, to his plea that she remain with him. In return he accepted and encouraged her withdrawal from the world in the cloister of their home, reassuring her that he would propose no marriage arrangements for her. And so she lived her two lives, the religious and the familial, confident that the familial was but an instance of her commitment to the religious. However, her religious life took more overt expressions as well: she began to use her literary gifts for the composition of religious poetry, translating the hymn of the Ascension, *Jésus, notre rédemption,* in verse form. Also, like her brother toward the end of his life, she ministered to the poor and the sick.

In this religious commitment up to the time of her father's death, she seems to have had the encouragement of her brother. In a brief letter he wrote to Gilberte at the end of March 1649, he seems cautiously to be referring to Jacqueline's secret visits to Port Royal: "I tell you no news, because the general news is just too much so and the personal must still be just that. I would have much to tell you that goes on in full secrecy, but I find it useless to send it to you; all that I ask is that you add pleas for grace to the prayers you say for me, which I ask you to multiply at this time." As Mesnard notes,[9] this plea for prayer on his behalf echoes the same plea made by Jacqueline in a letter to Gilberte at the very same time, March 24, 1649: "Pray God for me, but earnestly: thank him for all, and for my brother special prayers and pleas for grace."[10] Mesnard believes the prayerful allusion in both letters refers to Blaise's health. Undoubtedly, but one wonders if a plea for prayer evinced earlier in the letter does not contain a veiled allusion to her own situation, on which she could pray for more than her brother's complicity of silence in the face of their father's opposition. She writes earlier in the letter: "I beg you only that one of the subjects of your prayers for the first Thursday be the public manifestation or at least the private manifestation to certain people of a thing of consequence that is hidden [occulte] and whose effects are astonishing, saying to God with Jesus Christ: 'My Father, if it is possible, that is, if it be for Your glory', and always adding: 'Thy will be done', in order that it please God to send his light into hearts rather than minds." Among the certain people whose hearts rather than minds she would have moved by grace on her behalf is, undoubtedly, her father. But the plural is tantalizing. Perhaps it already includes her spiritual director, M. Singlin. Almost two years later, as we shall learn from Mother Agnès on the occasion of a retreat by Jacqueline at Port Royal, he was opposed to her entering the choir during the ceremony. Again, in the course of her spiritual tutelage in the long years before she was finally received into religious orders one senses in her relations with Singlin (as reported by both correspondents in her exchanges with Mother Agnès) a certain reserve on Singlin's part. But perhaps the plural includes her brother Blaise, whose support for her vocation she hoped would take the form of an intervention with their father to allow its realization.

Whatever the degree of support by her brother at this time, it abated considerably after the death of their father. Given the hold of Etienne Pascal on his children, particularly on Blaise and Jacqueline, his death could not but be an unusually traumatic event in each of their lives. Pascal's letter on his father's death to his brother-in-law (and, as its terms show, to Pascal's older sister, as well) anticipates, as Mesnard has noted, many of the major motifs of the later, famous religious writings.[11] Generously, humbly acknowledging that the consolation he offers is but a repetition "of what I have learned," Pascal majestically orchestrates the Christian theme of the death in the body that is the return of the soul of God. As many scholars have pointed out, the sources of Pascal's learning here are principally Augustine, Jansen, and Saint Cyran. The sources are also more personal and immediate. He notes toward the end of the letter that, had he lost his father six years ago, "I would have lost myself, and although I believe to have presently a less absolute need for him, I know that he would have been necessary to me another ten years, and useful all my life." In the reference to "six years ago," the event of the family's "first conversion" through the father, we see that the father is the very foundation of the scholarly sources on which he relies. There is perhaps another family source too, and, in the years just prior to Etienne's death, one even more intimate for the Christian view of death Pascal elaborates in the letter: Jacqueline.

Both informally through her secretarial services to her brother and formally through her own reflections on the Christian view of death Jacqueline may have influenced her brother. In the spring of this same year (May–June 1651) Jacqueline had composed a short reflection on *The Mystery of the Death of Our Lord Jesus Christ*. The form of this reflection is a series of fifty-one relatively brief, two-paragraph entries (ranging in length from three to twenty-five lines) with the first paragraph giving a universal or general perspective on an aspect of Christ's death and the second drawing a personal lesson. Thus:

I

Jesus died for love of his Eternal Father, because he died to repair in an infinite offering the infinite offense that had been done to him. He also died for love of us, because he satisfied our debts through his death; so that the little that we can do, that we cannot do without him, suffice to pay for all of them.

I learn from this that I must die to the world for love of God, to

render him what I owe him, in giving him all my heart without division, and satisfying all my sins through penance, which is locked into
this death, and for love of myself of the same kind.[12]

The first reflection is not only typical of the remaining, but, in its
form and its content it suggests both short-range and long-range paral-
lels with Pascal's own reflections on the significance of Christ's death.
In the long range, both form and content here anticipate Pascal's
Abridgment of the Life of Jesus Christ (nearly half on Christ's death and
the events just preceding) and *The Mystery of Jesus* (on Jesus's torment
in the Garden). In the short range, Jacqueline's first reflection posits in
its terms the central motif of Pascal's letter on the death of his
father—the view of death, Christ's and man's, as a sacrifice:

> We know that life, and the life of Christians, is a continual sacrifice
> that can be realized only in death. We know that, as Jesus Christ,
> entering the world, considered himself and offered himself to God as a
> holocaust and a true victim; that his birth, his life, his death, his resur-
> rection, his ascension, and his presence in the Eucharist, and his eternal
> seat to the right of the Father are but a single and unique sacrifice; we
> know that what happened to Jesus Christ is to happen to all his
> members.
>   Let us therefore consider life as a sacrifice; and let not the accidents
> of life make an impression in the spirit of Christians except in the
> proportion that they interrupt or accomplish this sacrifice. Let us not
> call evil that which renders the victim of God the victim of the devil,
> but let us indeed call good that which renders the victim of the devil in
> Adam victim of God; and according to this rule let us examine the
> nature of death.

Like his sister, Pascal posits a general or universal perspective on the
death of Christ (Jacqueline: an infinite offering; Blaise: holocaust, true
victim, single and unique sacrifice) and then makes a personal comment on this aspect.

There are differences of tone, emphasis, and strategy, and we might
note that this form is a familiar one in religious literature of the period
and especially in the milieu to which Blaise and Jacqueline belonged.
Nevertheless, we can sense in Jacqueline's statement of the Christian
view a "source" or "resource" very different from the one he had used
in the first familial reflections on religion we know him to have composed: his report of the troubling encounter with M. de Rebours at
Port Royal early in 1648. In the three years since, he had had the ex-

ample of his sister's mystical defense of Christian truths that, in his exchange with Rebours, he had insisted were largely if not exclusively susceptible of demonstration by the light of *reason*. Toward the end of this letter, he tells the Périers that he prays God to have for them and Jacqueline "more tenderness than ever," so we may reasonably conjecture that the shift in this letter from the rationalistic to the mystical is in part due to the mystical model of belief represented at his side not only in those three years but especially in the very moment of mutual loss in which he composes this letter.

Capital in its expression of the theology informing the letter is the point of view in which Pascal writes. The letter is composed and written in Blaise's own name. A portion of the manuscript is in his hand, the rest in a secretary's, not Jacqueline's this time. "We" had written an earlier letter, Pascal begins, but Jacqueline had sent if off before it was completed. It contained reflections on "God's actions on life and illness that I would like to repeat to you here, so much do I have them engraved in my heart, and so strongly do they bring solid consolation." However, relying on the first letter or on Jacqueline's possible more exact repetition of them, he writes that:

> I shall speak to you here then only of the consequences that I draw therefrom, which is that his end is so Christian, so happy, so holy, and so desirable that except for the people interested in natural feelings, there is no Christian who should not rejoice in it.
> On this large foundation I shall begin for you what I have to say by a discourse truly consoling to those who have enough freedom of spirit to conceive of it in the throes of sorrow.
> It is that we must seek the consolation for our troubles, not in ourselves, not in men, not in all that has been created; but in God.

The third paragraph continues for a full page, leading into the statement of the major motif of sacrifice whose premises are developed throughout the remaining ten pages of the letter.

As a token of development of the motif, the "I" becomes "we," but not the "we" referring to himself and Jacqueline as in previous letters written to Gilberte, although that "we" is mentioned once, in the second line of the letter as Pascal speaks of the unfinished letter sent earlier. Now "we" means the cobelievers, who are different from "people interested in natural feelings" and who "have enough freedom of spirit" to conceive of his discourse here "in the throes of sorrow." The effect of this formulation is to act retroactively on the very "I" who will make this discourse. Anticipatively, the "I" becomes one of the "we" who, as the next paragraph begins, "must seek consolation." It is the "I who is part of the we" that says it will speak here only of the consequences that it draws from the earlier letter presumably written on behalf of the restricted "we" of Jacqueline and Blaise. "I is another" for Pascal here, but not the alienated "I" in that famous formulation by Rimbaud more than two centuries later. The "I" who is now "another" for Pascal is the "I" who would have prevailed in the debate with Rebours and in the letter of January 1648 reporting the debate. To be sure, in the following two letters to Gilberte in the same year (April 1 and November 5), the "I" had begun to speak as a "we." But that "we" spoke didactically, stating there in a schematic, intellectual fashion the Christian viewpoint that he develops with profundity of thought and feeling in this letter. The letter of April bespoke a "we" in the tones of the "I" who would surpass the younger sister in her undeflected commitment to the order of the heart; the letter of November framed its theological "we" in the chiding tones of a supercilious fraternal "I" who finds the older sister deflecting from the order of the heart.

It is the world that Pascal chides for its deflections from that order. This letter is in part a release upon the world, an unleashing of a Godlike fury at the world without Christ, the world of Seneca and Socrates, who are the best the world has to offer and yet who have nothing "persuasive" to tell us on the subject of death. Their discourse is founded on the erroneous belief that death is natural to man, and thus all they have to tell us only demonstrates how man "in general is weak, since the highest productions of the greatest of men are so lowly and puerile." The letter is a preamble, we might well say, to some of the more searing and sustained attacks on man's pride that Pascal will unleash in the *Provincial Letters* and in the *Thoughts.* But the world is not so much with Pascal in this moment of the consolation he would bring to those who seemed to have suffered the most grievous of losses. Rather, he insists on the *seeming* of that loss in order to indicate the reality of a gain: the gain of heaven by his father and the gain in Christian wisdom that the father's gain brings to his survivors.

The father's gain and the survivors' gainful lesson lie in the truth of Christ's *mediation* of man's fear of death and hope for life. The figure of Jesus Christ begins to emerge in Pascal's theology with some of the force it will assume in his later writings. From a theological point of view, it is possible that the father's death is itself the occasion of the *maturation* of the son. On his own in considering the premises of the religion he had learned from the father, the son becomes less patricentric, less concentrated on God the Father, and shifts to an emphasis on the Son. The shift is the more compelling for the son, Blaise, in that the Son of God survived death. In this perspective, the father, Etienne Pascal, himself becomes a son who is received in God the Father. To understand the nature of death, Pascal writes, "we must return to the person of Jesus Christ; for all that is in men is abominable, and, as God considers men only by the Mediator Jesus Christ, men should also look upon others and themselves only through the mediation of Jesus Christ; for, lest we pass by this milieu, we find in ourselves only real miseries, or abominable pleasures; but if we consider all things in Jesus Christ, we will find all consolation, all satisfaction, all edification."

The edification that Pascal sees in the mediating death of Christ is not without Jansenistic overtones. In certain of its premises Pascal's letter on the death of his father is far more Jansenistically inflexible than those of the *Apology for the Christian Religion* he will later undertake. There is none of the bending toward the world implicit in the famous wager, for example; there is none of the seductive generalization of the audience to whom he addresses the projected *Apology* with its appeal to the capacity of "man" to heed the salvific lesson of Christ's death. Rather, there is a potentially harrowing constriction of the audience, a principle of exclusion in the "we" who are capable of the consolation he brings:

> There is the state of things in our Sovereign Lord. Let us consider them in us now. From the moment that we enter the Church, which is the world of the faithful and particularly of the elect, into which Jesus Christ entered from the moment of his Incarnation by a privilege special to the only Son of God, we are offered and sanctified. This sacrifice is continued by life and is completed upon death, in which, the soul truly leaving behind all vices and life of the earth, whose contagion always infects it throughout this life, achieves its immolation and is received in the bosom of God.
>
> Let us not therefore afflict ourselves like the pagans who are without hope. We have not lost my father in the moment of his death. We had lost him so to speak from the moment that he entered the Church through baptism. Since then he was God's. His life was dedicated to God. In his death he detached himself totally from sins; and it is in this

moment that he has been received in God, and that his sacrifice has
realized its completion and crowning. He has thus done what he
vowed; he has completed the work for which he was created. The will
of God is completed in him, and his will is absorbed in God. Let not
our will then separate what God has united; and let us stifle or moderate, through knowledge [*intelligence*] of the truth, the feelings of corrupted and disappointed nature, which has only false images and which
troubles by its illusions the sanctity of the feelings that the truth and
the Gospel should give us.

The world without hope of Christ is pagan. The paganism Pascal attacks includes not only those who have not heard and thus do not
know the Gospel. It includes many of those who have heard and
known—at least through their eyes and their ears—that Gospel. For
Pascal in this letter the communion of the faithful is made up not of
the believing (*les fidèles*) and the infidels but of the elect and the
nonelect, of Christians and pagans. The father's baptism had been
meaningful because he was of "the world of the faithful and particularly of the elect." He had received that special grace of the elect not only
to have been baptized in election but to have persisted in that election:
"he has completed the work for which he was created."
    It is a difficult position for human beings to accept: that some of
them are chosen before birth to be saved. Both logically and psychologically it is repugnant to many modern minds. However, this position cannot be dismissed as merely the elucubration of a neurotic
religious view, presumably outdated by "modern" advances in the sciences of man and nature. The same premise emerges, for example, in
the contemporary theories of Arthur Jensen on genetic differences in
intelligence between races.[13] Jensenism is more than a close ho-
monymic reprise of Jansenism, the theology of restrictive grace. Educational disputes over the influence of nature versus nurture parallel
the terms of dispute between Jansenist and Jesuit, Christian and pagan
in seventeenth-century France. For three centuries the sciences of man
have wrestled with the moral implications of, and the sociopolitical
rules to be applied to, the concept of *gift,* whether it be of the gift of
grace, talent, or disposition. In these disputes the *liberal* insistence on
each human being's giftedness and the moral necessity of providing
equal opportunity for that giftedness to realize itself is anchored in
belief, or faith, in the sanctity of the human creature. The liberal may
well reproach Pascal for finding the warrant for this sanctity in a

transcendent God, but where will the liberal find the warrant for the belief in that sanctity: in nature, in history?

Still, granting the anchorage in God or in whatever life force, the liberal may well reproach the Pascal of this letter for so severely limiting the human capacity to do something with or about the gift of grace—to use the terms of the liberal canon, for restricting opportunity. There is something to the charge as it applies to this letter, to Pascal's dogmatic position at this moment. Yet, there is opportunity: for prayer. Not for self-improvement; to borrow that liberal category would be to falsify the theological and moral position of Pascal. Rather, the opportunity exists for self-reprovement, for the reminder to the self, the elect, of their fallen state in which the horror of death bids to seem final except that "we draw an advantage from our own imperfections, since they will serve as the matter of this holocaust; for it is the purpose of true Christians to profit from their own imperfections, because all cooperates in good for the elect." Thus, "prayer and sacrifice are a sovereign remedy to pain." As Pascal tells his correspondents, this is what his father would have counseled them were he still in the world.

He himself prays that God will "form and maintain these sentiments in us and will continue those that it seems to me he gives me, to have for you and my sister more tenderness than ever." One senses the conservative, restrictive theology of Pascal at this moment: God gives even the capacity for prayer. But more striking in this formulation is its tone both theologically and psychologically. The believer is tentative in a new way, saying, "that it *seems to me* he gives me." The troubled debater of Rebours, hurt in his rationalistic pride during and after the debate, is as tender in his dependence on God as he is in his tenderness toward his sisters. He goes on to state how "it seems" to him that they should not "lose the love we had for our father" and that they should principally "inherit the affection he had for them in order to love each other more cordially if possible." One senses that, in this moment of sorrow, Pascal becomes more flexible, more humane than we have seen him thus far. Particularly striking is the use of the terms of love—*tenderness, affection, cordially,* even *love* itself—in a horizontal rather than a vertical direction. From the distinction he made between two kinds of tenderness, as reported in Gilberte's *Life* of her brother, we know what the theological rules of charity are for Pascal. Indeed, he has reformulated one of them in this letter: the sacrifice of death is meaningless unless God accepts the sacrifice, and it is this acceptance "that crowns the oblation; but it is rather the action of God toward the creature rather than of the creature toward God, and does not prevent that the last act of the creature is death." Conversely, charity is the love the creature owes God and not God the creature. In all this there seems little of the love creatures owe one another, the kind of love Pascal is expressing for his father and his sisters, unless, of course, we read this human love as indeed illuminated by faith and an action of the rule of the love *owed* to God. The language of "owing" is not the tone of this direct expression of affection for his sisters, however. The tone is not of an assessor or a collector of debts, like the tone of the Pascal who collected the debts of scientific priority that his confrères had refused to pay, of the Pascal who put his older sister into psychological debt with her earthly father and the logical debt with her Heavenly Father.

The adversarial spirit has abated in this moment of consolation, as the soul of the antagonist moves toward more positive postulations, but not fully. In the passages on Seneca and Socrates, on the pagans, on the horror of death, that fierce antagonism still makes itself felt, even as the dependency on reason characterizing Pascal the scientific adversary still makes itself felt. He concludes this magnificent letter with an allusion to Augustine, whose premises he would later elaborate into the conception of the three orders we know and rightly think of as being as much Pascalian as it is Augustinian.

> Saint Augustine teaches us that there is in each man a serpent, an Eve, and an Adam. The serpent is the senses and our nature; the Eve is the concupiscent appetite; and the Adam is reason.
>
> Nature tempts us continuously; the concupiscent appetite desires often; but sin is not realized if reason does not consent.
>
> Let us then allow this serpent and this Eve to act; but let us pray God that grace fortify our Adam so that he remain victorious; and that Jesus Christ be the conqueror and that he reign eternally in us. Amen.

Amen: the letter is an application of its own final lesson, the injunction to pray; for it is a prayer. But it is a prayer in keeping with the spirit of the petitioner, particularly his confidence in the powers of reason. Earlier in the letter, Pascal postulates the power of prayer as essentially defensive, a power to retain a state of being that is constantly menaced by the pagan forces of the world's "true miseries and abominable pleasures" in which the elect soul finds itself. In the second paragraph just quoted, as the factor of reason is introduced in contrastive exaltation at the end of the sentence, it is as if the reason alone, unaided by the rules of charity, could accomplish the work of salvation from sin. In the final paragraph Pascal does return to the source of reasons's power: "let us pray God that grace fortify our Adam"; but the relationship seems more Cartesian than Pascalian: God seems to give only a flick of the finger, to throw a switch or provide the fuel while the engine of reason does the work. In the three orders, the order of mind seems the highest. It is as if the order of the heart were to the side of the other two and less in scope and power. In the second paragraph, Pascal separates what he will later coalesce: serpent and Eve, nature and concupiscent appetite, temptation and desire. In the infusion of grace into the order of mind, the order of charity does not seem as radically discontinuous with the order of the mind as in later formulations. To look at the same relationship from another angle, the separateness of the orders both in their processes and in their objects does not characterize this formulation of the concept of orders. Rather, the object of the order of charity and of the order of mind are the same here: salvation of the soul, with charity in a supportive rather than primary role.

REASON WILL fend off sin for Pascal, even as mind will address itself to those objects of knowledge more evidently within its sphere: mathematics, physics, mechanics, science in general, and, now for Pascal, society. The death of his father does not betoken for Pascal a release into the world; it is not the occasion or cause of his so-called worldly period. In her memoirs on the family, Marguerite Périer, Pascal's niece, indicates that her uncle's going into the world began before the death of his father.[14] Like her mother's, Marguerite's explanation of this turning to the world is medical. But there are significant differences in the agency, so to speak. According to Gilberte, in the first version of her Life of Pascal,[15] her brother was only following doctor's orders and he did so with some reluctance because he saw "some danger" in doing so. In her second version she again gives the medical grounds, but she now adds a number of observations that indicate a more complex explanation of Pascal's going into the world: Pascal let himself be persuaded that he had to give in to worldly pleasures for the sake of his health, a gift of which God wants us to take care. Gilberte tells us that her brother behaved as if he were born to the elegant ways of the world. As if embarrassed at this side of her brother's character, she goes on to depict him almost as a social scientist, studying the world's ways in order to learn how to adapt himself to it, "to the extent that he would find it reasonable." Yet even Gilberte cannot but look on this worldly period as "the worst used time of his life." It was not that her brother gave in to vices, but he was in the way [*air*] of the world "which is very different from that of the Gospel." Through the agency of their sister Jacqueline, Pascal was rescued from the world; she spoke to him with such force that he came to look upon his concern with his health as shameful. He withdrew from the world definitively at this time, and, as Gilberte's first version puts it, "it was from this time that he embraced the way of living that he followed up to his death."

Marguerite Périer's account of Pascal's worldly period gives us a very different view of her uncle's character. The decision to go into the world would have been not the doctors', but Pascal's and apparently with no reluctance or reliance on persuasive theological grounds: "This state in which the doctors found him obliged them to forbid him any kind of application to work; but this spirit, so lively and active, could not remain idle. When he was not occupied with things of science or things of piety, which bring along with them their application in work, he needed some pleasure; he was constrained again to see the world, to play, and to divert himself." The constraint to worldliness came from within the character of Pascal himself; he needed it. The need is still related to the medical condition, but it is the patient who is his own physician. Just as significantly, Marguerite notes that it was in the nature of her uncle to be occupied with either things of science or things of piety. He himself gave to each of these orders what it was appropriate to give to each of them. This is consistent with the dichotomy that Pascal had lived since the Affaire Saint Ange, with only rare lapses during which the orders interpenetrated. It is in this light that he could, within a year after his father's death, write what is one of his most prideful defenses of the order of the mind, his famous letter to Queen Christina of Sweden.[16] He draws for the queen a distinction between the order of the mind and what he calls the "empire of power," clearly an analogue of the "order of the flesh" posited in the *Thoughts*. What really brings him to write to Christina, he tells her, is the union that is found in [your] sacred person of two things that seem to me equally worthy of admiration and respect, which are sovereign authority and solid knowledge [*la science solide*]; for I have a very particular veneration for those who are raised to the highest degree either of power or knowledge. The latter can, unless I am mistaken, pass as much as the former for sovereigns. The same degrees are to be found among people of genius as among people of rank. And the power of kings over their subjects is, it seems to me, but an image of the power of [certain] minds over those that are inferior to them, over which they exercise the right of persuasion, which is to them what the right to command is in political governance. This second empire seems to me even to be of a higher order, since the mind is of a higher order than the body, and all the more justly so in that it cannot be made manifest [*départi*] and maintained [*conservé*] except through merit, while the other can be done so by birth or chance.

It is in such a spirit that, even before his father's death, he can begin to give himself to a third order, the world (or in the term he will later use: the flesh [*chair*]), with all that it demands. Marguerite continues her account:

In the beginning his worldliness was moderate; but unconsciously the taste for it comes, one no longer uses it as a remedy, one uses it as a pleasure. That happened to him. He went into the world, without vice or unruliness, but in uselessness, pleasure, and amusement. My grandfather died; he continued to go into the world with even greater facility, now being master of his fortune; and then after having ensconced himself therein somewhat, he resolved to follow the common route of the world, that is to take on an office and to marry. He cast his eye on both a girl and an office, and taking steps on one and the other, he spoke of it to my aunt, who was at that time a religious, who groaned to see him who had made her know the nothingness of the world plunge himself into it by such commitments. She often exhorted him to give them up; but the hour had not yet come, he listened to her and still did not cease developing his plans.

The death of his father may not have been the cause of Pascal's worldly period; it may merely have facilitated a worldly period that had already begun.

It is a period in which he was to turn to the order of the flesh as involving just that: the flesh. The idea of Pascal not only turning to but "turned on" by the flesh is inconsistent with the image of him that emerges from those two works by which he is principally known to us, the *Provincial Letters* and the *Thoughts*. With their searing condemnation of the "sins of the flesh," those masterpieces have been read by most Pascalians as quasi-confessional confirmations of their author's absolute and lifelong celibacy and presumably lifelong virginity. Thus much doubt has been cast on Marguerite Périer's account of her uncle's projected marriage. Nevertheless, the perspectives on her uncle's worldly proclivities at this time, coupled with her mother's evident dismay that this period "was the least well spent time" of her brother's life, make it difficult to dismiss completely the possibility that Pascal may have contemplated marriage, doing so (to take Marguerite Périer's lead) with the purposefulness and care, not to say cunning, we have seen him take in many of his commitments to science and theological inquiry.

Morris Bishop has suggested that the conjugal commitment Pascal contemplated at this time was to Charlotte de Roannez, younger sister of the Duc de Roannez whom Pascal was to persuade to adopt the religious ways of Port Royal just as, later, he would persuade Charlotte herself.[17] (For Bishop this relationship even becomes the grounds for attributing to Pascal the *Discourse on the Passions* that most Pascal scholars refuse to see as by the author of the *Thoughts*.) Though suggestive, by concentrating on the girl rather than both the "girl and the office," Bishop's interpretation misses the full import of the contradiction both in itself and in its relation to the future strictures on *both* the lower orders, flesh and mind.

That Pascal was preoccupied with the order of the world in things other than the flesh has been clear to us since his dedicatory letter of May 22, 1645, to Chancellor Séguier on the "arithmetic machine" (quoted in the Introduction). Not only the tone of that letter but the worldly advantages that Pascal hoped to derive from that invention show his persistent and consistent concern with "offices." True, since that time we have seen him become more deeply aware of the depradations of the world without Christ. But nothing, not even the death of his father, suggests that he found it impossible to live in the world as if Christ had not existed. He lived as his father had, and, knowing his admiration for his father, it is not a contradiction for him to have followed his father's example. He had not had the vocation to live in Christ without the world that his younger sister had.

If we are looking without judgment for contradictions in Pascal's psychological and religious makeup, a more significant terrain of feeling lies not in his relations with Charlotte de Roannez but in his relations with his younger sister. Their father dead, he now assumes toward Jacqueline the domineering and hostile role Etienne Pascal had played toward her. Given the acknowledged closeness cum jealousy that we have seen characteristic of their relationship, it is possible that his feelings toward Jacqueline were incestuous. His later spiritual direction of Charlotte de Roannez may well have been at once a reprise of those feelings and a guilt-laden effort to sublimate those feelings. Like Etienne, he finally resisted his sister's efforts to realize her vocation, but not for the materialistic reasons that some scholars have seen in the disposition of their father's estate just after his death. As Jean Mesnard has shown, that dispositon provided little if any material advantage to Blaise over Jacqueline.[18] Blaise is not thus incriminated even by those clauses that, upon Jacqueline's death as a religious, redounded her portion to her brother. As Mesnard cogently observes, Jacqueline's projected religious vow of poverty explains this codicil. The reason that she entered at all into the complicated legal process of the exchange of her due from the estate with Blaise was to enable him to take advantage of increased capital. Of greater interest in these documents are the conditions affecting Jacqueline's share should she marry, for given the intensity of Jacqueline's vocation, there was little possibility of that. We may also conjecture that, should she not have been accepted as a religious, her brother would have accorded her the same secular retreat from the world that her father had accorded her in the last two years of his life.

This conjecture is grounded in the motive of his continuing opposition to her vocation as reported by both sisters. In her *Life of Jacqueline*[19] Gilberte reports that, upon the death of their father, Blaise had not only been greatly comforted by Jacqueline but that he had assumed she would postpone her decision to enter the convent and "remain with him at least a year, in order to help him resolve himself to her departure." Jacqueline told Gilberte that she would enter the convent as soon as the estate was settled and that she would tell Blaise she intended only to make a retreat on the occasion. Even this detour upset Blaise greatly when it was reported to him in the terms Jacqueline wished. She made the retreat early in January 1652, and, as is evident from a letter she wrote to her brother from the convent four months later (May 7–9, 1652), he was still not reconciled to her departure.[20]

She begins by reminding him that she is free to realize her vocation, thanks to the removal of the only obstacle through God's taking of her father (whose death she cannot bring herself to name). Nevertheless, she pleads with Blaise to grant his "consent and avowal" lest her joy in this "most glorious and happiest action of my life" be marred by his refusal. As in her letter to her father on the same subject four years earlier, Jacqueline shows at once courage and wile. Knowing the pull of family calls to "tenderness," she realizes she must take the utmost "precaution to make you consent to a totally holy and just thing, because the natural and supernatural graces that God has given you should lead you to encourage me in my plan if I were unfortunate enough to weaken in it." Nor is her tone without an edge of reproach if not bitterness as she goes on: "I dare not expect that from you, although I have the right to hope for it given the knowledge that you have." The reproach is not without a kind of spiritual blackmail as she goes on to reiterate it in larger moral terms: "but I do expect that you will make an effort on yourself not to put yourself in a state to make me lose the graces that I have received, and to answer for it before God, to whom I protest that it will be you alone that I shall blame and that I shall ask for them [the graces] back: May God spare us one and the other from falling into this misfortune!" Having begun with her strongest weapon, Jacqueline relents in this reproachful tone. As she does so we sense that in her brother's attitude toward her vocation there is a reprise of her father's attitude: each needed her humanly. "I know that nature arms itself with everything in these situations and that, to avoid what it fears, everything seems to it just and that, to foment what it will suggest to you, everyone will not fail on this occasion to exercise that sort of charity of fervor that is usual and that opposes only the good." She has too recently left the world, she writes, not to know its ways, the ways of "our enemy" (the devil) who uses praise of virtue as one of his chief weapons to weaken virtue in a soul under the pretext of communicating virtue itself to another. So she urges her brother:

> Resist this great temptation courageously if it come to you, and, when the world will express to you some regret at no longer seeing me, assure yourself that it is an illusion that would disappear immediately were it not a question of opposing a good; since it is impossible that there be a true friendship for a person who does not belong to it, who wishes

never to do so, and who presently has no greater desire than to destroy it with respect to herself, in abandoning it forever, by a solemn vow and by the commitment to a life totally opposed to its maxims, and who would with good heart give up all that it holds most dear to imprint a similar sentiment in all the souls that she knows.

Jacqueline's remarkable letter of farewell to her brother has the tone of a love letter of the final kind, in which one lover tells the other that he or she has found someone else more attractive and more worthy than the lover being abandoned. Given the religious nature of Jacqueline's new love, this is to say that she finds her brother too given to the world precisely in the tenderness through which he would cling to her. Undoubtedly he was the one above all in whose soul she would imprint "a similar sentiment" of renunciation of the world. But, for him, *she* was the world he would not renounce. We can imagine the anguish of his soul and his flesh when, near the end of her letter, she tells him that he must work against his dependence on her and prays to him—as if to God himself—"for my engagement" (*mes fiançailles*), the taking of the veil. It was to her with whom he was of one flesh that he clung in the world until the very moment of her "engagement."

That moment, we learn from an extract of a letter Jacqueline sent Gilberte the very next day, May 10, 1652, he would have postponed in the face of Jacqueline's fierce resolve.[21] We learn too that it had not been a year's postponement, as reported by Gilberte, but two years. Moreover, undoubtedly with symbolic awareness of the dates, on the feast of the Ascension, May 9, 1652, she had a friend carry the news to her brother that she intended to take the veil two weeks later, on May 26, 1652, the feast of the Holy Trinity. (The letter of May 7–9 just reviewed, containing the same news, was undoubtedly sent after, suggesting that it was long mulled over and undoubtedly written and rewritten by the anxious correspondent.) When he came the next day, Jacqueline tells her sister, their brother had a terrible headache but was considerably "softened," though still not resolved to the loss of Jacqueline: "instead of two years that he had asked of me the last time, he no longer wanted me to wait any longer than until All Soul's Day." That is, he wanted her to postpone the ceremony by another five months. In the face of Jacqueline's adamancy, though, "he softened completely and took pity on the trouble that it gave me to put off again a thing I have wanted for so long." As we can glean from Jacqueline in the final

lines of this letter, however, both his words and his actions on this occasion indicate that he would have postponed and postponed were it
within his rather than Jacqueline's power. She writes that "he did not
show up on time; but M. d'Andilly, at my behest, had the goodness to
have him fetched Saturday and went about things with such warmth
and astuteness that he made him consent to all that we wanted; so that
we stayed at this point, that he asked me to my utmost to surmount
myself such that I put off considerable time and that, if I did not wish
to, he liked it as well that it be the feast of the Trinity as two weeks
later." Jacqueline was too intelligent not to have understood the hurt
and resentment lying beneath the surface of this final consent. For
him, the sooner the better—which is to say the worse.

The worsening was renewed for him as the moment of Jacqueline's
profession of final vows approached one year later. During that year he
continued his worldly ways in both science and society with captains
of the earth (in this case, the Queen of Sweden) and figures like the
Chevalier de Méré, becoming a kind of precursor of those worldly intellectuals of the eighteenth century whom we now call *philosophes*. He
also pursued his scientific work. Concerning his worldly relation with
his younger sister, it is important to reiterate once again that there is
no contradiction between this worldliness and the reprise of resistance
on his part to her vocation as the latter was about to be sealed forever
through her final vows. For his later religious views to be understood
in their full force we must understand first the full extent and force of
his fierce attachment to his sister. In that worldly and possibly sensuous attachment we can all the more know the depths of fear and anguish from which he would have come to see such concupiscence as
sinful. He perhaps knew the temptation to break the strongest taboo
of religion and civilization. Being a man who, in his other desires for
scientific preeminence and for worldly attention, succeeded almost
without fail in realizing his will, we can understand the anguish of the
frustrations to his will in the sensuous realm. As he had learned from
his concern with the imperious "I" in his relations with his father that
the "I" is hateful, so he would have learned in his worldly and possibly
sensuous attachment to his sister that the will is corrupt.

That he had corrupted that attachment as she understood it is clear
enough in Jacqueline's report of her brother's behavior as the moment
of her final vows approached.[22] Written to the prioress of Port Royal
in the Fields, Mother Marie-Dorothy of the Incarnation, under the

title, "Relation of Sister Euphémie, that must be kept secret because of the people it touches on," and dated June 10, 1653, the document is a review of the opposition by her relatives to the disposition she wished to make of her inheritance upon taking final vows on June 5, 1653. "Relatives" this time includes Gilberte (and possibly Gilberte's husband) along with Blaise, but the brunt of the report on this opposition is borne chiefly by Blaise.

As the taking of vows approached, Jacqueline had decided to make the monastery at Port Royal the beneficiary of a substantial portion of her inheritance if not, as some have conjectured, of the entire inheritance. Blaise and the Périers wrote separately (copies have not survived) in protest against this act by which they would be "disinherited"(as we remember, in case of Jacqueline's entry into the religious life or her death, Blaise was actually to be the sole inheritor). As Mesnard points out, both religious and civil law were on their side, for a religious could not make such a disposition of her fortune as she "died to civil life."[23] Both Church and society thus prevented the most obvious kinds of abuse to their institutional integrity. Jacqueline understands this argument from the religious side quite well in her "Relation." She reports how she came to understand this need for both institutional and personal religious integrity through the wise counsel of a Mother Angélique, who happened to have come to the Paris site of Port Royal where Jacqueline resided. The older nun advised her to write to her relatives that she relinquished purely and simply her inheritance, but even after doing so, by her own report, Jacqueline had clung to the regret at the injustice that the convent suffered through not receiving a donation of whatever scale through her offices. The older nun then made Jacqueline see that she still clung to the world in many ways. In her continued preoccupation with the matter, in her shock at the world's self-interest, she showed that she had not fully understood the rule of charity by which the world's self-interest was an expected thing. Beyond this pride, she was perhaps guilty of the paradoxical pride of a humility and submissiveness assumed only to demonstrate to her adversaries that she was spiritually their better. Even in wishing to create in her relatives and in her brother in particular the desire to give something to the monastery on their own, she may still have been guilty of trying to use a worldly understanding of human nature to achieve an otherworldly purpose. In writing to her brother again, Jacqueline reports Mother Angélique warned her in particular that it was necessary "to avoid on the one hand doing it by pride and courage, saying: 'We shall have more generosity than you.' If we do it by that principle, it would be worth nothing at all. There must be charity alone that obliges us to it; otherwise it is as if we did nothing. And on the other, we must guard against wishing by that to pique them through friendship, in order to oblige them to do what we want; for that would be to take back on one hand what we leave aside on the other."

The terms recall the paradoxes of the code of generosity by which Cornelian heroes and heroines lived. One thinks of *Le Cid*, of Chimène's amorous combat with Rodrigue, in which she leads her lover to see that if he does not fight to the death in the duel he must fight with the champion she has chosen to avenge her lover's slaying of her father, her lover will have shown himself unworthy of her love in the first place. On the lips of Mother Angélique, the word *générosité* is informed more with the softer senses it has increasingly gained since the time of Corneille, kindness and eleemosynary giving. Apposite as she makes it to "pride" and "courage," the word may nevertheless have been chosen by Mother Angélique with an awareness of its etymological overtones of narcissistic concern with a self both essentially and existentially superior to any adversary. Certainly, in the deed that is at the root of the dispute between Jacqueline and her relatives there are signs of such a prideful self in Jacqueline. Against the code of the institution into which she was entering, she dared to assert her own rule. In clinging to that desire even after she has been advised by Mother Angélique to abandon it, she shows the tenacity and sense of self that characterized her brother in his defense of his scientific priority in the experiments on the vacuum and that he had manifested only the year before in his letter to Christina of Sweden with its reversal of the presumed inferior relation of men of science to the captains (and queens) of the earth.

The confrontation of two such prideful spirits, particularly in light of the tender feelings he felt she has rejected in entering the religious life, was bound to be explosive on this occasion. Jacqueline's account of the confrontation confirms this expectation.

A few days later [after her final conversation with Mother Angélique], that one of my relatives who had the greatest interest in this matter [her brother, as the masculine demonstrative of the French makes clear although the circumstances hardly require such evidence] having come to town, I tried to treat him according to the intentions of our Mother. But whatever effort I could make, it was completely impossible entirely to conceal the sadness that remained with me after all the trouble she had taken to make it cease. That is so unusual with me that he sensed it immediately, and he needed no interpreter to learn the cause; for although I put on the best face that I could, I am convinced that he quickly judged that his conduct had put me in this state. Nevertheless, he wanted to be the first to complain, and it was then that I learned that they [he and the Périers] considered themselves so offended by my conduct. But he hardly continued, seeing that I made no complaints from my side, even though I might destroy with a single word all their reasons, and that, on the contrary, I declared to him with all the gaiety that my state of mind could allow that, since the convent was willing to grant me the charity of accepting me freely without a donation and since my final vows would not be deferred, I was no longer troubled by anything but to take them [the vows] well and to acquire the grace I needed to be a true religious.

The passage tells us much about Jacqueline and about her brother. It shows her pride, her strength of will, her shrewdness. For all the counsel of Mother Angélique, she admits that she could not approach this encounter with the disinterestedness that the Saint Cyranian concept of charity imposed on her. As she refers to Mother Angélique's counsels, the counselor is herself not spared the jabs of Jacqueline's pride. Jacqueline reports her sadness as if Mother Angélique were wrong to counsel against such sadness. From the older nun's perspective, Jacqueline's thinly veiled reproach justifies the charge she had made "in smiling" to the postulant that she was not yet fully in the spirit of the convent because "you have not yet unaccustomed yourself to see yourself as belonging more to your family than to it, since you are jealous of their honor and their advantage to the prejudice of ours." Proud, righteous, ambitious in religion as she had been in poetry and society, Jacqueline will be proved right even as she seems to report the correction of a conduct she had been told was wrong. The self-love that Mother Angélique had told her was the engine of the world drives her own thought and feeling in the lines where she so shrewdly perceives its operation in her brother's behavior on this occasion: "Nevertheless, he wanted to be the first to complain" and "even though I might destroy with a single word their reasons." She pride-

fully clings to her complaint even as she represses it, both in the encounter and in reporting the encounter. For she was determined to
become a nun. She reports her joy in not having her vocation deferred
for the want of the donation.

We remember that in her first reflections and discussions of the matter, with Mother Agnès and M. Singlin at Port Royal, as reported
early in the "Relation," her chief concern seemed to be that this deter-
mination would be frustrated by the litigious situation she had created. She *willed* to be a nun. Was her vocation the religious prolonga-
tion of her rivalry with her brilliant brother? Was she moved not by
God but by a desire to outshine him in a domain where his apparent
commitment to science (and, later, the world) implied no possibility of
rivalry? Was she also pridefully moved to demonstrate the superficial-
ity of his purported commitment to the things of religion? Mother
Angélique had warned her against the danger of using her submissiveness thus. She reports in this passage that she needed only the
"charity" of the convent, that it was taking her in "freely." As these
two words commingle in a single sentence in the report (and as they
probably did in the encounter itself), the Saint Cyranian thrust is taken
from the "charity" and the word "freely" resounds of simony. We remember how Jacqueline had similarly used the vocabulary of market
exchange a year before, as she was about to take the veil, telling her
brother: "It is not reasonable that I prefer any longer others to myself,
and it is just that they do to themselves a little violence in order to re-
pay me that which I have done to myself for four years." Her ministrations to her father and to her brother had indebted them to her. As she
writes of that debt on the two crucial occasions, first and final vows,
she casts her sacrifice in the terms of a promissory note.

The letter of the late spring 1653 had the ring of a mistress abandoning her lover. The encounter of late spring 1654 and its report have the
ring of a lovers' quarrel or a divorce. Handmaiden to her father and
then to her brother, secretary to the latter, comforter to him in his fe-
rocities, Jacqueline found herself in a position in which women have
found themselves since time immemorial: helpmeet whose own personality must be subordinated to the realization of the other's self. In
later centuries women would divorce themselves from such a trial—
quite literally, in the legal sense. In seventeenth-century Catholic
France women took the only route to self-realization open to a woman
who did not wish to or could not abandon herself to the world: reli-

gious vocation as a form of legal divorce. In the encounter here Pascal behaved like many a husband or lover confronted with a wife or mistress's self-assertion: he put his own feelings first: "he wanted to be the first to complain." Both before the law and in light of his personal situation in the world, he was not wrong. Mother Angélique had reminded Jacqueline of her brother's financial and social need in this respect. Given her intelligence and her oft reiterated disdain of the worldly needs that she had herself known, Jacqueline may not have needed the reminder. Perhaps she foresaw the difficulties her intended disposition of the legacy would create for her brother but went ahead with it precisely as a way of protesting the priority that the man in a family traditionally and, as she perhaps saw it, unjustly enjoys.

Jacqueline may have been even more rebellious than her brother. Unlike him in his ambivalent rebellions against his father, however, she was both more consistent and more persistent. In the end, after her final vows, he did make a substantial donation to the convent. The insights into both his and his sister's character to be gained from this gesture lie not in the donation itself but in its large size. The donation itself was to be expected, for the family of any postulant finally accepted usually made such a donation, or dowry, as it was called. The convent did not have to persuade Pascal to make a contribution; he would have done that anyway and told his sister so as their bitter encounter came to a more or less peaceable end: "he was moved to confusion, and, by his own motion he resolved to put this matter in order, offering to take upon himself all the costs and risks of the legacy, and to do for the convent what he readily saw one could not omit in all justice." This gesture by her brother led Jacqueline to become concerned and to express her concern to her superiors about the size of the donation her brother was to make. Given the lesson of living by Saint Cyranian rules of charity she claims to have learned and to have applied up to this point, Jacqueline might just as well have left the matter in God's hands. But neither she nor on this occasion those who had taught her these lessons could leave well enough alone.

We may wonder if her brother did make so handsome a donation in a genuine spirit of disinterestedness. Perhaps he was uninformed by the sin of pride against which Mother Angélique in a final counsel had warned Jacqueline it must not be made, though Jacqueline reports that she repeated this caution "word for word" to her brother. Among the words used by the older nun and reported to Blaise were these: "I

would much prefer that he give nothing at all than give a great deal
out of a human principle. All that we can do, you and I, is to exhort
him not to do it; for we do not have his conscience to govern so as to
see by what motive he acts, it is up to him to examine it; but to contribute by our discourse, or by our looks, or in whatever way, to make
him take a bad one, would be not only to participate in his sin, but to
be the cause of it." Jacqueline's repetition of these counsels may well
be read as an example of the question posed to the married man:
"When did you stop beating your wife?" She and Mother Angélique
in her complicity to exhortation of Blaise here were perhaps shrewd
enough to see that, were it posited in this way, Blaise could not but
make a generous donation.

   This is not to see Pascal as Jacqueline's dupe and victim in this interesting encounter with her. If Jacqueline's report gives us certain insights into her character, it also provides equally interesting insights
into her brother's at this time. The adversary still prevails in his
character. Jacqueline's remark that "he wanted to be the first to complain" is of general as well as particular value. It recalls Gilberte's
general observation on the impatience and vivacity with which Blaise
behaved in his encounters with almost everyone. More especially, it
shows those traits as they manifested themselves in any difficult situation. For all the justice that lay on his side in the matter of Jacqueline's
outlandish proposal on her legacy, the pattern of his relations with her
since their father's death is too consistent not to see on this occasion,
too, that Pascal's right-thinking head is the dupe of a heart wounded
by his sister's abandonment of him.

   As he mounts this final opposition to the way in which his sister
would conduct herself as a religious, we cannot help wondering if he
had not hoped that it would disqualify her for acceptance. His accession to her first vows may have seemed easy once he had accepted it the
year before, but he well knew that those were only *first* vows, not
binding, and in the year that had elapsed he could have counted on
something to prevent the absolute loss of Jacqueline. He loved her as
much as he hated her in this moment. We do not know the terms in
which this love/hate *on both sides* expressed itself on the occasion. Jacqueline tells her correspondent that the colloquy was not so worthy as
the earlier one and that it was neither pretty nor useful. Given this
ugliness and futility one must wonder what moved Blaise to such
promptitude and generosity on the occasion "by his own motion."

The motion *is* characteristic of Pascal, if the social image of him depicted by Gilberte is to be our guide. Being told or perceiving for himself that he had upset people by the impatience and vivacity of his spirit, "He immediately repaired his fault by dealings so decent [*honnêtes*] that he never lost the friendship of anyone thereby." Perhaps in this moment he feared to lose that friendship most dear to him, his sister Jacqueline's. Nevertheless, in the promptness and resolution and sense of justice so close upon so much ugliness and futility, it is as likely that it was pride and the competitive desire to "go her one better" that moved him. The match between the quarreling and quarrelsome younger Pascals thus seems to have ended at best in a draw if not with a slight advantage to Jacqueline. Each would go the way he and she had chosen: Jacqueline out of the world and into the religious life, Blaise into the world.

Did going into the world mean, for Pascal, going away from the religious life? There is no evidence of that. That he should have given himself with his usual fervor, impatience, and vivacity to the world is not a *necessary* sign of a loss of faith. It may have been so for some at Port Royal but, to anticipate one of the famous formulations of the *Provincial Letters,* he "was not of Port Royal."

· 3 ·

THE
ADVERSARIAL
BELIEVER
AND THE
WORLD

As PASCAL now made his way in the world of science and society, he was not of Port Royal. The latter was a world apart, and its rules were not to intrude in the worlds of rulers in science and government. He had been living in that world when the first strains had begun to show between the two younger Pascal children. In June 1652 as we have seen, he had written a letter to Christina, Queen of Sweden, as revealing of his religious position in what it does not say on the subject as his letters to his sisters for what they do say thereon. It is useful to return to other portions of that letter.

He had been prompted to write to the queen by a famous physician with whom he had been in contact, Bourdelet, who had lauded the young scientist's achievements, particularly the calculating machine, to the monarch. Pascal took the occasion to expand, as quoted earlier, on the "two things that fill me equally with admiration and respect, which are sovereign authority and solid knowledge [*science*]." These are premises of what he would later call the two orders of flesh and mind, with no mention of the third and supreme order, charity or heart. In the letter to Christina he elaborated and emphasized the motif that he had barely sketched at the end of his letter to Gilberte and Florin Périer on the death of his father, the superiority of reason. There, it was as if the order of charity were supportive if not subordinate to the order of reason. Here, it is the order of the flesh that is subordinated to the order of mind, for, he goes on in the letter,

> It must thus be admitted that each of these empires [sovereign authority and knowledge] is great in itself; but, Madame, if Your Majesty permit me to say so (she is not offended thereby), one without the

102

THE ADVERSARIAL BELIEVER AND THE WORLD   103

other appears to me defective. However powerful a monarch be, there is something missing in his glory if he does not have preeminence of mind; and however enlightened a subject be, his condition is always reduced by dependency.

Tone and concept are equally important for an understanding of Pascal's psychological and religious state of mind in the so-called worldly period to which this letter belongs. Conceptually, in his use of the term *glory* to summarize the two things or powers or conditions that are his concern here, we are struck by his failure to mention the third order, the supreme one as he would see it later in a reprise of some of the very language he uses here (for example: "genius . . . empire" and the idea that each is "great in itself"). The language of this passage might easily have led into a discussion of the third and specifically religious order: for example, veneration, supreme degree, and knowledge in the French form *connaissances,* a word particularly frequent in the religious milieu of the Pascals. Yet, the lesson of the exclusion of the order of charity here in the letter to Christina lies precisely in the appropriateness of the occasion.

I do not mean that Pascal did not broach the matter of religion because he knew he was dealing with a non-Catholic monarch. Such a consideration would not have prevented him from discussing the order of religion, in an abstract way at least. Moreover, at one point he addresses the queen as "sacred person" (*personne sacrée*), which not only shows his awareness of another domain or order but also suggests the immanence of that order in the vocabulary he uses in the letter. However, he excludes that order here just as, on the occasion of his father's death, he had excluded the order of knowledge to which Socrates and Seneca belonged, because the occasion does not call for it in the terms in which Pascal had conceived of the operation of the three orders. At this time, however, the order of reason seems superior to both the order of the flesh (or power) and the order of the heart (or charity). I have already demonstrated this with respect to the order of the flesh (concupiscence and natural temptation) in the letter on the father's death. Here, the superiority of reason over the order of the flesh is even more patent: "the power of kings . . . is but an image of the power of minds." Reason is an all-embracing concept that is at once an order and a function, while the other two orders—flesh explicitly and, here, heart implicitly—seem to be only containers, sources or objects of action and knowledge on which reason operates as effectively as it does on objects appropriate to its own order in the tripartite distinction among orders that Pascal would elaborate in the *Thoughts*. At this moment, both linguistically and, by implication, theologically, Pascal is at one with the scientist-philosopher-mathematician whom he would later dismiss as the proponent of "the God of the flick of the finger," Descartes. Both relegate God and the things of religion to a transcendent realm, treating the power of reason as immanent to the human condition. Reason creates rational models by which the world is ordered to human ends, both personal and social. Language itself is such a model or a seemingly endless series of such models manipulated to express the changing conceptions of reason or mind as it seizes, in Descartes' case, upon "clear and distinct" ideas, and as it discovers, in Pascal's case, the workings of nature or of power. Little wonder that *this* Pascal should skeptically (or aporetically, in Louis Marin's term) dismiss Christina's station in the world with the derisive "but an image." Royal station is an inferior application of the power of mind. Significantly, both Pascal and Descartes are not only pure scientists but applied scientists as well. The very occasion of this letter, Pascal's calculating machine, is a case in point. Similarly, Descartes envisaged the application of many of his principles to medicine. In this commonality of pure cum applied science, the translation of an immanent power of reason to the natural world, Pascal, like Descartes, expresses a long-standing adversary attitude toward nature: it is there to be exploited, manipulated to human ends. This is evident in Pascal's concept of the "figural" relation between mind and body; its political and psychological implications are apparent in the way in which Pascal relegates the social and political superiority of monarchs to the realm of birth and accident, to the realm of nature. "Reign," Pascal tells the queen near the end of the letter, "by right of birth, by a long series of years, over so many triumphant provinces; but reign always by the force of your merit over the entire expanse of the earth." There are intimations of immortality here: the combination of temporal and geographical hyperbole evokes the religious formulation throughout the centuries *ad secula seculorum*.

Merit of mind reigns and shall forever reign over earth. Some thinkers see this adversary relation between mind and nature as particularly Western, emanating with the Greeks but given exploitative and hostile impetus by the Judeo-Christian tradition in particular. Perhaps this is true, but one must recall that many non-Western cultures also believe that the earth is a gift of the gods to be exploited by their chosen people. Moreover, within the Western and more particularly Judeo-Christian tradition one would have to make certain crucial distinctions. We have already noticed how, in his strictly religious writings thus far, Pascal insists on the Augustinian equation of Judaic and carnal. In the projected *Apology for the Christian Religion* he will elaborate this equation into a major motif of the difference between Christian and Jew in the Judeo-Christian tradition, explaining that the very immanentist concern with the order of flesh that has not been gainsaid by grace is what merits the exclusion of the Jews, as it does pagans, from salvation in the order of the heart. Before he reaches that explanation, the equation between carnality and Judeo-Paganism is, like the objects of science itself, susceptible to the control of science, what he calls in his letter to Christina of Sweden, "solid science."

Like others in this letter that formulation is as revealing tonally as it is conceptually. The tone of this letter looks forward not to the tone of the projected *Apology,* in which the "I" will be "hateful." Rather, it looks forward to the tone of the *Provincial Letters,* in which the "I" does "not content myself with the probable, but the certain." The "I" and its needs are very much to fore here. The rigidity and inflexibility of Pascal's temperament, manifest in his religious differences with Saint Ange and Rebours as in his scientific differences with Noël and Descartes, finds its corollary in his admiration for the solid, the supreme, and the sovereign. His need for certitude made him admire unambivalent states of being and often casts him, until the period of the *Thoughts,* into an adversary and intolerant attitude toward ambiguity, imperfection, and inferiority. Even in this letter of gratitude and spiritual fealty to the queen he cannot resist the adversary thrust of his being. The queen might well have found inadequate his brief parenthetical assurance that his exaltation of mind over throne was not intended to be offensive. As monarch she is made out to be a monster. Her real superiority lies in her power of mind, and the chief evidence of that power seems to lie in its capacity to recognize *his* power of mind. His compliments to the queen on this power are very dubious: throughout the long duration of the world, Pascal tells her, one has hardly seen a king even "moderately knowledgeable; this masterpiece was reserved to your century." As he takes account of the fact that this "masterpiece of moderate knowledgeability" is also a woman, he portrays her as a monster in that relation as well: in this young queen he mentions a number of seemingly contradictory states and qualities, among them "the eminence of knowledge with the weakness of sex." With such admirers the young queen needed no detractors.

Male chauvinism was undoubtedly being voiced as well as a larger temperamental chauvinism that characterized Pascal: an assertive, rushing-in-where-angels-dare-to-tread spirit with confidence that his mind could take charge where others could not or had failed to. He had proven his power of mind since he was a small boy, amazing his father-teacher by the speed and brilliance with which he learned and at times by the self-teaching he had undertaken—for example, creating on his own many of the proofs of Euclidean geometry when he was but nine years old. He was mentally gifted and accepted the gift without questioning its source. He does not raise with Christina the question of the source of his and her mental superiority. His opposition of "merit" to "birth and fortune" might suggest to some an existentialist explanation: nurture is more important than nature, and one is what one does. In light of such an interpretation we might well read the letter as potentially revolutionary, as if Pascal were protesting as politely as possible the injustice of a world in which birth prevailed over merit, accident over necessity, brute power over spiritual power. Morris Bishop sees existentialist protest in many of Pascal's scientific and personal relations, for example in his "religious seduction" of Charlotte de Roannez once his presumed "proposal of marriage" had been frustrated by her noble cousins, who considered Pascal a social upstart.[1] I think such interpretations miss the point of Pascal's views on the relations between the orders of mind and flesh. If any philosophical position is to be applied to his concept of merit, it would be the Platonic mind set of seventeenth-century France in general and, more particularly, the essentialism of his religious mind set: his merit shows him to be of the elect in the order of the mind; his genius is his birthright. Such concerns do not occur to Pascal at this time, however, precisely because of the separation of orders that he expresses in this letter and he has expressed in previous contexts.

What is of greater interest in this letter is the familiar psychological posture in which it shows Pascal. He baits the queen of Sweden as he had baited his father on the matter of Jacqueline's vocation, but he does not go all the way. Pascal is anything but a revolutionary. In her *Life*, Gilberte reports how politically conservative he was: conservative not reactionary, for he believed that the governance in which a state found itself (a republic in Venice, monarchy elsewhere) should be the one that its inhabitants should retain, because this was the state of things created by God, and he believed especially that to rebel against a monarchy was a "kind of sacrilege" with its consequence being civil war, "the worst evil that one could commit against the charity of one's neighbor." He cannot forsake the stability, the durability, the approbation of established authority. It is this psychological pattern, combined with his remarkable powers of mind, that gives special poignancy to the rebellious position in which he would find himself after his conversion. In fighting the Jesuit fathers he would insist that they were only seeming "fathers," false to the true fathers of the Church, especially Augustine and Paul. Through the intermediary of the true and faithful *Son,* whom he felt he had rejected and with whom he would again rejoin, he would identify with the Father whom he would have half-rejected all his life.

The conversion was still more than two years beyond the letter to Christina of Sweden. In his family life he was to spend the first of those years resolving his relations with his sisters, particularly Jacqueline. In science and the world he would cut an even finer figure than he had before. The letter to Christina announces the ambition and self-regard with which he would pursue science in this year, to the extent that the legal matters attendant on Jacqueline's legacy and his own practical needs would allow. In late October he moved from Paris to Clermont, where he was to stay until late May of the following year. It may have been at this time that, in the words of one memorialist of Port Royal, he courted "the Sappho of this region." Such a courtship may never have occurred, according to some scholars. Were he to have courted someone at this time, that it was a Sappho, a poetess, suggests again the nature of the attachment I have suggested he felt for his sister. On the rebound, the rejected "lover," like so many rejected lovers, would have found in this other poetess a way at once of hurting and recapturing (Jacqueline had taken only her first vows, we remember) the mistress who had abandoned him.

His return to Paris coincided with the occasion of Jacqueline's final vows with all the bitterness of a final rejection. If there is any family development that may be said to have triggered Pascal's worldly period, it was Jacqueline's profession of vows rather than his father's death. Not only is her profession quickly followed by the letter to Christina, which reveals a worldly rationalism, it is also followed, in the summer of the same year according to Mesnard, by his close liaison with the Duc de Roannez and through him with the worldly intellectuals, Méré and Miton. Some have conjectured that Pascal accompanied these three on a journey in Poitou in September of that year, although Mesnard thinks it highly unlikely that he did so.[2] With or without the voyage, as seen in the celebrated fragment of the *Thoughts* that I quoted in the Introduction, the encounter with these worldly intellectuals led Pascal to serious reflection on the relation between the self and the world. This fragment of dialogue between Miton and Pascal does not belong, for many modern editors of the *Thoughts,* in those sections presumed to make up the notes (if not, for some, the text itself) of Pascal's projected *Apology for the Christian Religion.* It is not unrelated to the themes of that project: through its famous opening line, "The self is hateful," it is obviously linked to the attack on self-love that is the very cause of man's "misery without God," the first part of the *Apology.* In this light, the most recent editor, Sellier, includes the fragment among the preparatory dossiers for the project, written between the summer of 1656 and late spring of 1658. It is obviously a recollection of discussions with the witty and argumentative Miton from the time when Pascal frequented him, Méré, and others before his conversion and may even be a recollection written just after the dialogue it reports.

The dialogue has much the air of a salon debate, a frequent entertainment of the period. Gamesmanship was almost without fail Pascal's stance in the world until his conversion, so much so that we are tempted to place his talent for empathizing with others, reported by his sister-biographer, only after that conversion. He had to take the lead and could not tolerate being one step behind. At the same time, he forgot none of the steps he had taken. What is remarkable about his scientific career, as Mesnard has noted, is its continuity. In 1654 he continued projects in physics and mathematics that had long preoccupied him. In physics he completed treatises (published posthumously) on the equilibrium of liquids and on the weight of air, summarizing researches on those subjects that we know him to have begun a decade earlier. Their conclusion shows the familiar prideful, adversarial spirit thirsting for personal vindication on the question of the value of his contributions to the new understanding of the vacuum:

Let all the disciples of Aristotle assemble all there is of any strength in the writings of their master, and of his commentators, to give cause [*raison*] for these things through the horror of the vacuum, if they can; otherwise, let them acknowledge that experiments are the true masters that must be followed in physics; that the one that was made on the mountains has overthrown [*renversé*] this universal belief of the world, that nature abhors a vacuum, and opened up this knowledge that can never more perish, that nature has no horror of the vacuum, that it does nothing to avoid it, and that the weight of the air is the true cause of all the effects that one had until now attributed to this imaginary cause.[3]

Beneath the seemingly objective, impersonal validity of experiment that is opposed to the subjective, personal fallacy of Aristotle and his commentators, Pascal's fellow scientists, like the later readers of the early exchanges in the controversy, can readily see that he poses himself here as the new Aristotle. This one will not perish like the first; he gives intimations of immortality through science, once again, even more clearly than in the letter to Christina.

His worldly period was not, however, simply a moment for vindictively catching up in the order of the mind. It also betokened a fresh start in mathematics. He continued the important work in conics and in arithmetic that had long interested him; in 1654 he published a treatise on conics as well as a treatise on the arithmetic triangle (with related treatises). Also in this period, as he reported in an address in Latin to an Academy of Mathematics at Paris in which he brought his confrères up to date on his researches, he was working on

a piece of research altogether new and bearing on a matter entirely unexplored, that is, on the combinations of chance in the games that are subject to it, what is called in our language *to play at games of chance,* where the uncertainty of fortune is so well dominated by the rigor of the calculation that, of two players, each finds himself assigned exactly what comes back to him in fairness. It is necessary to research it all the more vigorously because the possibilities are lesser in being taught by experiment *or* experience. In fact, the ambiguous results of chance are rightly attributed rather to the hazard of contingency that to a necessity of nature. This is why the question has moved about uncertainly until this day; but now, if it has been rebellious to experiment, it has not been able to escape the empire of reason. For we have reduced it to art with such a surety, thanks to geometry, that having participated in the certitude of the latter, it progresses henceforth with audacity, and, by the union thus realized between the demonstrations of mathematics and the uncertainty of chance, and by the conciliation between apparent contraries, it can draw its name from one side as the other and arrogate to itself this astonishing title: *Geometry of Chance.*[4]

Pascal announces probability theory here. The demonstrations of the theory are made by Pascal in letters to the mathematician Fermat in the summer and early fall of the same year and in the treatise on the arithmetic triangle. The mathematical, scientific, social-scientific, and technological import of this new theory has been enormous but is of less concern to us here than the bearing of Pascal's remarks (here and in the letters of Fermat) on his psychological and religious state.

The religious implications of the theory may well have already suggested themselves to the reader: one of the most famous (and for some, infamous) fragments of the *Thoughts,* the wager, applies the rules of chance to the question of the salvation of the soul. In discussing the *Thoughts* as the project for an *Apology for the Christian Religion* I shall return to this relation; here it is illuminating to note that the theory of probability is a theory of that worldly period that he purportedly renounced after his conversion. He came to the theory as a result, in part, of a parlor game that Méré had set him. (*In part* because the theory obviously continues the kind of interest Pascal had long since consciously shown in mathematics and of which he had unconsciously been aware in what might be called the "chanciness" of Jansenist theories of grace.) Méré had set two gambling problems to Pascal. First, suppose that one plays several times with two dice. How many throws are required at the minimum so that one can bet with advantage that, having played these throws, one will throw double six? Second, suppose two players agree to stop play before the end. How could they effect an equal distribution of the stakes according to the probability that each had of winning. With his usual dispatch and ingenuity Pascal provided the answers that have been recorded in the publications I have noted. Informing his dispatch and ingenuity was the by now familiar need to achieve, to lead, and *to be sure.* The very nature of the problem shows especially this need to be sure. Enabling him to satisfy this need was the supreme faculty of reason. As in proving his new views on the ancient and seemingly unshakeable views on the vacuum, so in resolving this equally ancient and seemingly unresolvable problem, he burned with the fires of reason.

Reasoning all the more fiercely and all the more purely was required in that this problem was not susceptible by its very terms to the method that his reason had dictated in the experiments on the vacuum, experimentation. Nature could not be his proof here; only human nature could—more specifically, that element of the human that distinguished it from the rest of nature, the faculty of reason. Of course, at base, the method was not so different in this mathematical research as distinguished from the physical research he had done. In the latter, it had been his reason that had guided him to experiment; he had *rationally tested* observation and hypothesis on the behavior of liquids and their relation to the weight of air. He had made a model and had applied it in the physical universe. Now he would make mathematical models and try them in games of chance (and, later, in the game of fates). The difference may seem one of degree rather than kind. In this very difference, however, one senses the import of reason for Pascal: it could demonstrate its power with unparalleled purity and absoluteness. Is there any wonder, knowing this scientist's confidence in reason, that he should announce this new field that *he* had discovered with such terms as "altogether new . . . entirely unexplored . . . empire of reason . . . with audacity . . . arrogate to itself . . . astonishing title?" And is there any wonder, knowing Pascal's need for certitude, his intolerance of ambivalences, he should announce the virtues of this discovery with such terms as "necessary to research all the more vigorously . . . ambiguous results of chance . . . moved about uncertainly . . . reduced to art with such a surety . . . the certitude of the latter . . . conciliation between apparent contraries?"

He was in the glory of reason; he was the cynosure of scientific and social attention. Fermat's letters are replete with compliments to his genius. (The noted mathematician had good reason to acknowledge that genius, for Pascal's contributions to the new field of probability theory that they were developing showed far greater potential for generalization.) Socially, he was lionized. One stream of Pascalian scholarship has him paying poetic court, possibly the versification of a more practical courtship, to still another lady. In the eighteenth century Condorcet published two short poems said to have been written by Pascal sometime in these two years. In a gallant style he presumably wrote in honor and flattery of the "young and charming hostess," as one verse puts it, of a chateau at which he would have spent some time. Condorcet and others date the verses at the period of the *Provincial Letters,* conjecturing that Pascal would have sought refuge in a bucolic retreat presided over by the lady. The eighteenth-century *philosophe* can only contrast these verses with the "mystic amulet" of the text of the *Memorial* that Pascal wore at the time. Mesnard rightly doubts this dating—at best they would be from 1653–54—and casts strong doubts on the attribution of the verses.[5] Such reserve on the attribution suggests the fear that the verses, even if from the period before his conversion, somehow do not agree with the image of the author of the *Thoughts,* a Pascal consistently and resolutely hostile to the order of the flesh. Whenever they were written, the verses could be by a Pascal given to the order of the mind. He would do the things done in that order, like paying poetic compliments to a charming hostess, and he would do them well.

As Marguerite Périer would have it, he did in fact intend to do another of the things of the order of the flesh: he would find a girl to marry. "Where is the harm of it?" he might well have asked of his coreligionists at Port Royal and of his scholarly hagiographers. This reported intention to marry, coupled with the verses reportedly written by him in the worldly period, bring us back to the end of the period as reported by his sister and his niece in their separate accounts. We remember that Gilberte saw it as the time of his life least well spent. The reproach, one of the few she penned that she did not somehow gainsay in one way or the other, need not imply a life of debauchery. It does tell us that Gilberte's conception of the relation between the order of the heart and the two lesser orders was less complicated that her brother's. She did not like the company he kept, because she did not understand *how* he kept that company. He did so in separate compartments or, in his terms, in separate orders, each to be kept according to its own rules as he saw the relation between them at the time. He could play moral games with Miton and mathematical games with Méré, court a Sappho of Clermont and a "young and charming hostess" of Poitou, correspond with the greatest savants of the international scientific community, and still keep the faith of his father with a purity that he, not Gilberte, would define. If later he came to see the bad "employment" of his worldly period, its "sinfulness" would not lie for him in the debauchery that may have been read into it by Gilberte and that has been read into it by a liberal, anti-Pascalian tradition that seeks to embarrass the literary saint of Jansenism in his religious stronghold. Rather, it would lie in the motives of self-regard that he perceived at its roots as he strove to shine in those lesser orders according to their own rules.

PART II

———◆———

Transition

· 4 ·

THE
CONVERT

Pascal's younger sister helped him to see the crucial role of pride as a motor of his own behavior in the period just before his so-called second conversion. Both Gilberte and Marguerite testify to the catalytic role of Jacqueline at this juncture.

> God [writes Gilberte] who asked of him a greater perfection, did not wish to leave him there in the world a long while, and on that used my sister to withdraw him from it, as he had formerly used my brother to withdraw my sister from the commitments in which she found herself in the world . . . she could not suffer that the one to whom she was indebted through God for the graces that she enjoyed was not in possession of the same graces; and, as my brother saw her often, she often spoke to him of this, and in the end she did it with such force that she persuaded him of that which he had first persuaded her, to leave the world and all the conversations of the world, of which the most innocent are but continual uselessness, altogether unworthy of the holiness of Christianity to which we are all called and of which Jesus Christ has given us the example.

Yet, we know too well the extent to which Blaise had resisted Jacqueline's desire to withdraw from the world to use this passage for its insight into the grounds on which Blaise finally did end his "worldly period." Marguerite Périer's account is more consistent with the complexity of her uncle's temperament and spiritual outlook at the time. Her report also gives continuing evidence of the special relation between the younger Pascal children. Gilberte would have the frequency of contact between Blaise and Jacqueline be a somewhat general matter, without specific cause. Given the bitterness with which they had

115

encountered each other just prior to Jacqueline's final vows, given Pascal's plunge into the worlds of science and the court, this seems a pietistic whitewashing of a relation that was especially strained by his feelings that Jacqueline had abandoned him. Marguerite's report that he went to see Jacqueline precisely on the matter of his projected marriage seems more consistent with the pattern of their stormy relationship.

He was his own man at this time. In his relations with his sisters after his father's death, particularly with respect to Jacqueline, he had conducted himself as pater familias (albeit a role he may have used, with Jacqueline, as a surrogate for the role of lover whose imperatives may have unconsciously caused him great anguish). If he was going to confer with any member of the family on a projected marriage, one would have thought it would be with the older sister on at least two counts: she was the older sister and she was experienced in the married state into which he presumably intended to enter. Instead, it was to the younger sister that he addressed himself, perhaps because of geographical convenience, both being in Paris. The motive would be pretextual. He could have conferred with Gilberte by mail, as he so often had before. He would thus have gone to tell Jacqueline of his proposed marriage out of an old longing and an old resentment. "See, now," his first conversation could be seen to have told her beneath its surface message, "what you have reduced me to by forsaking me." It was after this first conference, as Marguerite reports this juncture, that the "frequency" of visits started: "She exhorted him often to renounce it, but the hour was not yet come." She goes on to report that the hour did not come until the feast of the Immaculate Conception—which is to say December 8, 1654, a fortnight after the brother's night of fire, November 23, 1654, the date of his second conversion from which tradition has marked his supposedly absolute break with the world. That the break was not so absolute, particularly in the hold of reason in the *Provincial Letters,* will be the sense of my analysis of much of that famous work. In the delay between the night of fire and his renunciation of the world two weeks later, one can already see the inadvisability of maintaining the simplistic, univocal conception of Pascal's character that has characterized both the hagiological mainstream of Pascal scholarship and the usually hostile liberal, skeptical, tradition that has relied on the hagiological simplicities chiefly in order to point to Pascal as a religious fraud, moral hypocrite, a schizophrenic, or even a psychopath.

Conversions are not simple affairs, especially in the stringencies of the Christian tenets to which Pascal himself converted. One of the principal tenets of the projected *Apology* as of the writings attendant upon it (particularly the *Writings on Grace* and his letters to Charlotte de Roannez) is the imperfection even of the elect, of the possibility and even probability that the elect will himself or herself be unable to continue in the assurance of salvation so long as one is in the world, even in monastic retreat from the world. Thus it is not surprising or disappointing, and certainly not scandalous, that the recently converted Pascal should still cling to the world. Nor is it unexpected that it should require, through the catalytic influence of his younger sister, an occasion as extraordinary in its timing and as personal in its content as the one reported by Marguerite to bring Pascal to as complete a break with the world as he or any believer of his persuasion could attain.[1]

The occasion was a sermon at Port Royal on the feast of the Immaculate Conception, in which the preacher spoke on

> the beginnings of the life of Christians, and on the importance of rendering them holy, in not committing oneself, as do almost all people of the world, by habit, by custom, and by reasons of a very human proper behavior, in offices and marriages; he showed how it was necessary to consult God before thus committing oneself, and to examine well whether one could thereby work one's salvation and whether one would therein find obstacles thereto. As that was precisely his state and disposition, and this preacher preached that with a great vehemence and solidity, he was deeply touched, and, believing that all that was said for him, he took that way, and making serious reflections on this whole sermon while he heard it, he saw my aunt immediately afterward and noted to her that he had been surprised by this sermon because it seemed that it had been made only for him, and that he was all the more reassured that, having found the preacher in the pulpit, she had let nothing on to him [the preacher]. My aunt encouraged as much as she could this new fire, and in a very few days, he determined to break entirely with the world; and for that he went to spend some time in the country in order to disaccustom himself and break the stream of the great number of visits that he had been making and receiving; that worked for him, for since then he saw no more of his friends whom he had been seeing only in connection with the world.

There is undoubtedly some romanticizing here, at least, if we are to understand "world" to mean more than the order of the flesh and of social or political ambition. In the order of the mind, Marguerite and Gilberte notwithstanding, we know that Pascal would continue to concern himself with such things as the mathematical problem of cycloids and the five-penny bus. But the psychological acumen of this report is nonetheless great. It records the by now familiar pattern of Pascal persisting in a chosen pattern with great fixity, going far down the path before reverting to its opposite and then pursuing that opposite with all the intensity of which he was capable.

Conversions are not simple affairs, either theologically or psychologically. His new state would be one that represents a redirection of energy rather than the substitution of one energy for another, a shift in emphasis; he would rely more on one current, the other still making its force felt. This pattern is manifest not only in his behavior after his conversion, completed as we have seen through the intercession of Jacqueline, but in the moment of conversion itself as he recorded it in the *Memorial*:

1   The year of grace 1654
Monday, 23 November, Saint Clement's day, pope
and martyr, and others in the martyrology.
Eve of Saint Chrysogonus, martyr, and others.
5   From about half past ten in the evening until
around half past midnight.
Fire
God of Abraham, God of Isaac, God of Jacob.
Not of philosophers and scholars.
10   Certitude, certitude feeling, joy, peace.
God of Jesus Christ.
Deum meum et Deum vestrum, my God and your God
Your God will be my God.
Forgetting of the world and everything, except God.
15   He can be found only by the ways taught in the Gospel.
Greatness of the human soul.
Righteous Father, the world has not known Thee,
but I have, O Righteous Father, known Thee.

Joy, joy, joy, tears of joy.
20   I separated myself from Him.
Delinquerunt me fontem aquae vivae, they have
forsaken me, the fountain of living waters
My God, will you abandon me?
Let me not be separated eternally from Him.

25   *And if this is life eternal, that they might*
          know Thee, the only true God, and Jesus Christ
                Whom Thou has sent
                   Jesus Christ.
                   Jesus Christ.
30   I separated myself from Him. I fled, renounced,
                  crucified Him.
         Let me never be separated from Him.
    He can be kept only by the ways taught in the Gospel.
             Total and sweet renunciation
35   etc. (S 742)

I have translated here the version of the *Memorial* in Pascal's hand written on a small fold of paper that was itself inserted in a parchment on which according to his nephew, Louis Périer, Pascal had written a slightly different version of the lines I have given here and which contained at the end the following lines:

       Total submission to Jesus Christ and to my
                  director
      Eternally in joy for one day of effort on earth
      Non obliviscar sermones tuos [I will not forget Thy
38   Word]
               Amen (L 913)[2]

During his life Pascal carried both parchment and insert in the lining of his jacket. It was obviously what Condorcet called it in the next century, a "mystic amulet." We need not accept Condorcet's derisive overtone, however, for we can understand that the imperious self who had "separated himself from Him" carried this amulet close to his heart throughout his life not out of some superstitious faith in any mystical powers. Rather, he carried it as an act of self-discipline or, more exactly, in the spirit of the text of the *Memorial* itself, of *anti-self* discipline. Pascal had come to know himself, his *self* in all its imperious narcissism. As much the record of a conversion, the *Memorial* is the record of a deconversion from self-regard by this son who has rebelled in his heart against his father and who had known the anguish of separation from that father. In the "God of Jesus Christ," in God through Jesus Christ, who had also seemed to rebel against the Father ("O My God, why has Thou forsaken me?"), Pascal became reconciled to the father. He thus found the certitude to appease the anguish of ambivalence, the love, and the respect for the father warring with the need for self-definition and transcendence of the father's influence. With certitude came "feeling" to buttress "reason," the feelings of joy and peace that assuaged trouble and confusion.

I say to *buttress* reason for the *Memorial* does not attack reason. Rather, its content, like the very act of carrying it through the rest of his life, shows a new relation between reason, the order of mind, and feeling, the order of the heart. This relation emerges most clearly in considering the differences between the version on the folded paper and the version on the pouch of parchment. The version on the folded paper in itself shows the operation of Pascal's memory, a cognitive function related to rational learning and intelligence. The biblical and liturgical texts, some in Latin, some in French (italicized in my translation) undoubtedly sprang to Pascal's spirit in the fire of grace that had moved him. But the meditative form of the *Memorial* shows that the fire of grace had not dampened the fires of reason. It had put them to its own votive use.

In neither version is the *Memorial* an adumbration of the Romantic or Surrealist form in which it was long believed Pascal later wrote the fragments of the *Thoughts*: acts of inspired or automatic writing in which the reflective self plays no part. In those parts that both versions have in common we clearly have the record of an experience that has been consummated and that is being recorded in a two-part meditation: a first part with a reflective exactness about date, time, and religious setting; a second part (beginning with the titular "Fire" in the center of the page on its own line) in which reflective ("God of . . . not of ") and objective (biblical and liturgical references) elements are orchestrated into a poem with three movements with distinct but related motifs. In the first movement (lines 7–16) the poet-convert identifies primarily with God the Father ("God of Abraham," and so on) but sounds the motif of the Son ("God of Jesus Christ . . . the ways taught in the Gospel"), which will later emerge as the principal motif of another movement. The second movement (lines 17–24) is intensely personal, a joyous affirmation of reconciliation with the "Righteous Father," an affirmation nonetheless haunted by the intense personal anguish of having been separated by his own doing ("Je m'en suis séparé"—the reflexive form of the verb has both personal and theological significance). In the third movement the poet reconciles the antithetical modes of the first two movements. The positive feelings of identification with the Father and the attendant feeling of certitude, joy, and peace are reconciled with the anguish at having denied the Righteous Father, an anguish compounded by the fear that the Father will now deny the poet-convert. In this movement there is not only reconciliation on the subjective level, that of feeling, but an important thematic shift: it is not the God of Abraham (first movement) nor the Righteous Father (second movement) but Jesus Christ (subordinated in the first movement to the God of Abraham) that the poet-convert apostrophizes.

The two-part meditation is common to both the fold of paper and the pouch of parchment. On the latter Pascal has varied certain lines through additions and omissions. Some additions give biblical references in conventional hermeneutic fashion, giving books of the Bible (line 12: *Jeh.* 20, 17; line 13: *Ruth*; line 18: *Jeh.* 17); some lines omit words (line 9 omits the second preposition of *des*; line 26 omits the name "Jesus Christ"), while others vary (line 10 reads: "Certitude, joy, certitude, sentiment, sight [*vue*], joy;" line 19 adds "and" after the third "joy"). Most important, of course, the parchment adds six lines that provide an even more reflective frame than the first. The preoccupation with the self is found here again, as in the poem itself, particularly in the second and third movements. Yet, whereas the lyrical dominated those personal moments in which the poet-convert and the Divine lived in the order of charity, in the last addition to the parchment it is more the convert than the poet, more the man of reason than the man of feeling who prevails. In line 34 the connotations of self-abnegation have shifted from the poetic to the reflective: "total and sweet renunciation" has become "total submission." *Renunciation* connotes an awareness of the world that the poet-convert was leaving behind and the oxymoronic play between it and "sweet" emphasizes the paradox of the conversion itself. *Submission* connotes an apodictic relation between signifier and signified. This becomes even more apparent as the line adds "and to my Director." The addition replaces "sweet," in fact, and thus suggests an awareness of the world to which the convert was returning, for, in the Port Royal tradition, spiritual directors served principally to reinforce the lesson of the difference between this world and the other world to which Pascal had been lifted in his conversion.

Like certain editors of the *Memorial* (the most recent, Sellier, for example) I speak of the *additions* on the parchment, as if that version were the second. Both the content of these differences and the circumstances of the two texts justify this interpretation. The largely referential and grammatical character of the differences suggest the reworking of an initial text of the *Memorial*: the version in Pascal's own hand that has survived. The idea of carrying it with him as a memorial, a *reminder* of moral discipline, occurred to him later (perhaps immediately after writing the version on paper) and he saw the chemical necessity of protecting it and even of having two copies of it, one on the more durable parchment, to safeguard its disciplinary value to him. This double guarantee of specifically disciplinary intent would explain the addition of the three lines at the end of the parchment version. If the rational faculties stand forth in their reflective aspect in the first of the three lines added, they stand forth just as clearly in their reflective *and voluntaristic* aspects in the last two added. The play between "eternally" and "one day of effort on earth" in line 36 returns us to the Pascal of probability theory and looks forward to his more extended application of that theory in the famous wager fragment of the *Thoughts*. He would have been the first to take his own bet. This is not to say that he thus could testify to prospective other bettors that he could guarantee success. He could not guarantee that to himself either in writing the fragment on the wager or even in writing the *Memorial*. This is clear from the third line of the addition at the end of the text here (line 37): "I will not forget Thy Word." He thus reminds himself that he has at times forgotten that Word and that both by knowledge of his own temperament and according to Jansenist doctrine, it is the human condition to forget the Word of God.

Forget it he would, as his recalcitrance before Jacqueline's exhortations to him at Port Royal two weeks later show. Perhaps he had been aware of forgetting and thus sought to concentrate on *not* forgetting even before the night of fire. In his last letter to Fermat on the theory of probability, we perhaps have the sign of the conversion he was to undergo less than a month later. In a letter of August 9, 1654, to their mutual correspondent on the matter, Carcavy, Fermat had proposed a three-way collaboration in the publication of some of their researches and reflections.[3] On October 27 Pascal wrote to Fermat to thank him but decline, saying, "For my part, that is far beyond me."[4] The formulation may be purely scientific in intent, although given Pascal's acumen, both in Fermat's and his own eyes, this seems unlikely. As he declined Fermat's invitation he may have already begun the kind of self-defense, defense against himself, that he would have to continue even after his conversion.

5

THE
CONVERT'S
AGONY

The convert would become his own adversary. In a short writing, on the *Conversion of the Sinner,* which it seems reasonable, both circumstantially and intrinsically, to place just after the conversion, perhaps as early as December 1654, Pascal reprises the dark side of the *Memorial*: the anguish of having separated himself from God, the fear of being abandoned by God.[1] However, he does so not in the lyrical, ecstatic mood of that text. Rather, he is reflective, strangely puzzled and curiously objective as he inquires into the differences between his present state of "just beginning to know God" and his previous state of intense "love of the world."

To convert for Pascal is to converge all the energies of the soul, diverted in "the things that made for its pleasures . . . that used to charm it," in order to look "in a new way" at the very means by which the soul looks at itself and those things. This convergence, this diversion from diversion, is the "first thing" that God inspires in the soul, and it is a new awareness, a "knowledge," rather than an annulment of knowledge. Here, of course, Pascal is expressing in an unscholarly way, without scriptural and doctrinal texts, the fundamental Augustinian tenet of the two states of man that he elucidated in the *First* and *Second Writings on Grace*: of man before the Fall and of man after the Fall. Emphasizing the second state with the "extraordinary look" at things that God has given him in the conversion, he "begins to consider as a nothingness all that is to return to nothingness." The notion of *beginning*, of the old soul making careful, almost gingerly steps in self-knowledge and self-abnegation, characterizes both the turning away from the world and the turning toward God: "It begins to be astonished at the blindness in which it had lived." The formulation is paradoxical: we usually think of astonishment as a sudden seizure of the psyche, a flourish of the soul to be expressed, as in the Cornelian hero, for example, in exclamatory sentence and, as the etymon of *astonishment* (thunder) suggests, thunderous imagery. Yet, psychologically, Pascal's formulation rings true, for it reminds us that old habits are hard to break. It is perhaps the very recollection of his own conversion that led him to be concerned in the projected *Apology* with the creation of new habits, of a "second nature."

I say "he" and "him" as if this text were written in the first person. Appropriately, it is not. The subject of this conversion, the sinner of its title, is the soul. Pascal is aware that his is one soul among others. But that he is thinking of his own sinful soul, of the "delights" (*delices*) to which we know he had committed himself, is clear in such passages as:

> So that the soul having amassed treasures of temporal goods of whatever nature they be, either gold, or knowledge [*science*], or reputation, it is an indispensable necessity that it finds itself denuded of all these objects of felicity; and that thus, if they have had anything to satisfy it, they will not have anything to satisfy it always; and that if that is thought to procure for oneself a true [*véritable*] happiness, it is not really to procure for oneself a lasting happiness, since it must be limited by the course of this life.

Gold that he had hoped to *amass* through his inventions and, according to some, through depradations on Jacqueline's legacy; *knowledge* he had amassed as a scientist; *reputation* that he had amassed not only as a scientist but as a man of the world. This passage, the entire reflection on the world in this text, seriously qualifies the presumably saintly indifference, the mere game-playing motives that Gilberte would have us believe motivated her brother in his worldly period. Pascal knows himself in that period better.

But now thanks to God's first gift, he has come to the beginnings of a thirst for the eternal. The logic and psychology of the famous wager are in germ here, of course, as they are, if my interpretation of the dating of the parchment is correct, in the last part of the *Memorial*. But there is none of the peremptory tone of the third line of that additon: "Eternally in joy for one day of effort on earth." Rather, Pascal, too, is aware that conversions are not easy things, the matter of one-day efforts. He is more aware of the *striving* toward the eternal joy than of the joy itself: "This elevation is so eminent and so transcendent that it does not stop at the heavens; they have nothing to satisfy it, neither above the heavens, nor with the angels, nor with the most perfect beings. It crosses all creatures and cannot stop its heart until it render itself unto the throne of God, in which it begins to find its repose and this good that is such that there is nothing more lovable, and which can be taken from it only by its own consent." The joy is more a promise than the stake it will become in the last part of the *Memorial* and in the famous wager, the promise of a joy that is repose. Psychologically, this motif shows Pascal moving away from the patricentric reality principle that had motivated him in so many of his scientific and worldly dealings. In terms of the concept of the will in the *First Writing on Grace,* the passage shows him moving toward the pleasure principle. However, for Pascal, steeped in Augustine, we could say that the distinction between a reality principle and a pleasure principle is meaningless, because as Pascal was to quote Augustine approvingly in the *Provincial Letter* 18: "Quod enim amplius nos delicate, secundum id operemur necesse est" ('Of necessity are we moved to that which most pleases us'). All is pleasure principle both before and after the Fall, with the difference between those two times lying not in the operation of the principle itself but in the objects of the operation: God before the Fall, the world after the Fall. If Pascal anticipates any modern psychological notions, it is in the theme of repose, a Christian manifestation of what Marcuse and others have called the nirvana principle found in certain of Freud's writings: the desire to return to a state of rest.[2] As Marcuse says in *Eros and Civilization,* for Freud this principle underlies both the pleasure principle and the death instinct and is linked to the self 's preentropic sense of comfort in the womb before the tensions of birth.[3] The concept seems pertinent here in that Pascal records what might be the death of the reality principle or, in his Augustinian terms, of the pleasure principle in Adam after the Fall in order to return to the first state of the soul, the pleasure principle in Adam before the Fall.

If the psychology of this passage is sound both on a general basis (the awareness of the difficulty of changing habits) and a Freudian basis (the nirvana principle), the theology *seems* to be less so in relation to other texts in which Pascal raises the question of the divine and human roles in the work of what Pascal here calls "elevation." To the contrary of his position in the first two *Writings on Grace,* that God's role is primary, in the *Conversion* he sees the individual soul's role as primary: "which can be taken from it only of its own consent." The motif is repeated in the following paragraph: "For although it does not feel those charms with which God recompenses the habit of piety, it understands nevertheless that creatures cannot be more lovable than the Creator, and its reason aided by the lights of grace makes it know that there is nothing more lovable than God and that it can be taken only from those who reject it, because to desire it is to possess it and to refuse it is to lose it." Miel sees this text as at odds particularly with the *Third Writing on Grace,* the letter to the unidentified correspondent presumably written in mid- or late 1655.[4] As Miel shrewdly notes, it does echo one of the most famous passages of *The Mystery of Jesus,* which probably dates soon after the *Conversion of the Sinner.* Miel ascribes the contradiction to Pascal's state of anxiety just after his conversion, a state in which he is "not altogether reconciled to the Augustinian theology or his own earlier views." Those earlier views are contained, of course, in the *First* and *Second Writings on Grace* and especially in the first portion of the *First Writing,* which, as Miel has cogently argued, dates perhaps as early as 1647. The development on the primacy of God's role in salvation in that portion and especially on the very matter of the "special graces" needed even for what he calls in the text on *Conversion* the "habit of piety" seems even more relevant to the problem Miel raises than the later writings, especially in light of the reflective mood of the text on *Conversion.* Yet, I suggest that the difficulties of reconciling the seemingly contradictory positions are resolved by the text of the *Conversion* itself.

That Pascal should have repeated this motif, in different language, suggests that he may have been aware of the implied Molinism of the phrase: "cannot be taken away from it except by its own consent." The repetition comes at the end of the very next paragraph, which begins in an explanatory frame: "For . . ." The first term of explanation in fact addresses itself to the question that he had so feverishly developed in the first portion of the *First Writing:* "but he did not will to give them this singular grace of perseverance without which one never uses the others well." As he raises the matter of perseverance under the phrase "habit of piety" in the present text, its recompense of divinely given charms is corollary to the awareness that the creature's amiability is less than the Creator's. This awareness is corollary to two other awarenesses that grammatically depend on the nominative "reason aided by the lights of grace," namely that there is nothing more lovable than God "*and*" that "to desire him is to possess him and to refuse him is to lose him." As we shall see, Pascal repeats this dependence on God's "means" at the end of the *Conversion*. Its theology strikes me as consistent with that of the formulations in both the *First Writing* and the *Third Writing on Grace*.

The formulation of this consistent position is rather pithy. Pascal is not writing a treatise of the kind he wrote in the earlier texts; he is writing a kind of confession, making an act of perfect contrition. The fear of the loss of the goods of heaven (the sign of an act of imperfect contrition or, as it is called in theological discourse, attrition) is real enough here, but it yields toward the end of this text to the perfectly contrite awareness that the greater harm that the sinner has done through his sin is not to himself but to God: "Then it, [the soul] acknowledges the grace that he has granted it manifesting his infinite majesty to such a spindly worm; and after a firm resolution to be eternally grateful, it enters into confusion for having preferred so many vanities to this Divine Master, and in a spirit of compunction and penitence, it turns to his pity, to stop his anger, whose effect appears frightening to it in seeing its immensities."

This act of confession ends with "ardent prayers" that God will provide the soul with the means that come from God alone to enable it to arrive unto God. Although Pascal does not look at the word *conversion* itself, his whole text, but particularly its final paragraphs, is informed with the etymological sense of that word not as a turn about but as a turning toward—a painful, difficult, and challenging act: "It resolves to conform to his wishes the rest of its life; but, as its natural weakness, with the habituation that it has in the sins where it has lived, has reduced it to the inability to come to this felicity, it implies from his mercy the means of coming to him, to attach itself to him, to adhere to it [presumably 'felicity'] eternally." The habit of sin is at odds with the habit of piety. In order to achieve felicity in God out of piety Pascal prays God for the means to achieve the habit of piety.

In *The Mystery of Jesus,* his prayer seems to have been answered. As already noted, the motif of having found for having searched is common to both texts, but the serene identification with Christ that *The Mystery* shows suggests that Pascal had come still closer to God as he had prayed he might be able to in the *Conversion*, to which, in this respect and others, it might be considered a reply. It is an even more intensely personal document that the *Conversion,* however, much more like the *Memorial* in this respect. Its structure also resembles that of the *Memorial;* like that text, it is made up of a two-part lyrical development, to which, on the other side of the last sheet on which it was written, Pascal added a more prosaic and voluntaristic reflection on the motifs of the first two parts. If any single text of Pascal may be said to record his conversion it is *The Mystery.* Of course, it too shows his doctrinal awareness of the instability of any conversion. The mysterious hiddenness of God, man's inconstant nature, the soul's dependence on God's grace for both the beginnings and the perpetuation of conversion—all these doctrines are to be found in *The Mystery.* They are rendered in a dramatic rather than discursive fashion, lived rather than pondered (except for the brief portion added at the end). The text is a dialogue of communion with Jesus expressing an inwardness that is unique among Pascal's writings on his conversion. With *The Abridgment of the Life of Jesus,* an obviously related text that he probably composed soon after, they show the adversarial believer whom we have met in earlier texts yielding to the advocate of faith whom we shall meet in that project for an *Apology for the Christian Religion* known as the *Thoughts. The Mystery* is at once so beautiful and so crucial to an understanding of Pascal's life that I shall comment on it in considerable detail.

The text is made up of forty separate and brief passages, all of one paragraph except the thirty-third (two paragraphs) and the thirty-ninth (four paragraphs).[5] These passages treat the mystery of Jesus's Agony in the Garden and may be divided into three movements. The first (passages 1–21) depicts Jesus in his human suffering in the Garden of Gethsemane, abandoned by his sleeping disciples. Pascal, using the first person singular, is writing a "history" of the Agony in the Garden, on which he sympathetically reflects at key points, a method of writing history that we have seen Jacqueline use in her text on the death of Christ, one that Pascal would use just as systematically as Jacqueline in his own *Abridgment of the Life of Jesus.* Thus, he writes in *The Mystery,* "He suffers this trouble [*peine*] and this abandon in the horror of the night," and "I believe that Jesus complained only this one time. But at the time [*alors*] he complains as if he could not contain his excessive pain. My soul is sad unto death." As Pascal records his reactions to the history the text begins to shift from history to drama, with Pascal the spectator of the drama. In the second movement (passages 22–37), this generic shift is fully realized: passages 22–32 are a dramatic monologue by Jesus, the tragic hero of the tragedy of the Agony in the Garden, addressed to the historian-spectator of the first movement; passages 33–37 become fully dramatic, with the tragic hero and Pascal both actors in a dialogue of the drama of man's agony on earth, but with Jesus now in the role of the sympathetic historian-spectator of the first movement and Pascal the tragic hero of the play. The third movement, (passages 38–40) is a dramatic monologue of self-flagellation and resolve by Pascal, in the spirit of the third section added to the parchment version of the *Memorial*.

If Pascal's self is very much to the fore in the third movement, it is none the less so in the first two. It is not a prideful self, but a humble self, rather. The dramatic form of *The Mystery*, the dialogue of communion with Jesus, seems to have enabled Pascal to penetrate one of the great mysteries of his own character, its incorrigible pride, which would make of humility itself a source of pride. The last words that he says to Jesus in the second movement are "Lord, I give all to Thee." Jesus replies that he loves him more ardently than he has loved his staining sins and then, seeing what Pascal will see reflectively in the third movement, Jesus warns, "Let the glory of it [your giving] be all Mine and not yours, worm and earth," and "Give witness to your [spiritual] director that my very words are an occasion of evil and of vanity or curiosity to you." In the second passage of the more discursive third movement Pascal writes, "I see my abyss of pride, of curiosity, of concupiscence." He has, in a certain sense, become the spectator once again, or, in the same vein, a dramatic critic who analyzes the play to draw its meaning out in the discourse of the world.

The world of man's "second state of nature," of Adam after the Fall. This is the world in which Pascal has so often felt abandoned and frightened that he would be without consolation. But, in *The Mystery*, which is like a memorial of a night not of fire but of horror for Pascal, he learns that Jesus' acceptance and transcendence of *his* abandonment and lack of consolation is the very reassurance and consolation that he himself longs for. "Console yourself," Jesus begins his monologue to Pascal, "you would not have searched for me if you had not found me." The paradox has meaning only because Jesus is at once man and God. In *The Mystery*, the abstract *word* of the doctrine of the two states that Pascal has read and written about becomes *flesh*. The Jesus of *The*

Mystery does represent the doctrine of God's primacy in the act of salvation:

> If you knew your sins, you would lose heart. I shall lose it, then, Lord, for I believe their malice on your assurance. No, for I by whom you learn it can cure you of it and what I tell you is a sign that I wish to cure you. To the extent that you will expiate them you will know them and it will be said to you: See the sins that are remitted you.

> Do penance, then, for your hidden sins and for the occult [*occulte*] malice of those [sins] that you know.

This is Jesus who is God, but Pascal can heed him because he has found him in searching for Jesus the man. The searching is the agony of remorse at Jesus' suffering, at making Jesus suffer by sleeping in sin like the disciples even though one has known that he is the Lord. As Jesus complained to God in his agony, so Pascal has complained to God in his. There is a kind of spiritual algebra at work here: souls equal, that is, capable of the same thing, are equal to each other. Jesus in his agony is equal to God, Pascal in his agony is equal to Jesus, therefore Pascal is equal to God. But the algebra is possible only because of the existence, the concreteness, the "enfleshing" (Incarnation) of God in Jesus.

The manhood of Jesus enables Pascal to resolve at once deep-rooted psychological as well as theological problems: "Let yourself [Jesus tells him] be guided by my rules. See how well I have guided the Virgin and the saints who have let me act in them," and "The Father loves all that I do." The Father against whom he had complained, even as Pascal had complained against his father in various rebellions. Not only were there excesses of a rationalistic defense of the faith with Rebours and his insidious encouragement of Jacqueline in her vocation against his father's wishes rebellions. No, the complaints, the rebellions, were deeper than that; they were the "hidden sins" and the "occult malice" of other sins that, as Jesus tells him here, he knows.

In distinguishing two kinds of secret sins, those that are hidden and those that are of an occult malice, Pascal shows an awareness of two states of the psyche, a conscious and an unconscious. The hidden sins are those the sinner may not confess but of which he is conscious. The other sins are buried deeper, as the very term Pascal used indicates: occult. Littré indicates two meanings that seem especially relevant to Pascal's use of it here: that "which is hidden under a sort of mystery";

and the "term of ancient geometry. Occult line was said of auxiliary lines that one traces on a plane to make whatever construction and that one erases afterwards."[6] As a geometer Pascal undoubtedly knew the term, and his use of it here may be a metaphorical application of this scientific sense of the first meaning indicated by Littré. The meaning, "sort of mystery," tinged with a strong tone of sensuality (or, in Pascalian terms, concupiscence of the flesh), emerges as "occult" and is adjectivally linked to "malice," as if the malice were a force itself, a deviated principle, the deviation of the Augustinian pleasure principle. In keeping with the workings of that principle I have sketched these secret sins are of the kind that Augustine himself, in his *Confession* and elsewhere, and that the Jansenists in Pascal's time were particularly to excoriate: sins of the flesh and of the mind, surrenders to the *libido sentiendi* and the *libido sciendi* (themselves, as we shall see through the *Thoughts,* variations or expressions of what for Pascal perhaps more than for Augustine, is the worst sin—of pride, the surrender to the *libido dominandi* or will to dominate, for it usurps God's authority). In Pascal's case, we have seen what these secret sins are: against father, mother, sister, scientific forebears and contemporaries, spiritual directors. In this connection, Pascal's evocation of a mother figure is especially significant in this text.

The *Mystery* contains one of the rare allusions in Pascal to the Mother of God, but, as seen, it is not as mother but as Virgin that she is identified. As the object of his love, his mother here is pure and, significantly, the very next passage (number 26) makes the point that "The Father loves all that I do." It is as if Jesus is telling Pascal that it is all right to love his mother, that his own father understands. But the later injunction to confess the malice of occult sins must be linked to this depiction of the mother as Virgin. Before coming to Jesus through her, he must extirpate the concupiscent desire he has felt for her as well as those feelings of anger for her abandonment of him in death—an abandonment that is itself linked to the concupisence, for in thus abandoning him she deprived him of the possibility of satisfying those desires. Psychologically, it is also possible that his evocation of the Virgin points, unconsciously, to Jacqueline as well, especially in light of the importance of the motif of abandonment in the first movement of *The Mystery* and of the motif of self-separation from those closest to oneself in the passage: "Jesus tears himself away [*s'arrache*] from his disciples; one must tear oneself away from those closest and most intimate, in order to imitate him." The addition of "most intimate" to "closest" might seem a poetic redundancy adding to the beauty of the passage, but psychologically it carries the overtones of the kinds of feelings that will be the object of Jesus' injunction against the occult malice. The kinds of feelings that must be rooted out, then, are not only the positive ones of love of those closest to one, but the negative ones for one's "most intimate."

With respect to Jacqueline, with whom he was closer than anyone else as Gilberte has told us, the negative feelings would have been sins of occult malice: anger for having been the cause of his loss of his beloved mother, followed by jealousy of her talents, followed by concupiscent desire now transferred from the mother to her daughter (if Jacqueline could be resented as the cause of his mother's death in childbirth, she was by the same token the reproduction closest to the mother). Both women had abandoned him (as perhaps Gilberte had, in his unconscious feeling, by marrying; his direction of his brother-in-law, especially in science, may well have been a way of reasserting his emotional claim on his older sister). He had abandoned them through anger even as he had the father. Now he can resolve all these ambivalences through Jesus, the son of God, who is at once gently human and divinely authoritative, sweet and stern, at once mother and father and sister. The depictions of Jesus in much of the Church art and hagiographical literature (sermons, texts) that Pascal was bound to have encountered were now of the sweet and girlish Lamb of God, now of the stern and forceful driver of the moneylenders from the temple, often a composite of both these feminine and masculine traits not unlike the picture that Herman Hesse's Sinclair draws and ultimately recognizes to be his friend Demian and, when he meets her, whom he recognizes more as Demian's mother than Demian himself: "something else, something unreal, yet it was no less valuable to me. It looked more like a boy's face than a girl's; the hair was not flaxen like that of my pretty girl, but dark brown with a reddish hue. The chin was strong and determined, the mouth like a red flower"; and later, of Demian's mother: "with a face that resembled her son's, timeless, ageless, and full of inner strength, the beautiful woman smiled with dignity. Her gaze was fulfillment, her greeting a homecoming."[7] It is in such a face, the face of Jesus, that the Pascal of *The Mystery* finds his homecoming. He returns to the home of the stern father and the sweet mother.

Two events of the infant Blaise's life, reported by Marguerite Périer, take on fuller meaning in relation to *The Mystery of Jesus.* The first I have already adduced in this context: that he cried when he saw, first, water and, second, his mother and father together. But, as Marguerite adds, he "suffered the caresses of the one or the other in private with pleasure." In Jesus, at once mother and father, he can at last "suffer" the combined caresses of mother and father. The second story reported by Marguerite is of an illness Blaise suffered at about two, brought on, according to Marquerite, by the crying and "excessive violence" of his reaction to seeing his parents together. Neighbors told the parents that the boy's illness was due to the curse of a local sorceress, to whom Blaise's mother had been quite kind. Blaise's father attributed the accusation to jealousy by others of these very charities, but grudgingly met with the sorceress to find out what truth there might be to the accusation. He pretended to believe she had put the curse on his son, says Marguerite, and threatened to have her hanged unless she told him the truth. The sorceress then admitted that the accusation was true, that because Etienne Pascal had refused to plead a case for her, she had cursed the child whom she saw that he "loved tenderly." The frightened father wondered what was to be done; the sorceress told him that another must die in his stead. Etienne refused, saying it was better his son die than that another die in his place. The sorceress then said it could be an animal. Etienne offered a horse; the sorceress said a cat would suffice. Etienne provided a cat, but the sorceress, cat in hand, encountered two Capuchin monks who accused her of preparing to do black magic with the cat. She threw the cat out the window and it died even though, as Marguerite notes, it fell only six feet. She asked for another; Etienne provided it, but apparently to no avail. Marguerite does not say as much directly but is concerned to exculpate her grandfather from doing the devil's work. Her explanation is revealing: "The great tenderness he had for this child made him pay no attention that all that was worth nothing, since it was necessary, to transfer this fate, to make a new invocation to the devil; never did this thought come to his mind, and it came to him only a long time afterward, and he repented for having let all that take place." Between that long time afterward and the child's illness, however, he did collaborate with the sorceress on her next request, which was to find a child of less than seven years old who would gather three leaves of each of three kinds of herbs. Etienne chose his daughter, Gilberte (then about five), whom he took to the apothecary the next day to gather the herbs. From these the sorceress made a poultice that she brought the next morning at seven to the father to be placed on the son's stomach. This done, the father went off to his practice. When he returned at noon he found his wife in tears, for the child had apparently died. Encountering the sorceress on the stairs as he rushed from the room, he struck her so hard she fell back a step. She told him she understood his anger, but that he should not worry, for she had forgotten to tell him that the child would appear dead until midnight and that if they left him in the crib until that hour he would revive. The father thus left the child—without pulse, without feeling, cold, and apparently dead—until that hour. The infant did not come to at that moment but between midnight and one o'clock, closer to one than midnight, says Marguerite in her report. He was given some sugared wine, and then the wet nurse fed him at her breast. He slept until six, and when he woke, seeing his mother and father next to one another, he began to cry as he used to. He now could stand the sight of water, however, so much so that, when the father came home that day, he found the boy in the arms of his mother, playfully pouring water from one glass to another. When the father tried to come to him, the child would not "suffer it." He did so a few days later, and in three days was otherwise cured and, says Marguerite, had no other illnesses.

The story is undoubtedly true at its medical core; the medical aspects suggest that Pascal's first illness as a small child was the first attach of the "weaknesses" that often kept him from working in later life. From the autopsy report given by Marguerite and other evidences physicians have concluded that Pascal's death probably resulted from a malady of the brain. The brain showed only one suture, and, as Marguerite herself says, this probably caused the great headaches he suffered throughout his life. Her report of the incident is equally true in its psychological and theological core. The report illuminates the relations of Pascal with his father and mother at that crucial stage of infancy when the child vies with the father for the affection of her who is at once the child's mother and the father's wife. Marguerite reports Blaise's very early rebellion against the father here. In the father we can see signs of sternness, his irritation at the sorceress, for example. But we also see his extreme tenderness for his son. Was the father as stern at times with the child, both before and after this illness? The son's "repudiation" of him when with his wife at *all* times before the illness but especially just after the illness may have made him act more distant in his attentions to the boy—still affectionate but more controlled and perhaps edged with hostility. And, given the gravity of the illness and the collaboration with the devil to which it had led the father, when the father repented of that collaboration, the son might well have suffered because of his sense of religious guilt. Out of that guilt, the father may have become more the intellectual and spiritual mentor than the tender father whose caresses the boy had enjoyed as a small infant. The attention and affection the mother gave the small child whom she had nearly lost may have been even greater in the short time that she had to live thereafter (barely a year). The sense of deprivation—or in terms he would use later in religious contexts, of abandonment, of being dropped—that the child would have felt upon her death would have been all the more intense. Pascal's later illnesses may in part have been psychosomatic reprises of this first great illness, thanks to which he won his mother away from his father. The ministrations he asked of Jacqueline may well be related too: she not only cared for him as secretary but also as a substitute for his mother. Her wit, kindness, and courage may have been like those of her mother, Antoinette Bégon, who, as Marguerite says, "had wit" and who did not care what the neighbors thought of her helping out the old woman sorceress. One can see how in *The Mystery of Jesus* these two witty, courageous, and tender women might be conflated psychologically into the image of Jesus. His mother was his lifeline to physical health even as Jacqueline became the lifeline to spiritual health on that feast day of the Mother of God, commemorating the theological paradox of her stainless birth, known as the Immaculate Conception.

From a religious point of view, Marguerite's story is probably more enfabulated mystically than it is medically. Yet, this very enfabulation sheds light on Pascal's later spiritual life, both subjectively in its probable personal impact on his struggle toward God and objectively in certain of his theological pronouncements. Subjectively: in a family so close-knit as that of the Pascals, especially after the death of the mother, the story of the sorceress is not one that Marguerite alone would have told (and, at that, some time after her famous uncle was dead). It is the kind of story that was undoubtedly the fare of many a family gathering, particularly when matters of faith came up, as they so often did after the first conversion of 1646. We can well imagine that the story had come up before, and it would be surprising if such a story did not leave a deep impression on its principal actor, Blaise himself. The story may have led him to feel himself to be somehow under the sign of the devil rather than of God. Again, the father's ambivalent behavior must have deeply reenforced a natural ambivalence toward the dynamic father on the part of the sensitive, strong-willed son. On the one hand, the story told of his father's initial willingness to let him, rather than another, die. The psychological impact of this paternal position is, of course, that the boy would have felt abandoned at his roots by the very father who was now raising him at once as father and mother. The religious implication counterbalances this potential sense of deprivation, for it suggests an identification with the Son of God, who was also abandoned and allowed to die for the sake of another from an illness that had come from the devil and thus was a sin of the flesh like the sin for which, as *The Mystery* puts it, "Jesus had made himself for me." In clearly indicating the diabolical source of the sin and thus of Etienne Pascal's collaboration with that sin as well as his tardy acknowledgment of guilt for that collaboration, Marguerite illuminates the awareness of what would be an explicit tenet of Pascal's theology: that the just can fall into sin as well as the reproved.

Both psychologically and theologically Pascal would have learned, or sensed, what he could not come to face and overcome until his second conversion: that the father is not all-powerful and integral, but, like the son, weak and contradictory. Again, the psychological and theological implications of the hydrophobia—the child cried not only at seeing his parents together but also at the sight of water—are equally significant, if we assume that Blaise had been reminded of the precarious beginnings of his life. It may be that the sickly child was a rather bad bedwetter and that, in the cultivated family to which he belonged, there was a convection of two strong taboos that made him suffer unusually when he gave in to this natural function: first, the insistence on orderliness and, particularly, of good toilet habits; second, the association in this pious family of excremental functions with the work of the devil. Combined with natural phallic tropism toward the mother, the strictures on this "weakness" might well have aggravated his conflict with his father. The specifically theological implications of this hydrophobia may manifest themselves in Pascal's ambivalent attitude toward infant baptism.

I shall elaborate on this connection in discussing his text on the *Comparison of the Early Christians with Those of Today,* but let me anticipate that discussion by noting that Pascal *tends toward* what might be called a baptismal conception of the Eucharist—of the abolition of the stain of original sin through direct adult confrontation with Jesus rather than through an institutional abolition through the Church before the onset of consciousness. Indeed, that his hydrophobia had been cured by what might be called a diabolical baptism, the poultice soaked in the herbs gathered at the behest of the devil's agent, may have made Pascal both psychologically and theologically leery of the idea of infant baptism. Why had it not protected him so soon after its administration from the devil's curse, a curse that had to be cured by another "curse" of the devil? The waters of the earth, all liquids, like the mercury in the tube of his famous experiments on the vacuum, may all have come to stand for the works of the devil for Pascal in the occult recesses of his being. In connection with the two-year-old child's playfully pouring water from one glass to another after his cure, some commentators have seen a symbolic attempt on Marguerite's part to show that his scientific genius (his contributions to hydraulics) was thereby predicted. The symbolic intention seems to me to be overshadowed by the theological or religious implications that Pascal himself might well have drawn from this story after his conversion: that his infantile adeptness in handling the water he had so feared was indeed a sign of his commitment to science, but science was a vanity, a curiosity, a concupiscence, the concupiscence of the mind through which he would try to exercise the worst of the libidinal drives: the *libido dominandi.*

"Know thyself, then, by knowing me," the Jesus of *The Mystery* tells Pascal, "bring peace—my peace—to the occult recesses of your being." He identifies with Jesus, a Jesus who speaks to him in the familiar form *tu*-(thou) and whom he addresses in the formal form *vous* (you) and as Lord (*Seigneur*). Jesus suffers his agony as a man, but calls out to his compassionate historian-spectator-fellow actor as God. Like Jesus, Pascal is an agonist in the garden, who suffers an *agon,* a passion that is not passive, but, as my dramatic metaphor for the text implies, a state of active suffering in which the actor is, as in Baudelaire's poem "Héautontimouroumenos," at once victim and butcher of himself. It is an agony that he creates as well as one that he accepts from him with whom he identifies as a son to a parent, the parent Jesus who is mother as well as father to him now. As the Son who is also the Parent, Jesus rightfully speaks in stern tones to the wayward son Pascal, who has

not yet looked upon his occult malice and who may well have an imperfect motive for coming to him: "It is to tempt me more than it is to
test yourself for you to think that if you were to do good, such and
such an absent thing would be given you; I shall do it in you if it [the
absent thing] is to come." This passage (number 24) seems to be the
dramatic expression of the warning Pascal draws in the first paragraph
of the third movement, a warning against the "false justice of [Pon-
tius] Pilate" and all the "false just" who "do good works and bad
works to show the world that they are not altogether with Jesus
Christ, for they are ashamed of him and finally in the great tempta-
tions and occasions . . . kill him."[8] Against these and against himself,
as he says in the second passage of this movement, he must be on
guard against adding any more wounds to Jesus in the future.

For all its discursive resemblance to the added portion of the
Memorial, this added portion of *The Mystery* is still attuned to the emphasis of the heart over the mind in the first two movements, of charity over reason. The charity is Saint Cyranian enough; that the
creature owes love to God is a clear motif, but it emerges in a uniquely
Pascalian framework of the love that the Creator *shows* the creature.
Both loves emerge in the last passage, with its reprise of the motif of
Jesus' humanity through the pluralization of the first person showing
that the communion of the self with Jesus has led to its communion
with other selves: "Do small things as if they were big things because
of the majesty of Jesus Christ, who does them in us and who lives our
life, and the big as if they were small and easy because of his om-
nipotence [*toute-puissance*]."

In *The Mystery of Jesus,* as in the *Memorial,* Pascal is fully in that
sweet phase of his self that has been expressed before only tentatively
and haltingly. The positive current emerges as well in an obviously
related text, *The Abridgment of the Life of Jesus Christ,* which came to
light through his nephew Louis Périer only in 1711.[9] Noting the text's
thematic connections with the *Spiritual and Christian Letters* of Saint
Cyran and especially Jansen's *Series of Events in the Life of Jesus Christ in
the Order of Time* (a follow-up to that author's *Tetrateuchus* that had
been reissued in 1655), most scholars date the *Abridgment* in 1655–56. It
is a more objective text than the *Memorial,* the *Conversion,* or *The
Mystery* inasmuch as Pascal clearly intends it as a possible instruction to
others. However, a number of passages reprise the motifs and feelings
of the earlier texts related to his conversion to such an extent that its

infrastructure is as subjective as those texts. The combination of subjective and objective, of repentant self-concern and tender concern with and for the other, suggests that it represents an intermediate step from the profound subjectivity of the *Memorial,* the *Conversion,* and *The Mystery* to the more objective, proselytizing objectivity of the later theological writings in the two years just after his conversion. In the latter, *The Conversation with M. de Sacy, The Comparison of the Christians of Early Times with Those of Today,* the *Third Writing on Grace,* the *Provincial Letters,* and the *Letters to Charlotte de Roannez,* the convert is more fully the adversary once again, more concerned with attacking the enemies of faith, than the serene advocate concerned with the feelings of joy, peace, and consolation that inform the first series of texts written after his conversion of 1654.

The *Abridgment* is composed of a brief preface (about two printed pages in the Pléiade edition) followed by paragraphs of varying lengths (one line to thirty lines), numbered 1 to 354, in which, as Pascal puts it in the preface, taking the life of Christ as recorded in the four Gospels, "we edit [the events] in the order [*suite*] of time, linking each verset of each evangelist in the order in which the thing that is there written happened, as much as our weakness will permit." However, as with his sister Jacqueline's text on the death of Christ and, to a considerably lesser extent, his own *Mystery of Jesus,* for many of the versets the author systematically adds a personal commentary expanding factual aspects or indicating the moral import of the verset or combining both the factual and the moral. The *Abridgment* is thus at once a history and a kind of autobiography. The autobiographical element prevails even in the history. The careful addition of Roman calendar dates (as in the very first verset: "1. During the empire of Augustus Caesar, *under the reign of Herod in Judea,* on September 24, fifteen months before the birth of Jesus Christ, *the angel Gabriel was sent*" — the italics throughout are scriptural) would seem to dampen the religious import of the selections. The effect easily yields to the subjective, poetic effect of the very arrangement of all the selections and of the commentary Pascal adds to many of them, however.

The emphasis of the arrangement and the commentary falls on the meaning of the life of Christ for the individual Christian, Pascal himself, and other Christians. If it is a chapter of Pascal's own autobiography, it is not a diary, a kind of memorial intended for the author alone. The meaning of the life of Christ for him is one that the author wishes to share with others: "If the reader finds herein something good, let him give thanks to God, sole author of all good. And what he finds bad, let him forgive it as my infirmity." The tone is, however, close to that of the *Memorial*. The willfulness, the self-aggrandizement, the need to prevail of earlier encounters are gone, replaced by a sweet submissiveness and identification with him who, as Pascal puts it early in his preface to the *Abridgment*, "has conversed among men, denuded of his glory and dressed in the form of a slave, and passed through many sufferings unto death and unto death on the cross, on which he bore our languors and infirmities, and destroyed our death by his, and, after, willingly left his soul, which he had the power to leave and take back; he resurrected himself the third day, and by his new life communicated life to all those who are reborn in him, as Adam had communicated death to all those who had been born of him."

In terms of the dichotomy of his personality, Pascal clearly gives himself to "feeling" as he had put it in the *Memorial,* the feelings of joy and certitude and peace that had made his night of fire so memorable. The *Abridgment* enables us to see that he has given in to other feelings as well, that he has found in the life of Christ ways of resolving the ambivalence of certain feelings he had long felt in the human realm, particularly those concerning his own father. The theology of the *Abridgment* is at once patricentric and filicentric, deicentric and Christocentric, as certain of the versets that he comments upon at length reveal:

279. *And around three o'clock,* or, according to the Hebrews, at nine o'clock, *Jesus cried out: "Eli, Eli, lamma sabbactani?"* that is: "My God, My God, why has Thou forsaken me?" namely: in his human nature, abandoned to all the torments of the butchers, and of his enemies, without consolation. And he calls to God to ask the cause of this abandonment; therefore one sees that it is the sin of men that he expiated in his innocent flesh. Nevertheless, this sin is not well known by men, and its horror is well known only to God. And even this discourse can be heard as a prayer that Jesus makes to the Father to remember the end for which he afflicts him and abandons him; as if saying: "My God, my God, why have you gone from me [*m'avez-vous delaissé*]? You know, my God, that it is for the salvation of the world, apply therefore the fruit of this sacrifice to the human species [genre humain] to which you have destined it." And these words are full of hope and not of despair, for he says: "My God, my God!"—now God is not the God of the dead nor of the despairing.

Abandoned, consolation, sacrifice, hope, dead: the language recalls Pascal's letter on the death of his father. In light of the present text the somewhat stern tone of that letter suggests that at the time of the father's death he did indeed feel abandoned by his father as Christ by his here. The tone in which the doctrines of uncomplaining acceptance of that letter are posited suggests as much self-bracing as haughty predication to his perhaps more humanly plangent sisters. The soul had repressed its despair, its plaint against the father on earth for having abandoned it and preached a tenet of laughter in heaven lest it cry too much on earth. At heart, of course, the doctrine of both texts is consistent: in the mystery of the Incarnation God is the ultimate source that consoles the soul by returning it to himself. Here, however, that he does so through the *human* suffering, physical and *psychological,* of his *Son* provides a basis for Pascal to overcome his own feelings of abandonment and rebellion against that father not only for his having died but for having dominated him in his own efforts at self-assertion. Jesus, too, had rebelled against the father.

Through the Son, through Christ, Pascal also learns lessons in "anti-self " discipline as marked as those he would teach himself by carrying the *Memorial* close to his breast. At the Last Supper,

> 197. *Then he predicts to them that they will all be scandalized that night in him, but that he would rise again, and that he will go before in Galilee.*
> 198. *Upon that, they disputed among themselves the primacy* (perhaps because they believe, as before, that his reign was approaching).
> 199. *Jesus reproaches them and tells them that the greatest shall be the least.*
> 200. *And* yet *prefers Peter* (perhaps because he was not among those who aspired to primacy) *turning to him, saying:* "Simon, Simon, here, Satan has asked that you be sieved like wheat, but I have prayed for you that your faith not fail." In order to make him understand that his perseverance in the faith would be a gift of God and not a pure effect of his own power [*force*].
> 201. *But Peter,* full of the feelings that nature inspires and not yet having received the Holy Spirit, *says to him,* assuring himself of his own powers, *that although the others might abandon him, he will follow him everywhere. But Jesus predicts to him his triple denial. And then orders them to carry buckles and swords, and then predicts again his death.*

Pascal's commentary on those who seek primacy is a repentance for his own preoccupation with priority and prevalence in science, society, and theology. His commentary that Christ preferred Peter perhaps because he did not seek primacy but that he nonetheless would abandon Christ is a touching reminder in which Pascal at once flagellates himself for not being like Peter in his best light but also hopes that, like Peter, having denied Christ and being likely to deny him still again, he will nonetheless ultimately be "preferred" by Christ.

The *Abridgment* shows the Christianization of a Christian. In it Pascal limns many of the motifs that would guide his thought in the elaboration of the *Apology for the Christian Religion* he would one day write not as an antagonist in science or faith but as an advocate of faith. Many of the commented versets already show his awareness of a motif he was to emphasize in the *Apology:* miracles as a touchstone of faith, enabling one to distinguish between Christian and Jew, Christian and pagan (versets 294, 339a, 353, 354). Others raise the thorny problem of election (the preface and versets 49 and 354). But the preoccupation with the relation between God the Father and God the Son is paramount. In its "total and sweet submission to Jesus Christ" the text may be read as the overflow of the first version of the *Memorial.* Consistent with his nature, Pascal would not usurp the primacy of the Son at the side of the Father. In the last verset that he comments, the very length of the commentary as well as its content indicate the tension in relation to paternal authority that always characterized his behavior in the order of the heart in its divine and human expressions:

347. *And he mounted above all the skies,* so that he might fulfill all (Eph. 4), *and was received in heaven and now sits at the right of the Father . . .* in an equality perfect with the Father, and in a plenitude of power. For this seating on the right is opposed to the ministry of angels as inferior, Hebr. 1 [13 and 14] Phillip. 2:9, Eph. 1:20 [I] Corinth. 15:25, etc. where the Apostle understands by seating on the right, the full power that he never failed to have, but that he has appeared to have received on this day. And although the Son be on the right of the Father, this is not to say that the Father is on the left of the Son. For in the psalm *Dixit Dominus,* where it is said that the Son is on the right of the Father, it is said also that the Father is on the right of the Son. But that is because speaking of each person it is necessary to give him all and almost more, lest one give him less. Ambr. . . . And from there he rules and conducts his Church with full power and Providence.

The struggle between Pascal's head and his heart, between theology and psychology, surfaces here. If the theology of the earlier passages was at once patricentric and filicentric, deicentric and Christocentric, their tendency was to emphasize the patricentric and the deicentric: the abandoned Son appealed to the all-powerful Father to keep their compact, to make his sacrifice meaningful in the Father's having sent him in the first place. Pascal is struggling to achieve not only an equality but a coauthority, to see the Son as powerful as the Father. Psychologically, the passage on Peter that I have quoted moves toward this final attempt at accession by the Son: he is at once Peter the denier and Christ the knower of denial, sinning son, and forgiving father. In this final commentary the identification is once again with Christ, the Son to whom "it is necessary to give him all and almost more." Pascal's language is as psychologically revealing as it is theologically complex. Language seems inadequate to Pascal for stating the paradox he wishes to render. As his father told Father Noël, in the order of religion one can only intimate through metaphor the truths appropriate to that order—thus, Pascal's hyperbolic "all and almost more." *Almost:* the reservation shows Pascal aware of the theological danger of the unqualified assignment of "more" to the person with whom he is most concerned, the Son. At the same time it shows his desire, his need to overcome the dependency, the inferiority, the submission to the father/Father. If the theology of *The Abridgment of the Life of Jesus Christ* is fundamentally patricentric, its psychology is fundamentally filicentric.

The fervent, pious self-abnegation of the four texts written after his night of fire suggests that Pascal has gotten out of that hellfire of reason in which he lived for so long in both scientific and religious discourse. In his warnings to himself in the "added" third movement of *The Mystery of Jesus* that the temptation to vanity and curiosity must be resisted, he reaches what might be called the limit or zed degree of writing and language, of thinking itself, of reasoning of the kind that he had sought to impose on Rebours in the famous encounter of early 1648 on the very subjects that have preoccupied him in *The Mystery*. In light of the mystery, his curiosity itself is a vanity, and it is no accident that *The Mystery* expresses best this insight that is also to be found more implicitly in each of the other three texts. Since it too is in language, it might be tempting to find in the difference between earlier, objective prose formulations and this poetic rendition of insight the distinction made by various formalist philosophical and critical theoreticians: that *The Mystery* (like the other texts on conversion, suggestively) is nothing more than a poetic text.

Nothing could be further from Pascal's mind and heart. Like James Agee in the prologue to his and Walker Evans' *Let Us Now Praise Famous Men,* Pascal in his epilogue to the first two movements of *The Mystery* is warning against the danger of letting the poetry (Agee's beautiful language; Pascal's dramatic form and his language) get in the way of the truth (the poverty of the Southern poor, better rendered, says Agee, in Evans' photographs than in his own prose; Pascal's discovery of Jesus in his Agony). Pascal uses poetry because it expresses his insight better, but, like his father in his remonstrances on language to Father Noël, he seems aware of the danger of poetry itself being a source of vanity and curiosity. He thus tells himself prosaically what he had told himself dramatically: that Christ's very words are to him an occasion of pride, curiosity, and concupiscence. The latter term brings the linguistic into the esthetic realm, the realm of pleasure. But in his discursive reflection on the poetry, Pascal underscores the secondary ontological status of his poem: it is pointing to a reality outside itself. For Pascal after his conversion poetic language, like prosaic language, is provisional and instrumental precisely because it is the greatest mistake, or sin, one can commit to regard it as permanent and absolute.

As if in spite of but actually in tragic keeping with his insight at the end of *The Mystery,* however, he will fall back into his "vanity" and "curiosity" — into the vanity of curiosity — in his more public expressions of the meaning of the truth he gleaned in the early stages of his conversion.

6

THE
CONVERT
AS
PRIVATE
ADVERSARY

I N RELIGION, no less than in science, the vanity of curiosity mo-
mentarily overcome in *The Mystery* would make Pascal a difficult
ally. If Christina of Sweden and so many others could testify to it in
science, his new coreligionists at Port Royal could do so in religion.
Among them, soon after the conversion, was Isaac-Louis Le Maistre,
the nephew of the great Arnauld, who was known under the name M.
de Sacy, which he bears in the text recording his conversations with
Pascal (probably in January 1655) on the Christian value of reading
Epictetus and Montaigne: *The Conversation with M. de Sacy (L'Entretien
avec M. de Sacy)*.[1] Translator of the Bible, writer in his own right,
priest and spiritual director of the solitaries and nuns at Port Royal in
the Fields, de Sacy was as imposing a figure in the world of religion
and letters as Pascal in the world of science and, before his conversion,
society. After that conversion it was quite natural that Pascal should
frequent the milieu of Port Royal. In particular, like any adept of that
milieu, he needed a spiritual director and, through the offices of M.
Singlin, it was in this relation that he sought out de Sacy. Their encounters are best known through the Pascalian text. I call it a Pascalian
text rather than a text of Pascal because it is, in fact, the summary not
of one conversation as the title suggests but of a series of conversations
between the two summarized by the abbé Fontaines, de Sacy's
secretary. Some scholars conjecture that the text may have been written by the secretary with notes provided by Pascal himself. In any case,
one recognizes Pascal in the *Conversation* on several counts: in the portrait of him given by Fontaines, in the style of his address, in his way

of relating to his interlocutor in the ideas he puts forth at this time. On each count the adversary reappears in the new convert.

The portrait of Pascal may be said to be the frame of the *Conversation,* with the portraitist-reporter giving different but complementary aspects of the subject: first in the general introduction recording the circumstances of the conversation and then, the conversation recorded, in the briefer but equally illuminating concluding remarks that confirm the first, general impressions of Pascal. That Pascal was known at Port Royal goes without saying, but what Fontaines notes is not the knowledge of him that we might presume came from his fairly recent stormy relations with one of their adepts, his sister Jacqueline. Rather, it is that Pascal was a man "whom not only France but all of Europe admired." The awe that fills Fontaines before this "elevated spirit" who seemed "able to animate copper and breathe spirit into bronze" does much to explain the diffidence that will be evident in Fontaines' later remarks on the way in which the directors of Port Royal, Singlin and Arnauld and de Sacy, received the new convert. Pascal seems to have been a mythic figure not only for the secretary of his new spiritual director but for all at Port Royal. That such a convert represented a great catch for Port Royal comes out in the text, but when one links this reflection on the catch to Fontaines' impression of Pascal after the conversation, it is not so much the convert who stands out in the record as the figure whose mythic powers made him able to animate copper and breathe spirit into bronze: "Thus it was that these two people of so fine a spirit finally agreed on the matter of the reading of these two philosophers and met at the same final point, where they arrived nevertheless in a somewhat different manner, M. de Sacy arriving all of a sudden by the clear view of Christianity and M. Pascal arriving only after many detours in attaching himself to the principles of these philosophers." Very likely, Fontaines does not know of the night of fire with its *Memorial.* The secretary is all the less likely to have known it if his remarkably full dialogue is the transcription with possibly only slight variation for literary purposes of notes written by Pascal and de Sacy themselves for the purpose of a record. He thus cannot know his man as fully as we know him, but what he does know of him is nonetheless consistent with the pattern of Pascal in his adversarial stance.

The general traits of Pascal's character as given by Fontaines are of capital importance. He is, Fontaines notes first of all, "lively, always active." One wonders if this characterization is not the author's anticipatory summary of the very style of address that Pascal shows in the dialogue with de Sacy. There Pascal seizes his interlocutor in the way that Gilberte Périer has noted as one of the faults of her brother. The personal as well as the scientific knowledge that the directors of Port Royal had of Jacqueline's brother may well lie at the root of the diffidence with which they met the convert's request for spiritual direction: "M. Singlin believed in seeing this great genius that he would do well to send him to Port Royal in the Fields, where M. Arnauld would put the bridle on him in what concerned the higher sciences; and where M. de Sacy would teach him to scorn them." Port Royal des Champs was where Mother Angélique was located, having left there, fortuitously as Jacqueline had seen it in her *Relation,* for the Paris house at just the moment that Jacqueline needed for counsel on her all too "secular" brother. It is not unlikely that Mother Angélique and others at Port Royal in the Fields knew the lively spirit of this new convert. M. Singlin, who had been Jacqueline's first counselor in that stormy period, knew what he was doing when he sent the new convert to that house for the ministrations of Arnauld and de Sacy. It was more than Pascal's presumed commitment to science that the directors wished to bridle: it was as well those other qualities that Fontaines records in awe here, "a range, an elevation, a firmness, a penetration and a sharpness" of spirit "beyond what one could believe." Those qualities may have left such a trace at Port Royal that not even de Sacy could hope to bridle them. As Fontaines implies, it was with a certain reluctance, overcome only by a sense of decency reenforced by a sense of duty, that he agreed to serve as Pascal's spiritual director: "M. de Sacy could not get away without seeing him out of a feeling of decency, especially having been asked to do so by M. Singlin; but the holy light that he found in the Scriptures and the [Church] fathers, made him hope that he would not be dazzled by all the brilliance of M. Pascal, who nevertheless charmed and carried everyone away." The reluctance was at once doctrinal and personal before this prepossessing, mythic figure.

De Sacy was disappointed neither in Pascal nor in himself. In this general introductory part of the *Conversation,* Fontaines reports that de Sacy appreciated the force of Pascal's mind and his discourse, but that he found nothing new there, for all the great things that Pascal had told him he had already found in Saint Augustine:

And doing justice to everyone, he said: "M. Pascal is extremely estimable, in that not having read the fathers of the Church, he had on his own, by the penetration of his mind, found the same truths that they had found. He finds them surprising, he said, because he has not seen them any place; but for us, we are accustomed to see them on all sides in our books." Thus this wise ecclesiastic found that the ancients had no fewer lights than the new and he held to them; and esteemed M. Pascal greatly in that he agreed [se rencontrait] in all things with Saint Augustine.

M. de Sacy did not want to be churlish, but he obviously could not spare himself the implied reproach on Pascal's naïveté. It is as if he tells Pascal here that he need not, indeed should not, have relied on his own penetration of spirit to find the truths to be read in the Church fathers. In Pascal's discovery of Augustinian principles on his own we are reminded of his discovery as a small boy of the principles of Euclidean geometry. It is as if de Sacy were reproaching all such exercises of mind precisely because they are exercises of *the mind*. The truth is at hand in the books of the Gospel and the books of the fathers. The director wished to leave little doubt that, in the conversation itself, he had found the convert still too much a man of mind.

He could not know that the convert was as aware of this as he, but that the convert could not help himself. Except by carrying in the lining of his clothing the *Memorial,* the first, as hair shirt and other such flagellations of the spirit, not the *body,* that Pascal would wear after this conversion. If de Sacy's summary comment on the conversations is of their failure for de Sacy, Pascal's parchment version of the *Memorial* may have been his summary comment of both its failure and its success for Pascal. He may well have perceived what de Sacy perceives here: that he had been too much a man of mind and that he had not yet submitted to the lesson the director had tried to teach him, total submission to Jesus Christ. So he would record the double lesson of the conversion and the *Conversation* and carry them on his person, emphasizing for himself the difficulties of his temperament, especially the temptation that mind represented to him.

The pathos of his state of mind does not gainsay the excesses of that mind in action. The excesses are rife in the *Conversation* itself. Pascal seems to have succumbed to what may have been a spiritual trap set for him by de Sacy, as Fontaines tells us, by way of explaining why the subject of those exchanges turned out to be Epictetus and Montaigne:

"M. de Sacy's usual procedure, in speaking with people, was to pro-portion his conversations to those with whom he spoke . . . He believed therefore to put M. Pascal on his ground and speak to him of the readings in philosophy that occupied him most . . . M. Pascal told him that his most usual books had been Epictetus and Montaigne; and he made great praise of these two spirits." Pascal's choice may seem surprising at first glance. From his letter on his father's death we know him to have read the Church fathers and from his introductory remarks in his Preface to the *Treatise on the Vacuum* we know him to have been as aware as de Sacy that the books of the Gospel and of the Church fathers are the first and the last word in the very matter that had brought them together. Why then Epictetus and Montaigne? The very domain provides and initial answer: de Sacy had put him on his own ground or what Fontaines "believed" to be that ground: philoso-phy, not theology. One might expect, however, that the convert would not accept this as his ground, that he would indeed prefer direct instruction from another ground, the one occupied by de Sacy. Pascal, though, is not yet the author of the fragment of the *Thoughts* who would find that "philosophy does not merit one hour of one's time" (S 118). Nor is it simple deference and submission to the director that leads him to occupy the ground of philosophy. Rather, in accepting to occupy that ground, he shows that it preoccupies him in the antagon-istic frame of mind that has driven him in so many of his relations to date. He would take on Epictetus and Montaigne as he had taken on Aristotle and Father Noël.

Why did he choose Epictetus and Montaigne and not, to recall two philosophers we know him to have taken on in another specifically religious context, Socrates and Seneca? They had been of no use, he wrote, on the questions of death that preoccupied him and his sisters in his letter on the death of his father. And why Epictetus and Mon-taigne as he addresses himself to the questions of life, of "how to live"? Because, as he tells de Sacy at one point, "I have found that they are assuredly the two greatest defenders of the two most celebrated sects of the world and the only two in conformity with reason; since one can follow only one of these two routes, namely, either there is a God; and then one places therein the sovereign good: or that it is uncertain, and then the true good is also, since one is incapable of it." He would take on the greatest examples of moral difficulties as he had taken on the greatest examples of physical and mathematical difficulties, such as the problem of the vacuum and the problem of games of chance. Epictetus and Montaigne are new father figures whom the convert must best even as the scientist would best Aristotle. These two figures are as mythic to Pascal as he was to the directors at Port Royal. He is taken with them in his familiar love/hate relationship in all its intensity, especially with Montaigne. The director listens to the new convert brilliantly summarize Montaigne's virtue in having demonstrated the susceptibility of all things, natural and rational, to universal doubt and the futility of all human hope for a just order in science, mathematics, law, and a "reason denuded of faith."

As he listens, Fontaines tells us, "M. de Sacy believing himself living in a new country, and hearing a new language, said to himself the words of Saint Augustine: 'O God of Truth, those who know these subtleties of reasoning, are they for all that more pleasing to you?' He pitied this philosopher, who prided himself and rent himself in all his parts with thorns that he himself formed, as Saint Augustine says of himself when he was in this state." Certain scholars have believed that by "this philosopher" de Sacy points to Pascal rather than the subject of Pascal's discourse, Montaigne. Other scholars deny this possible allusion in view of de Sacy's comparison of Montaigne and Augustine "in this state." Yet, one connection does not preclude the other. As de Sacy concludes his first remarks at this point, his language suggests the possibility that he may have had Pascal as much as Montaigne in mind as a philosopher who had just uttered subtleties of reasoning that were not very pleasing to God: "He acknowledged with what wisdom Saint Paul warns us not to let ourselves be seduced by these discourses; for he admitted that there is a certain attractiveness that carries one off; one sometimes believes things true only because one says them eloquently: these are dangerous meats, he said." We may wonder how Fontaines knew what de Sacy was saying to himself before his reply to Pascal here. The spirit of that wonder as reported, however, is very much in keeping with what de Sacy is reported as saying: that Montaigne's discourse is pleasing and seductive, that his eloquence is capable of carrying one off. He obviously thought Pascal had been pleased, seduced, carried off. Having thanked Pascal for his summary of Montaigne's views, having slyly noted that he himself had not read Montaigne, and that Montaigne should hope that his writings should be known only by Pascal's account of them, de Sacy notes that "this man did have wit, but I do not know but that you lend him a bit more than he has, by this very fine running link that you make of his principles. You can judge that, having spent my life as I have, I have been little advised to read this author, all of whose works have nothing that we must principally look for in our readings, according to the rule of Saint Augustine; because his words do not appear to come out of a great depth of humility and piety."

The director's lesson in humility seems clear enough in Fontaines' spare report, but Pascal missed it. He would not be denied priority, not even by de Sacy and, in a certain sense, not even by Saint Augustine. De Sacy tried to go on in this vein: "upon which M. Pascal said to him, that if he was complimenting him on possessing Montaigne well and knowing how to shape him [*le tourner*], he could as well tell him, without compliment, that he knew Saint Augustine better and that he knew how to shape him much better, although with little advantage to poor Montaigne." The new convert is more new than convert: he tells de Sacy that he is extremely edified by what de Sacy has told him. However, "being still all filled up with his author, he could not contain himself" and he launched into an equally brilliant demonstration of the vice of Montaigne's "pagan" laxity of morals, with its exclusion of God from ethical conduct and its facile reliance on an easy come, easy go ethics of personal comfort and self-indulgence.

In his long second discourse (four pages in the densely printed Pléiade edition of Pascal) Pascal himself acknowledges his being carried away in an inappropriate way on this occasion. About halfway through his discourse he admits to de Sacy that the latter has "admirably" made him see the "little usefulness" of philosophical studies for Christians: "I shall nevertheless with your permission, not cease to tell you my thought, though ready to renounce all lights that will not have come from you; in which I shall have the advantage either of having encountered the truth by good fortune [*bonheur*] or to receive it from you with assurance." And toward the end, " 'I beg your pardon, Sir,' said M. Pascal to M. de Sacy, to have let myself get carried away in this way before you, into theology, instead of remaining with philosophy, but . . . " and he continues to be "carried away," words pouring out in a brilliant exposition of the superior truths of theology to which, as he puts it, he has been "unconsciously [*insensiblement*] led."

We might also translate *insensiblement* "insensitively" in the context. Pascal has been insensitive to the fact that M. de Sacy is beyond rhetoric, beyond the ways in language and the world in which excuses are proferred as preemptive ways of forgiving the fault to be excused. In these, his final remarks on theology in the *Conversation,* Pascal is only reaching the ground he had wanted to reach even in accepting M. de Sacy's assignment of the ground of philosophy: de Sacy's own ground, theology. On that ground, from the point of view of his new coreligionists, exhibitionistic behavior may be understood as the sign of his reluctant submissiveness, the sign of the enduring force of his belief in the power of mind in a realm where they affirm it has no place. In the very theology that he posits here it is the grasp of the mind that one sees at work, not the surrender to grace. Grace is the rationale that he sees as the reconciliation of the antinomies he posits between, on the one hand, Epictetus with his belief in God sans awareness of corruption and, on the other, Montaigne with his belief in corruption sans real awareness of God. The advantage of grace does not seem to come to him all of a sudden as it did in his night of fire.

De Sacy did not believe that it was he or any human being who gave the advantage of truth and grace. And he certainly did not believe that one received it by good fortune. Pascal's polarity takes no real account of God's action as his interlocutor understood that action. In spite of Pascal's evocation of the mysteries of the Incarnation and the Eucharist in his final intervention (not unexpectedly he has had to have "the last word"), one does not feel their impact on his heart as one feels the impact of such mysteries in the first text of the *Memorial.* Rather, it is more the author of probability theory who moves these tokens on the gaming board of philosophy and theology, more taken with the game itself than with the hope of winning. He has no more heard de Sacy's final warning about the danger of reading the philosophers than he had the earlier. The spiritual director observes that his interlocutor resembled those skillful doctors who use certain dosages of poison to effect cures, but he adds that the dosages of poison from Montaigne and Epictetus that Pascal has used would not be so advantageous for many people *as Pascal told him they were for him.* Pascal cannot hear this skeptical note on his own readings, nor can he hear the implication that, however really useful, such readings could be useful only to a very few people. Instead, Pascal launches into a final discourse on the general usefulness of the readings of Epictetus and Montaigne. He concedes that their separate reading must, indeed, be carefully adjusted to the reader's condition and mores. He concludes in a generalizing tone that shows he has missed completely de Sacy's countergeneralization: "Only it seems to me that, in joining them together, they could succeed pretty well, because the one opposes the evil of the other; not that they can give virtue, but only trouble one in vice, the soul finding itself besieged by these two contraries, of which one chases pride, the other laziness; and not being able to repose in any of its vices by its reasoning nor also to flee all of them." The seed of the strategy of the projected *Apology for the Christian Religion* has appeared: the confrontation of contraries to demonstrate man's need to appeal to a higher source of reconciliation, the negative use of reason, so to speak. Yet, the sower seems more bent on weeding the soil than on planting the seed itself. The adversary is still on the attack; the advocate of faith has not yet emerged to emphasize those more positive, poetic, and proselytizing accents that had seemed to emerge in the shorter version of the *Memorial.*

He has not emerged, at least in public or, as with de Sacy, in settings calling for social intercourse even as limited and unworldly as the dialogues with his spiritual director. The antagonistic tendencies of his personality still sought to prevail, even in those moments of most intensely positive expressions of personal faith and communion with others of that faith. The presence of another, including another of his own faith, became an occasion for Pascal's old Adam of self-regard and self-priority to spring forth and to seek to prevail as it had in his first conversation with Rebours in early 1648.

As THE ENCOUNTER with Rebours seems to have sent him back to the theological drawing board in the *First* and *Second Writings on Grace,* so the encounter with de Sacy seems to have sent him back to that board in *The Comparison of the Early Christians with Those of Today.*[2] Like so many texts written after his conversion, this text (published in 1779 by Bossut on the basis of manuscripts discovered posthumously) has an uncertain date. Most editors place it between 1655 and 1657. Its subject matter and its somewhat polemical and proselytizing tone suggest to me that it is early in that two-year period, probably shortly after the encounter with de Sacy. Pascal, perhaps with some suggestion by his spiritual director, might well have reasoned that, if one is going to go back to antiquity, better to do so with those ancients who were of the faith than with those who, like Epictetus, were not. Because of his serene, if naïve, belief in God, Epictetus had been less burned by Pascal's fiery reasoning. Nevertheless Pascal may have come away from the encounter with de Sacy convinced that he had made an error of judgment in looking back in antiquity to a pagan, however potentially pious, rather than to the truly pious who were waiting at hand there, the early Christians.

The organization and the style of the text suggest some resemblance with the *First* and *Second Writings on Grace*: a contrastive lining-up of positions, with a briskly logical and almost peremptory tone, reminiscent of the letter of late 1648 in which he read the holy book to his older sister. Here he reads the holy book to the flaccid practitioners of "today's Christians." In this tone and design Pascal seems as sure of himself as in the encounter with de Sacy; gone is the agonistic anti-self discipline of the *Memorial* and *The Mystery*; gone, too, is their sense of a lyrical communion in Jesus who salves life's occult sins and saves one from the final sin of death. Rejoined to his mother, Pascal bosses her around a bit here. The good mother Church (*la bonne mere*) he invokes in this text is somewhat formulaic, not someone who sets the example Jesus posed in *The Mystery* in pointing to the Virgin and the saints but an institution that *sets up* the examples to be followed by the Christians of the day, whose religious laxity stands in such stark contrast to the purer faith of the early Christians. Finally, the reasoning by which Pascal defines this difference suggests that his curiosity, the vanity of reasoning, has gotten the better of him once again. As so often when it does, he becomes something of a scold.

He defines the difference essentially by a review of the question of baptism. Pascal *tends toward* a Protestant suspicion of infant baptism in particular:

> In the time of the Church aborning, one taught the catechumens, that is, those who were to claim baptism, before conferring it to them, and they were admitted only after a full instruction in the mysteries of the religion, only after penance for their past life, only after great knowledge of the grandeur and excellence of the profession of faith and of the Christian maxims into which they wished to enter forever, only after eminent marks of a true conversion of the heart, only after an extreme desire of baptism.
>
> These things being known by the whole Church, one conferred on them the sacrament of incorporation and regeneration by which they became members of the Church.
>
> Whereas in this time, the sacrament of baptism, having been ac-

corded to children before the age of reason, for very important considerations, it happens that the negligence of parents lets Christians age
without any knowledge of the grandeur of our religion.

Pascal goes on at some length in this vein before he gives the "very important considerations" that nevertheless seem unresponsive to the
negligence of parents, biological and, in this context, those who may
serve as godparents. Those considerations are as follows:

> Her [the Church's] real spirit is that those whom she withdraws at
> such a tender age from the contagion of the world might take on feel-
> ings altogether opposed to those of the world. Thus she anticipates the
> age of reason in order to anticipate the vices into which the corrupted
> reason would drag them; and, before their spirit can act, she fills it
> with her spirit, so that they might live in a great ignoring of the world
> and in a state all the more distant from vice in that they would never
> have known it.

Even as he introduces this justification of infant baptism, Pascal has
hedged it on the foreside with the rehearsal of laxities into which today's Christians fall in spite of having received it. In the sentence just
preceding the passage quoted Pascal sees the Church as having the
same reservations about infant baptism that he has expressed: "And
this good mother sees only with extreme regret that what she has pro-
cured for the salvation of her children becomes the occasion of the loss
of adults." He therefore recommends that today's Christians imitate
the early Christians: they "must submit themselves to receive the instruction that they would have had, if they were beginning to enter
into the Church." Further, "it is necessary to make them understand
the difference in the customs that have been practiced in the diversity
of times." He has hedged his begrudging acceptance of infant baptism
by these categorical injunctions.

The importance of reason in relation to this hedging cannot be underestimated here. Baptism before the age of reason appears to be inadequate to Pascal. His injunctions threaten to annul a sacrament of the
Church. Even his call for a more rigorous fidelity by godparents to
their baptismal duties of instruction of their godchildren are assimilated into the overarching injunction to imitate the first Christians.
The principal characteristic of the latter for Pascal is precisely that they
were of the age of reason before they were admitted to baptism. It is
the reason that must be cured through the agency of reason, through

instruction in the faith rather than by the mysterious agency of grace coming from God himself. In the only mention of grace in this text, it is the Church who grants grace: "If the early Christians evinced [*témoignaient*] so much gratitude to the Church for a grace that she accorded only to their long prayers, they of today evince so much ingratitude for this same grace that this good mother accords them even before they have been in a state to ask it of her." Pascal storms against the "spirit of the world, the spirit of ambition, the spirit of vengeance, the spirit of impurity, the spirit of concupiscence" as much as he does in earlier texts. The ground of God's will seems curiously circumscribed, however, as Pascal makes grace more a gift of the Church than of God.

What is striking is the peremptoriness of tone, the very failure to take account of complexities in a matter where Protestant doubts on infant baptism were a sore point of the theological history with which Pascal is dealing here. Pascal is not the convert, but the catechist, the instructor, the rule-giver, and once again the scientist (of theology, this time). He seems to be saying to the Christians of today: Do the experiment and you will see that, indeed, the waters of infant baptism do not rise to fill the vacuum of your sinfulness. He will provide a logic that the Church itself was not applying. Still, he would do so within the bosom of the Church. Pascal's misgivings on infant baptism are only a *tendency* toward Protestant positions he had excoriated in other writings. Theologically, he stays within the family of the Church, but, psychologically, the good family man will now act like the good husband to the good mother Church. He will keep the books, be less indulgent than mother has been with her wayward children. It is a role we have seen him act with his sisters and that we shall see him act again with Christians close to him and not so close to him.

If Miel is right in his dating of the letter known as the *Third Writing on Grace* and in his identification of Pascal's correspondent there, Pascal will play the polemical catechist first with someone close to him: in the late summer or early fall of 1655, with the Duc de Roannez. Miel's reasoning on the date seems cogent and the spirit of the letter seems further evidence for placing it at this time; it is the spirit of a Pascal scrupulously and ingeniously reasoning his assured way through a maze of theological pronouncements on the same question that preoccupied him in the *First Writing on Grace,* the Council of Trent's meaning in the article, "The commandments are not impossible to the

just." It is not only "on the possibility of the commandments," however, but also on "the apparent contradictions of Saint Augustine, the
theory of the double abandonment [*délaissement*] of the just, and the
proximate [*prochain*] power."[3] It is a response to the first of these matters, raised by his correspondent in a letter we do not have, that Pascal
writes here. The correspondent is one to whom he has, as he puts it at
one point in the letter, told certain things "often." This suggests a
closeness that supports Miel's identification of the correspondent as the
Duc de Roannez. The latter had served as Pascal's worldly director a
few years earlier, introducing the scientist into the society of court and
salon during his so-called worldly period. Now, the convert will serve
as the spiritual director to his friend and former director in worldliness.

He was to serve more as spiritual director than as friend. It is clear
from the letter that the correspondent had expressed another concern
beyond the one that Pascal identifies at the beginning as the reason for
his reply: the friend's inquiry on the Council of Trent's article that
"the commandments are not impossible to the just." At later points in
the letter, Pascal also brings out that the friend is also concerned with
another, related matter. Having dealt at some length with the apparent contradictions of Saint Augustine that derived from the answers he
has given on the friend's doctrinal question, Pascal writes,

> No more is needed to make you see in what way one can accord these
> apparent contraditions. I shall then not extend myself any further on
> this subject. But because it has unconsciously [*insensiblement*] led me to
> speak of the abandonment of the just and because I know that this is
> the only difficulty that holds you back and the only thing of all the
> points that people contest today, that you have difficulty in believing
> that it is from Saint Augustine, I shall not finish this letter without
> clarifying this point perfectly for you, if God gives me the power.

He then goes on to clarify the point in Augustine, but not without
first reentering, at some length, into a discussion of the possibility of
the commandments to the just. Then, as if aware of his digressive re-
entry into that matter, he writes, "I come now to the question that
touches you the most. And I want to make you see that, in the doctrine of Saint Augustine, the commandments are sometimes impossible to some of the just." He then reiterates the Augustinian notions of
the two perseverances that are to be considered: the one in prayer, the

other in charity (that is, in doing justice by good works) and reempha-
sizes the point made in many ways earlier (both here and in the *First
Writing on Grace*) that the first underlies the second inasmuch as to persevere in prayer one must have a special help (grace) from God. From
this it flows, he then points out, that God does then abandon some of
the just before the just abandon him, those to whom God does not
give the special help to ask him to persevere.

Pascal answers this question that touched his friend the most in but
one of a total of forty-six pages in the Pléiade edition of the text. The
question rightly touched the friend the most, for it is the very kind of
question that had so disturbed Pascal himself in the agonistic texts on
his conversion, bringing the sense of abandonment, the fear of being
dropped by God even before one had come to know him and, what is
worse, the anguish of being dropped by God even after one has come
to him. Pascal does not offer the friend consolation on this question.
Instead, he demonstrates the logicality of Augustinian theology with
great intricacy and rigor. As Miel rightly notes, Pascal's theology here
is not very original, but his method is new and, within it, his reasoning brilliantly keen as it elaborates and refines the fundamental position
of the first two *Writings on Grace.* The method is not only new but, as
Miel illustrates, it strikingly anticipates certain methods and concerns
of contemporary linguistic philosophy, the examination of ordinary
language. What Miel calls Pascal's "contextualism" is very much to
the fore: we must examine the way statements are made, the way
words are used, in light of the way people understand those statements
and those words in ordinary usage: "There is what I had to say to you
on this subject, where I am glad to have entered in order to have you
see that propositions that are contradictory in the words, are not
always so in the sense." And:

> *The commandments are possible to the just.* And yet, who does not see that
> the word *puissance* ["power" or "ability"] is so vague, that it contains
> all opinions? For finally, if one deems a thing *to be in our capability*,
> when we do it when we want, which is a very natural and familiar
> way of talking, will it not follow that it is in our power [*pouvoir*],
> taken in this sense, to keep the commandments and to change our will,
> since, from the moment that we want it, not only does that happen,
> but there is contradiction if that does not happen, But if one deems a
> thing to be in our power [*pouvoir*], when it is only in the power that
> one calls proximate [*prochain*], which is also a very ordinary way of us-

ing the word *power* [*pouvoir*], in this sense we will no longer have this power except when it will be given by God. Thus this expression of Saint Augustine is Catholic in the first sense, and Pelagian in the second.

He will not leave Augustine hanging on this Pelagian petard, for he goes immediately on to quote at some length Augustine's "retraction" of the implied Pelagianism: "That is in no way against the grace of God that we preach, for it is in the power [*puissance*] of man to change his will for the better: But this power of man is null if it is not given by God: For since a thing is in our power, which we do when we want, nothing is so much in our power as our will itself. But the will is prepared by the Lord."

Pascal goes on and on in this vein of speculative theology, peppering his developments in what follows as in what preceded with such locutions as "a thing so clear . . . who could . . . is it not clear . . . is there anything clearer . . . without equivocation . . . is it not indubitable . . . a necessary consequence . . . the same nicety . . . it is absurd . . . here are some proofs thereof . . . is it not visible . . . who does not know that . . . who does not see . . . does it not suffice . . . let us examine it according to the principles . . . how will one say with boldness . . . will we not have reason to conclude . . . in what abyss of absurdity . . . this comparison explains." Hardly a page of this long letter lacks one or more of these argumentative formulations. Moreover, although he notes at the outset that he does not have the books at hand to support his arguments, he quotes at great length from the Council of Trent and Augustine and others. After his brief exposition to his friend on the question that touches him the most, he refers him to a recent book by the Jansenist Bourzeis as making it unnecessary for him to treat the disturbing question any further. Naturally, Pascal had some books at hand and he remembered those he did not have at hand well enough. It is not Pascal's intellectual honesty that is at issue here. It is his intellectuality. The logical armature of the *Third Writing on Grace* is as imposing, if not more, than the theological lessons it frames. Pascal has turned the power of his mind on theological questions in the same spirit in which he turned it on physical questions: in an argumentative, antagonistic spirit. Like a modern linguistic scientist, he demonstrates the relations between the deep structure of grace and the surface structure of its linguistic expression. However, he is less concerned with the deep structure than with the transforms.

By the very definition of the deep structure, he cannot talk about it very much, one might say. As in the earlier *Writings on Grace,* he writes of God's hiddenness and impenetrability. These crucial aspects of God are, he recognizes, at the core of the problems raised by his friend's letter: "For who does not know that it is an indubitable principle in the doctrine of Saint Augustine that the reason for which, of two just, the one perseveres and the other does not, is an absolutely incomprehensible secret?" Pascal's friend might well have replied to him: "Well, I am one of those who does not know it." The level of patristic authority at which Pascal puts the human concern of his friend's difficult question differs radically from the level of communion in Christ at which he put it in the advocative writings after his conversion. Here, he is more the author of the Preface to the *Treatise on the Vacuum,* who, in distinguishing between two kinds of reasoning, had insisted on experiment in science and on authority in matters of faith. This rationalistic approach to deeply moving human concern about abandonment, deprivation, and loss of the approval by God dehumanizes the reassurance Pascal would give his friends. God does not emerge as the Father who gives the certitude and peace and joy of the *Memorial;* Jesus does not emerge as the androgynous consoler of *The Mystery* who reconciles one to one's occult sins. The word occurs here, too:

> And if one asks why, being just as well as the elect, God leaves them to their free will and not the elect, he [Augustine] declares that it is by a hidden judgment. From which it is seen that it is not for having badly used the grace that was in them, nor for having attributed to themselves the effect of the grace, for in this case the discernment would not have been a hidden [*occulte*] cause, but well known. In sum [*enfin*] it is for no reason which can be known to us, since it is by an occult judgment; which is of such a great force that I leave it to you to exaggerate it.

Here, *occult* cannot have any of the carnal overtones that informed it as Jesus used it with Pascal in *The Mystery*: God is by definition without libido. Rather, in this rationalistic context, it has the geometric sense of a line that the Great Geometer drew in preparing his plan and then erased. The human import of the abandonment (*délaissement*) that so disturbed Pascal's correspondent has also been erased as Pascal assimilates it into an explanation concerning double cessation, substituting a term rife with concrete feeling for one with an abstract and analytical force.

Even as Pascal adopts a familiar figure he drops it for a rationalistic explanation. He asks his correspondent to imagine (*figurons*) the relation between the divine and human wills or delectations as that of a man placed between two friends, each holding him by a chain, for fear that he will pull away from each the more. This is the image of man caught between his two freedoms, the one of his state before the Fall of Adam, the other of his state after the Fall. The chain of grace pulls with more "force," he says, quoting a beautiful line of the Psalms (115:16): "Lord, you have broken my bonds." But he goes on himself to raise a "metaphysical supposition" that the two "covetousnesses" pull the man equally and proceed to leave him immobile. He destroys this argument with brio, by denying the appropriateness of the very figure he has imagined: "This comparison almost explains his state, but not perfectly, because it is impossible to find in nature any example, nor any comparison that fits perfectly the actions of the will." There follows the by now familiar doctrine of the will as containing its own motive power. Yet, Pascal cannot let the figural and the biblical be; he assimilates the beautiful image of the chain and the beautiful verse from the Psalms into the logic of speculative theology. As in the *Comparison* he had interposed the "good mother Church" between "today's Christian" and God's grace, so here he interposes the, for him, first father of the Church between God the Father and his anguished son on earth. *Quod est demonstrandum.*

The theology of the future *Apology for the Christian Religion* may be rather fully formulated in the *Third Writing on Grace* and in the *Fourth*, which, applying the methods of linguistic analysis on the same questions even more rigorously, may well have been written around the same time. As Mesnard has noted, it is around the second half of 1665 that Pascal began to be concerned with linguistic problems (witness his influence on the *Port Royal Logic*, for example). Miel has also noted that Jacqueline Pascal's letter of October 1665 concerns a related interest, her brother's devising of a method for teaching the children at Port Royal to read by relating the sounds (the "ordinary" sounds, we might say) of the letters of the alphabet to the sounds of words themselves before asking the child to spell the words. In these purely linguistic matters as in the linguistic analysis of theological questions, the applied scientist has taken over in Pascal once again. However consistent the "theo-logic" of these writings be with that of the projected *Apology*, its intellectually rigid framework may work *against* it in the same way that the much looser framework of that text works *for* that theo-logic. Pascal may well have thought that his friend had already been converted and thus had no need of the kind of consolations that he himself had had in his own conversion. They would both be beyond those beginnings. Moreover, as he puts it at one point in the *Third Writing*, the ways in which God acts on the just after those beginnings are different from the ways he acts long after. Presumably, Pascal sees himself as acting in consonance with God's actions in that after stage, cooperating with God's grace. Yet, often sounding like the God of Job ("Where were you when I made the thunder?"), Pascal attempts to push language beyond the zed degree, the limit he had earlier acknowledged in the poetic expression of the same truths in *The Mystery of Jesus*. Both God and Jesus seem less mysterious as Pascal defines them not only as hidden but also as forbidding.

· 7 ·

THE
CONVERT
AS
PUBLIC ADVERSARY:
PROVINCIAL LETTERS
1–16

THE *Provincial Letters* are more fully known as *Letters Written to a Provincial by One of His Friends,* and eighteen of them, with a fragment of a nineteenth, were written by Pascal in the fourteen months between January 14, 1656, and March 24, 1657.[1] The first ten might be even more fully entitled by the addition to each of the phrase their author added to the first: *on the Subject of the Present Disputes at the Sorbonne.* With the eleventh, in various formulations, Pascal changes correspondents, from the provincial, his brother-in-law Florin Périer, to those who now have become his adversaries in theological matters as they had been in scientific matters, the Jesuits.

The *Provincial Letters* have been variously and justly celebrated as brilliant journalism, as one of the foundation stones of modern French prose, if not the primary one, and as dramatic comedy of the highest order. The letters also mark Pascal's entry into the world in a way that makes his more touted worldly period seem tame compared with the passion with which he enters in them into a concern with worldly ways. The concern on this occasion is, however, of a very different order from that of his own worldly period. He is concerned with another order, the order of the heart, of charity that stands for him in the course of these letters at such a remove from and, at times, in such stark contradiction with the abominations of the order of the world, yet not with the order of the mind. It is chiefly on mind that Pascal relies in order to combat the degradations and derogations of faith that he finds so flagrantly propounded by those who would all too easily make peace with the disorders of the world. Thus, responding to the appeal of his coreligionists at Port Royal—an appeal, it is reported, made specifically by the great Arnauld himself—the new convert turns his enormous energy of mind to a public defense of the faith. The adversary becomes advocate, a public advocate, albeit it a somewhat ambivalent one. The addressee of the first letter is genuine enough, of course. That Pascal should be writing privately on religious disputes to the brother-in-law who has been both his scientific and religious confrère is not wholly pretextual. The letters were clearly intended for publication, however. They were meant to be made public, to become open counteroffensives in the disputes in which, up to this point, the defenders of Jansen had been very much on the defensive.

Jansen's defenders had begun very much on the offensive. Jansen's famous book, the *Augustinius,* had been published in 1640 (two years after its author's death) in clear opposition, as its subtitle indicates, to the adaptation of Pelagian postulates over the course of a century and more, an adaptation associated chiefly with the Jesuits. In the 1640s, however, abetted by the papal condemnation in 1641 of the *Augustinius* as part of a bull condemning the position of the theologian Baius, on whom Jansen had relied, and infuriated by Arnauld's persistent defense of Jansen (*Defense of M. Jansenius,* 1644, and *Apology for the Holy Fathers,* 1651), the Jesuits themselves counterattacked by positing seven (later reduced to five) propositions "drawn from" the *Augustinius,* clearly condemned as heretical in the papal bull of Innocent X issued May 31, 1653:

> 1. Some commandments of God are impossible for just men, even when they want and strive to accomplish them according to the powers that they have; and the grace by which they [commandments] are possible is lacking to them [men].
> 2. In the state of corrupted nature one never resists interior grace.
> 3. In order to merit or lose merit in the state of corrupted nature, freedom that excludes necessity is not required of man, but only that freedom that excludes constraint.
> 4. The semi-Pelagians admitted the necessity of interior grace bearing on each act in particular, even for the beginning of faith, and they were heretical for wishing that this grace be such that human will could resist it or obey it.
> 5. It is semi-Pelagian to say that Jesus Christ died or that he shed his blood generally for all men.

Arnauld and his coreligionists responded to this counterattack (published under the auspices of the Sorbonne's faculty of theology) by ac-

cepting the propositions as heretical in principle but denying that they
were to be found in fact in the *Augustinius*. The disputes warmed up
throughout the year 1654, coming to a head in early 1655 when a par-
ish priest at the Church of Saint Sulpice refused to grant absolution to
the Duc de Liancourt because he was suspected of supporting Jansenist
positions. The great Arnauld leaped into the fray, publishing in late
February a *Letter to a Person of Condition* and then in early July a *Letter
to a Duke and Peer,* supporting the duke in terms of the familiar distinction between fact and principle, denying that the propositions were to
be found in Jansen. He thereby exacerbated the quarrel still further,
however, maintaining that, in the matter of principle, grace had been
lacking to one just man: Saint Peter himself. In early January 1656 Arnauld was condemned by the Sorbonne for denying the fact regarding
the five propositions, and the Sorbonne was in fact considering the hereticality of his thesis concerning Saint Peter when the first *Provincial
Letter* appeared. It begins:

> We were altogether misguided. I was undeluded only yesterday. Until
> then, I thought that the subject of the disputes at the Sorbonne was re-
> ally important and of extreme consequence for the cause of religion. So
> many meetings of a company as celebrated as the Faculty of Paris, and
> where there occurred so many extraordinary and unparalled things
> give one such a grand notion of them that one cannot but believe that
> there must really be something truly extraordinary at stake.
>
>   However, you will be quite surprised when you learn by this ac-
> count what all this great show comes to, and this is what I shall tell
> you in a few words, having thoroughly informed myself.

We: in the first word of the first letter Pascal indicates the linguistic
and rhetorical strategy that will be central to all of the *Provincial Letters*: an appeal to the public, to the generality of readers, to all those of
whom he and his correspondent are but a part. That correspondent is
his brother-in-law and thus has a certain speficity that is not wholly
pretextual. The specificity becomes more and more a generality as the
reader observes the various rhetorical threads that Pascal weaves to create for *any* reader the impression that the disputants on the Sorbonne
side of the questions at issue have been guilty not only of dubious theological positions but also, if not chiefly, of an *abuse* of language.

    The topical organization of the *Provincial Letters* indicates the preoc-
cupation with language and its abuse. Tactically, each of the eighteen

letters and the fragment of a nineteenth concentrates on a single term, pair, or series of related terms drawn from the arsenal of the adversaries of Arnauld and his coreligionists at Port Royal. This is not to say that the author of the *Provincial Letters* was without a grand strategy Initially, as the tone of the first letter indicates, he writes as if he assumes that the matter would be disposed of in a relatively short series of letters, each disposing of key terms at the heart of the dispute. This assumption is implicit in the appeal to the general public not to tolerate the abuse of language that is characteristic of the Sorbonnard adversaries of Port Royal. However, the counterthrusts of the adversaries forced a change of strategy from the offense to the defense. This creates a two-part organization of the *Provincial Letters*:

I. Letters 1–10, Pascal on the offensive
   A. Letters 1–3, the pseudonymous author as impartial reporter
      1. On proximate power: differences between the Jansenists, on the one hand, and the Jesuits and even more the Dominicans on the other.
      2. On sufficient and efficacious grace; differences between the Jansenists and the Dominicans or "new Thomists"
   n.b. Letter out of the series, written in the name of the correspondent in comment on the favorable public reception of the first two letters.
      3. On the censure of M. Arnauld by the Sorbonne. As "impartial reporter," the author summarizes the disputes through the focus of a review of the censure action and a discussion with a "neutral" observor.
   B. Letters 4–10, the author as impartial interviewer of the Jesuits (the interlocutors are the interviewer and a Jesuit)
      4. On grace: sufficient, efficacious, actual
      5. The Jesuit doctrine of probability
      6. The Jesuit doctrine of confession and other accommodations in ethical matters
      7. The Jesuit doctrine of the direction of intention in private sins, especially murder
      8. Jesuit tenets of accommodation to sins affecting the public weal, such as usury, bankruptcy, and theft
      9. Jesuit tenets of accommodation to religious devotion and the distinction between venial and mortal sins
     10. Jesuit doctrines on the love of God
II. Letters 11–19, Pascal on the defensive

A.   Letters 11–16 the pseudonymous author as self-defender of pre-
     vious letters addressing the Jesuits (the company as such)
     11. On the validity of mockery in theological disputation
     12. On charity and simony and other materialistic concerns
     14. On homicide.
     15. On calumny in general and specifically against the author
     16. On calumny against the Jesuits' adversaries at Port Royal
B.   Letters 17–19, the pseudonymous author in self-defense in re-
     ply to a single Jesuit critic, Father Annat
     17. On heresy and papal infallibility
     18. On grace and human freedom
     19. On the piety and forgiving spirit of the community at
     Port Royal

Axiologically, Pascal proceeds from a position that is clearly sympathetic to the theological positions of the Jansenists. This is not to dis-
count his repeated disclaimers throughout the *Provincial Letters* that he
is "not of Port Royal." Rather, he proceeds from an independent
theological position, one arrived at well before his ironic assertion in
the letters (in obvious mockery of theological disputation as such) that
he has become a theologian in the short course of time since the
disputes at the Sorbonne began. Thus, it is not he who agrees with the
Jansenist positions; it is those positions that agree with his. If there is
any point at which he is not in accord with those positions, it is in the
final accommodations he seeks with Father Annat in the last two completed letters on the operations of divine grace with respect to human
free will.

Pascal does not so much elucidate a coherent theological position as
attack an incoherent one. He does so chiefly through the focus of
language. I do not mean the use of language as a weapon to destroy his
adversaries through mockery. The brilliance and pertinency of Pascal's
language in this celebrated work have been sufficiently noted. Nonetheless, it is important to stress an aspect of language in these famous
letters that has been obscured by the attention to Pascal's language.
The emphasis on Pascal's stylistic brilliance is ironic, for it has sought
to gainsay the value of the work in an esthetic appreciation, which,
presumably, transcends the provincial and historically moribund, if
not actually dead, theological issues that gave rise to this literary excellence. As he himself deconstructs the first ten letters in discussing the
relevance of mockery to theological dispute in the eleventh letter, he

indicates an awareness of this danger of estheticizing the subject or substance of his own writing. Literary history has ignored this caution by the writer himself, for, although undoubtedly aware from the outset of the power of his own language, it was not his own that pre-occupied him from the outset but the language of his adversaries and the question of language itself. "But, now now [he says, having heard out his Dominican interlocutor near the end of the first letter] . . . that is to play with words to say that you are in agreement [with the adepts of Father Le Moyne] because of the common terms that you use, when you are contrary to them in meaning." It is not only the certainty of his theological position that enables the impartial reporter to react with such promptness to this game of words on the part of his interlocutor; it is his confidence in the validity of an unconditional ref-erential concept of language. For the Pascal of these famous letters, one is not morally obliged to say what one means; language being what it is, one can say only what one means. That one does not—in fact, most people do not—achieve this accord of word and thing, of signifier and signified, is a lesson that will not impinge upon the author of the *Provincial Letters* until he is well along in this duel with the gamesters of the word.

At the outset of the duel he assumes that his concept of language is that of the wide world for which he writes. That world, he is con-vinced, will readily see the fatuity, futility, and falsity of the Domini-can distinction between the power to observe the commandments, a veritable power pure and simple, as the Jansenists maintain, and a proximate power, as the Dominican theologians argue. To expose the purely rhetorical nature of the Dominican position, however, Pascal does not pit Jansenist against Dominican. In this first letter, his Jan-senist interlocutor serves chiefly to sound the note that will become more insistent as the *Provincial Letters* proceed: that the adversaries of Port Royal, both Dominican and Jesuit in this instance, are not so much in disagreement on the issues in dispute as they are in agreement to create a majority opinion that will condemn the Jansenists in the eyes of the public on the exclusive and superficial level of words. Pascal thus opposes Dominican to Jesuit, bringing out through his inquiries of the smug disciple of Father Le Moyne and then (and primarily) of the timid Dominicans that both Jesuit and Dominican use the same term, "proximate," but that they understand different things by it. The neutral reporter's own referential conception of language emerges most clearly when, in pursuing Father Le Moyne's notion of power, he asks of his Dominican experts:

> Is it [proximate power] . . . not that which lacks nothing to enable action? No, they told me. But, how now, Father, if something is missing in this power, would you call it "proximate," and would you say, for example, that a man at night, without any light, has the *proximate power to see*? Oh indeed, he would have it, according to us, if he is not blind. I grant it willingly, I said to them; but Father Le Moyne understands it in a contrary manner. It is true, they said to me; but we understand it thus. I grant that, I said to them. For I never argue about the name, provided that I have been advised of the meaning that one gives to it; but I thereby see that, when you say that the just always have the *proximate power* to pray to God, you understand that they are in need of further help in order to pray, without which they will never pray.

Pascal's use of a naturalistic simile, the man at night without any light, is revealing not only of the conception of verbal language that is at issue but of his general theory of meaning. He (or his Jansenist interlocutor in the early letters) frequently uses such naturalistic similes (dealing with vision, with eating, with sickness) to emphasize the basic point not only that signifier and signified must be in a one-to-one correlation but, more important, that the signified exists, ontologically, apart from and prior to the signifier. To proceed otherwise is not only confusing, it is to give rise to the most immoral religious, social, and political consequences. Nevertheless, the subject of the first letter, the topic of proximate versus veritable power, is somewhat esoteric. The concept of the proximate is rather specialized and it is in the quasi-hermetic realm of expert theologians that Pascal maintains his inquiry. It has taken Pascal's enormous polemical skill, dialectical verve, and verbal irony to give that somewhat specialized topic the public import of the first *Provincial Letter*. The letter ends with a witty play on words in which Pascal makes, seemingly in passing, a point that will become more and more central—that the common or ordinary meaning of words (here the word *prochain*, which I have translated as "proximate," but which might well be translated "neighboring," in its scriptural overtones) is to be preferred to alambications of them by theologians or scholars: "I leave you then at liberty to stand by the word *neighboring* or not, for I love my neighbor too much to persecute him under this pretext."

The subject of the second *Provincial Letter*, the distinction between sufficient and efficacious grace, lends itself more readily to his overall strategy of demonstrating that the positions of the adversaries of Port Royal are no more than verbal. He uses basically the same narrative procedure of going first to his neutral friend and fellow observor of the disputes, Monsieur N. (who is to be distinguished from the other Monsieur N., who is a brother-in-law to the Jansenist interlocutor of the first letter), then to one of both of the opposing parties among the adversaries of the Jansenists (again, Dominicans and Jesuits). This time, he however, varies his visit to the Dominicans by bringing along a Jansenist friend (as he says, "I have friends in all parties"). The variation of procedure permits a two-pronged attack exposing the vacuity of the Dominican position: the reporter speaks as the "confused," inexpert reactor to the purely verbal manipulations of the Dominicans; the Jansenist interlocutor speaks as the expert reactor scandalized by those manipulations.

Let us trace two of these key reactions:

> *The Reporter*: . . . In sum, Father, this grace given to all men is "sufficient?" Yes, said he. And nevertheless it has no effect "without efficacious grace?" That is true, he said. And all men have "sufficient" grace, I continued, and all do not have "efficacious?" It is true, said he. That is, I said to him, that all have enough grace, and that all do not have enough; that is, this grace suffices, although it does not suffice; that is, it is sufficient in name and insufficient in effect. In all good faith, Father, this doctrine is really subtle. Have you forgotten in giving up the world what the word "sufficient" means there? Don't you remember that it contains all that is necessary in order to act? But you have not lost your memory of it: for, to use a comparison that will be more meaningful [*sensible*] to you, if one served you at dinner only two ounces of bread and a glass of water, would you be happy with your prior, who would tell you that that would be sufficient to nourish you, on the grounds that with something else, that he would not give you, you would have all that was necessary to you to eat well? How then can you let yourself say that all men have "sufficient grace" to act, since you admit that there is another that is absolutely necessary to enable action that all do not have?
>
> *The Jansenist*: . . . Tell me, Father, in what way you are in conformity with the Jesuits. It is, said he, that the Jesuits and we acknowledge that "sufficient graces" are given to all. But, said he, there are two things in this word "sufficient" grace: there is the sound, which is

but wind, and the thing it signifies, which is real and effective. And thus, when you are in accord with the Jesuits on the word "sufficient," and contrary in the meaning, it is apparent [*visible*] that you are contrary in the substance of this term, and that you are in accord only in the sound. Is that to act sincerely and cordially?

Language, for the Pascal of the *Provincial Letters,* is not a purely internal phenomenon, unrelated to the objects and actions that it designates. As the reporter indicates in his confusion, it is grounded ontologically in the correspondence between the world as given and man as user of that given. As the Jansenist indicates in his indignation, it is grounded morally in the need for sincerity and cordiality if the ontological compact is to have any bearing on men in interaction with one another. The "separate" positions of the inexpert reporter and the expert theologians are continuous.

Strategically, what Pascal does in this letter is to allow his Jansenist colleague to draw out even further than the reporter the general implications of Dominican equivocation on what might be called the "linguistic contract," which, to repeat some of the terms of the purely theological quarrel here, applies to all men at all times. Language, if not grace, is always sufficient in its denotative function; its efficacity depends on this designative and essentially denotative function. The Jansenist does speak from a particular point of view, but that point of view is not that of the Jansenist as distinguished from Jesuit or Dominican or secular (presumably the point of view of the author of the *Provincial Letters*). Rather, that point of view is that of the respecter of the referential character of language as he applies language and the notion of language to ethical and doctrinal situations. Speaking on matters of faith as he does here, the Jansenist friend is thus speaking as one of and for the majority; strategically, he is assimilated into the general theological position that Pascal considers the only sound one in these disputes. This is basically the strategy with which Pascal had concluded the first letter, but there it was the reporter who stated the sound general theology, in a series of flat propositions declaratively lined up in their résumé of what were really the Jansenist positions on the dispute about man's power to observe the commandments. It is now the Jansenist who has the last word, at least theologically:

Believe me, Father, your order has received an honor that it has respected poorly. It abandons this grace that has been confided to it and that has never been abandoned since the beginning of the world. This victorious grace awaited by the patriarchs, predicted by the prophets, brought by Jesus Christ, preached by Saint Paul, explained by Saint Augustine, the greatest of the fathers, maintained by those who followed him, confirmed by Saint Bernard, the last of the fathers, sustained by Saint Thomas, the angel of the school, transmitted from him to your order, supported by so many of your fathers, and so gloriously defended by your religious under the popes Clement and Paul: this efficacious grace, which had been put as in deposit in your hands so as to have, in a holy order enduring forever, preachers who would publish it for the world until the end of time, finds itself as if cast aside for such unworthy interests. It is time that other hands arm themselves for the cause. It is time that God raise up intrepid disciples of the doctor of grace who, ignoring committments of the time, serve God for God's grace. Grace can no longer have the Dominicans for its defenders, for it forms them itself through its all-powerful force. It demands hearts pure and detached, and itself it purifies them and detaches them from the interests of the world, incompatible with the truths of the Scriptures. Heed these threats, Father, and beware lest God remove this candle from its place and leave you in the darkness and without a crown.

This prophetic tone is one to which the author of the *Provincial Letters* will himself come when he is obliged to shift to a defensive strategy in later letters. Nevertheless, in spite of the difference in tone here between the Jansenist and the reporter (who cuts him off out of concern for the intimidated Dominican), the stamp of Pascal's own thought is not absent from this fiery discourse. In particular, the emphasis on the *traditional* defenders of the faith (and of their possible successors in the present time) as opposed to the current supposed defenders is a key aspect of his theological thought. That the Dominicans are identified in the present controversy as the *new* Thomists" is, in the eyes of Pascal, hardly a recommendation. Pascal has a compulsive suspicion of the new and the modern in theological matters. His is the faith of the fathers. As we have seen, it is the faith about which he learned from his own father, Etienne Pascal, that he defends here (he had, of course, received faith itself from the Heavenly Father). And it is on the father's linguistic grounds, pushed to an even greater purity and rigidity, that he defends that faith here. Where Etienne had allowed for a metaphorical or connotational use of language only in matters of describing or explaining man's relation to God, the son applies in this theological dispute those principles of denotational exactitude that the father had insisted must be applied in scientific discourse. Yet, both father and son agree on the primary validity of the fathers of the Church, especially the early ones and still more especially of St. Augustine, in settling matters of meaning and intention in ethical and doctrinal interpretation. Thus, for all the wit of the son's conclusion to this second letter, one senses in it some of the spirit of a geometric demonstration, a kind of Q.E.D. indicating that the "demonstration" has been fully and convincingly made: "Thus you see by this that we have to do here with a political 'sufficiency' similar to the 'proximate power'. However, I shall tell you that it seems to me that one can without peril doubt 'proximate power' and this 'sufficient grace', so long as one is not a Jacobin." For all his courtesy and sympathy toward the beleagured Dominicans, the neutral reporter is less axiomatic about the precision and sincerity with which language must be used than his Jansenist friend.

This axiomatic, conclusive tone is, of course, in part strategic, as if the author were telling the public that the disputation really should be put to rest in the face of such demonstrations as he has provided in the two letters he has written. The tone is reminiscent of the peremptory tone with which Pascal dismissed his disputants in scientific matters. Just as in those disputes he believed that his "reports" of his investigations were unerring in their propositions and conclusions, so in these matters his "investigations" should, for any and all, conclude the discussion of the matter. Why then did he go on with the letters? In part, of course, he did so because he was too intelligent and too aware of the stakes in this exchange and of the power and resilience of his adversaries. However, more circumstantially, as he indicates in this very letter, in the form of a postscript added to the letter just as he was sealing the envelope ("in closing my letter"), he has learned that the censure of Arnauld has been made, but that, since he does not yet know in what form, he will not speak of it until the next mail pickup. The letters will continue.

The series will be interrupted, however, by the publication of a *Reply of the Provincial Friend to the First Two Letters of His Friend*. In his edition of the letters, H. F. Stewart sees little doubt that the reply is also written by Pascal, a possibility that raises interesting considerations concerning Pascal's psychological stance during this period, particularly with respect to the egocentrism shown at its height whenever he has been engaged in dispute. However, before turning to that question, it is important to stress that this brief letter confirms the tactical and strategic postulates of the first two letters. It begins: "Your two letters have not been for me alone. Everybody sees them, everybody understands [*entend*] them; everybody believes them. They are esteemed not only by theologians: they are withal pleasing to men of the world, and intelligible even to women." The "easy" thrust at women might put off certain modern readers, but the mid-seventeenth century is not the mid-twentieth and it would be to miss an essential point to fail to see this thrust as part of the overall strategy of appealing to the public rather than to the specialists: *everybody* includes even those who, in the nature of the society of the time, could not be expected to concern themselves with such matters. The effect of the formulation here is to obliterate the distinction between this and that "condition," this and that "expertise"—indeed, between expertise and inexpertise. For, the letters have appealed both to those experts who are theologians and those nonexperts who, in the instance, make up the rest of the world. Moreover, the key terms of this brief paragraph—*see* (*voit*), *understand* (*entend,* which in French comports both hearing and understanding), *pleasing* (*agréables*), *intelligible* (*intelligible*)—return us to Pascal's referential, mimetic, and naturalistic conception of language. One and all naturally *see* the sense (to say "good sense" would be redundant in the Pascalian linguistics of the letters). In the formulation, the word "see" has the same bivalence as the word "understand": it means at once to "read" and to "understand."

The awareness of the linguistic strategy and a further advancement of it inform as well the report of the two concrete instances of the good (and intended) effect of the *Provincial Letters* in the world at large. The provincial reports, first, the remarks of one of the most illustrious of the members of the French Academy in response to the first letter and, second, the remarks of a woman who writes in reply to a lady who had passed on to her a copy of that same letter. The member of the Academy wishes that the Sorbonne recognized the jurisdiction of the Academy in this dispute, for, in his quality as member, "I would condemn with all authority, I would ban, I would proscribe, I am on the verge of saying I would exterminate with all my power this 'proximate power', which creates so much noise for nothing, and without knowing what it would have." The academician regrets that the Academy has only a distant and limited power in the matter. In the context of the time, the remarks are extremely relevant to what I call Pascalian linguistics. One of the principal activities of the Academy at the time was the establishment of a dictionary of the French language, which would not be merely comprehensive but prescriptive, fixing meanings and recommending correct usage. It is as if the academician were congratulating the author of the first letter (the only one he has had a chance to see) for making a contribution to the Academy dictionary. The remarks of the female reader of the first letter also confirm the validity of Pascal's strategy of appealing to the general public on the grounds of linguistic clarity and coherence; that letter, she writes, "is altogether ingenious and extremely well written. It narrates without narrating; it clears up the most complicated things in the world; it rails with finesse; it instructs even those who do not know these things very well; it redoubles the pleasure of those who understand them. It is moreover an excellent defense [*apologie*], and, if one wishes, a delicate and innocent censure." Although the lady's reaction is less linguistically explicit than the academician's, its key terms underscore no less the linguistic philosophy based on language as necessarily referential to something outside of language underlying Pascal's strategy in the *Provincial Letters: clears up, instructs, pleasure, understand.* That a woman of high society should so respond to the letters (indeed, to the first, however esoteric) is perhaps an even greater confirmation of the wisdom of Pascal's strategy than the response of the academician.

The response of the female reader casts certain shadows across that strategy, for counterbalancing the demonstrative and ethical effect of the letter upon her is an esthetic effect that would increasingly complicate Pascal's strategy. The letter narrates without narrating, it rails with finesse, and, if it is an excellent apology, it is also a delicate and innocent censure. Pleasure bids to outweigh instruction in the impact of the letters. However much Pascal might appreciate the compliment on the delicacy of his censure of the adversaries of the Jansenists, one senses that he might regret its characterization as "innocent." It is with a will to do harm to those who do greater harm that he writes these letters. He might appreciate the observation that he narrates without narrating, for that would indicate that he is telling his story more like a good reporter than a portentous theologian. Yet, the lady's pleasure in the storytelling seems to outweigh for her the instructive value of the story itself. Her pleasure predicts the literary destiny not only of the first but of all the *Provincial Letters*.

At this early stage the author of the *Provincial Letters* is convinced of the ethical impact of his appeal to the general public along the lines of a linguistic philosophy that is at once instructive and pleasing. In this respect, the *Reply of the Provincial Friend* constitutes a further instance of that philosophy and it may well have been written by Pascal himself, as Stewart believes.[2] The narrative strategy is similar to that of the first two letters: the author of the letter interviews others, so to speak, and reports their remarks at some length but more briefly than in the other letters, and then the author concludes in summary fashion on the validity of the tactic in general. He urges the author to continue his letters in spite of the forthcoming censure of Arnauld, for "*we* are very predisposed to receive it," the implication being that the *Provincial Letters* put that censure in its proper place. And much of the Q.E.D. tone spirit of the conclusions to the first two letters informs the final sentences: "These words 'proximate power' and 'sufficient grace' with which we are threatened will frighten us no longer. We have learned all too well from the Jesuits, the Jacobins, and from M. Le Moyne the numerous ways in which they twist them and just what is the solidity of these new words for us to give ourselves any grief." The call in the first two letters to a use of language that is solid, sincere, and tested by time is re-sounded with confidence and hope.

If re-sounded by Pascal himself as author of the *Reply*, one might wonder at the danger of self-gratulation in such a tack as well as at the degree of sincerity possible by their publication under a pseudonym, Louis de Montalte. Both issues are not easily disposed of. Undoubtedly, a certain amount of pride informs the *Reply*. The pride is to some extent modified by the clearly strategic intent of driving home the point that the issues at stake not only have been but must continue to be brought out of the cloisters of academic dispute at the Sorbonne. Not only the careers and fortunes of respectable prominent citizens (the Arnauld family and others) are at stake but the integrity of the commonwealth and the fate of each and every individual before God as well. Similarly, the seeming insincerity of resorting to a pseudonym is understandable in view of the juridical power of the Sorbonne in a state where cross and crown interact so directly on the lives of individual citizens. The *Provincial Letters* were written and published very much in the spirit of a pursued minority that challenged not only the authority of the "school" but the state itself. In fear of police detection, Pascal had to change addresses; the successive letters were spirited to the publisher; and a witch-hunting atmosphere pervaded the social and political scene as the Jesuits mounted their engine of the "big-lie" in their pursuit of Arnauld and, eventually, the unknown author of the *Provincial Letters* themselves. Within these understandable explanations of the pseudonymity, one can detect in the very name Pascal invents for himself signs of the pride that has informed his prose in earlier disputes: pride in the very source from which, according to Jovy, he had borrowed the name: an Italian author, Luigi Montalto author, in Latin, of *Revision of the Sentence of Pontius Pilate against Jesus Christ.*[3] Like the original Louis de Montalte, his namesake rises up in prosecutorial pride to correct an injustice done in the court of men to those Christians now being abandoned by the courts of justice in being handed over to their executioners. Underscoring this erudite source of Pascal's prideful pseudonym there might also be other prideful identifications; "Louis de Montalte" might be read as an identification with or an appeal through the homonymy to the king of France who ruled under that name, Louis XIV, with the partitive portion indicating that the king in question spoke from on high, from atop the mountain. Again, the pseudonym might be *heard* if not *read* as *lui de montalte,* a closer reference to that "him who speaks from on high," the Pascal who had supervised (if not actually carried out) the experiments on the vacuum atop the mountain, the Puy de Dôme, in Auvergne (the site as well of Mons, a fief of his mother's family). In this interpretation, the *lui* might also suggest a prideful presumption on the part of Pascal that he speaks for him who is atop the highest mountain, God himself. We have seen instances of this conflation of self and Godhead in earlier writings by Pascal.

The third letter makes up the last of the preliminary encounters with the theologically vapid Dominicans, of whom the author of the *Provincial Letters* easily disposes, before challenging the seemingly more serious adversaries of the Jansenists, the Jesuits, in letters 4–18. Although ultimately in this letter he will consult and report the reactions of another party, this time a neutral commentator on the censure of Arnauld, the author now writes at greater extent (slightly more than half of the eight pages in the Stewart edition) in his own name and with an increasing loss of the nonpartisan spirit that informed his reactions in the investigative stance he had adopted in the first two letters.

The subject of the letter is the censure of Arnauld and in the extended first portion of the letter, in which the author writes of his own reactions to the censure, he now constitutes himself more the reader than the listener of both the censure and of the writings of Arnauld. From the former he expected of Arnauld, as of all the Jansenists as described by their theological enemies, the most perfidious, the most contradictory, the most corrupted and heretical person imaginable. Instead, he discovers a writer whose consonance with the most sacrosanct documents of the Church, the writings of the early fathers, especially of Saints Augustine and Chrysostomos, could not be closer. The brunt of the censure had been that Arnauld had contended that a just person in the person of Saint Peter himself had lacked grace and that he had done so because God had removed that grace from him (in the instance of Peter's denial of Christ). Pascal lines up a series of texts from the early fathers positing the same view of Peter's religious state. He thus shows that not only, as his Jansenist friend had put it in the second *Provincial Letter,* are "words . . . inseparable from things," but words are inseparable from words when the words in question are those of the ancient fathers. "If," he addresses the authors of the censure, "it is against the words [*paroles*] of the fathers of the Church that one thus acts, what becomes of faith and tradition? If it be against the proposition of M. Arnauld? Show us how it is different, since it appears to us to be in nothing but perfect conformity." The tone is plaintive and borders on a defeatism and frustration on the verge of erupting into anger and rebellion (as if to say "That's the way they carry on; they are people who are too penetratingly finicky"). Confused in his own inexpertise and simplicity, the beleagured believer in Arnauld's orthodoxy goes to see an observer whom he knows to be neutral in the quarrel.

The latter reassures the author, laughing at him for believing that there is really a substantive difference between Arnauld and his censors. The quarrel is at heart a political one provoked by the Jansenists' doctrinally sound challenge to the Jesuits' abuse of both Scripture and doctrine for the purposes of winning over to their theological direction the credulous people. The author at last understands and so reassure his correspondent that Arnauld's is a "heresy of a new kind. It is not the sentiments of M. Arnauld that are heretical; it is only his person. It is a personal heresy. He is not heretical in what he says and writes but only in that he is M. Arnauld. That is all one finds to say and resay about him. Whatever he do, unless he cease to exist, he will never be a good Catholic. The grace of Saint Augustine will never be the true one so long as he will defend it. It would become so if he brought himself to combat it." So the reassured author concludes his letter with an enjoinder to his friend to have no more to do with the disputes of the theologians, for they are "disputes of theologians and not of theology."

The reassurance is curious. In the course of offering it, the author's neutral friend cautions him that, in his confusion and indignation, "if you knew the spirit of the people better, you would speak in a different fashion." Here again, much more explicitly, is the warning contained in the reaction of the female reader to the first letter (in the *Reply*): the author's confidence in common sense, in the public's capacity to understand the necessity of the consonance between word and meaning is ill-founded. It is Pascal himself who incorporates this caution in the letter, even as he had incorporated the awareness that the Dominicans were acting out of fear of Jesuit power and out of materialistic self-interest in their use of words like "proximate power." Yet even in reporting these reservations on his strategy with its anchor in a referential conception of language, it is as if Pascal, in logical extension of that conception, were saying: I have only to call attention to these reservations, these cowardly and credulous behaviors, for my readers [presumably everybody] to cease and desist in those behaviors. The prover of the existence of the vacuum in nature writes here as if his proof of the mind's abhorrence of a vacuum in language should destroy that vacuum and put an end to all controversy.

Provincial Letters 4–10

I shall not comment in the same detail on each letter of the series that constitutes Pascal's offensive against the Jesuits themselves. As he writes in the first sentence of the fourth letter, "there is nothing like the Jesuits." It might also be said that there is nothing like Pascal writing about the Jesuits in this particular series of the *Provincial Letters*. My schematic summary of their subjects should not mislead the reader unfamiliar with them or knowing them only in excerpt to regard them as an essayistic and doctrinaire break with the first three letters. These letters are at once more dense (proportionately, in the Stewart edition, for example, they occupy three times as many pages as the first three letters including the *Reply* to the first two); richer in texture (much of it citation of texts, primarily from the Jesuits, with the placement of citation at once skillful in its argumentative relevance and brilliant in its wit); shrewder in characterization of the personalities involved (not only the interloctors, Pascal and his Jesuit friend, but also others invoked in the course of the exchanges between the two); more forceful in their rhetorical development of the central topic of each letter and the concomitant issues raised thereby; and even more amusing.

Rhetorically, it is as if, over the course of these seven theological duels where Pascal is on the offensive, he paces himself very deliberately, feeling out his opponent at the beginning of the encounter before attacking him with a series of heavy blows at the end, with the degree of pressure mounting in each encounter. (Until the tenth letter there is no real desire to finish off the adversary, since that would leave certain of the weaknesses or, theologically speaking, abominations of the adversary unexposed.) Thus, Pascal proceeds from the "least abominable" of Jesuit derelictions to the most abominable: from Jesuit manipulations of the somewhat specialized concept of grace, through the horrors of their doctrines of probabilism and intentionalism, which will lead to the absolution and indeed authorization of murder by anyone, including priests, on to the Jesuit abdication of the need to love God. I should like to trace this progression, both in the overarching development of the series and within individual letters by examining three in particular: 5, 7, and 10.

The Jesuits as Pascal presents them in the *Provincial Letters* are among the earliest proponents of situation ethics and the earliest semioticians, as can be seen in their interpretation of the respected concept of probabilism in arriving at ethical decisions in the most latitudinarian terms. Historically, the concept has to do with the opinion or judgment that a confessor is to give on an ethical situation (or, more specifically, a particular action) to determine its moral character with respect to the law of the faith. The issue arises in those instances where the confessor is in some doubt about the specificity and pertinency of the law or when there is doubt about the very existence of a law affecting a particular situation. In either case (should a law be discovered in the second) there may be some difference of opinion respecting relevancy, with some opinions going one way, some the other, and still other opinions another way. The confessor must thus take a chance. Should he not take a chance and stick to the letter of the law or, in view of the dubiety at issue, stick as close to it as he can conceive the law's applicability, he is what theologians call a "tutiorist," or, so to speak, a "least probabilist." Should he lean toward an opinion that is less clearly responsive to the law but that has more probability than another opinion of conforming to the law, he is a "probabiliorist" or, again so to speak, a "less probabilist." Should he lean toward an opinion that has less probability than another of conforming to the law, he is a probabilist pure and simple.

For the Pascal of the fifth letter the Jesuits are much too purely and simply probabilists. It is not that he is himself a tutiorist. As one of the earliest inventors of probability theory in mathematics, and (perhaps more pertinently here) as a champion of the Scriptures and the texts of the early fathers over any subsequent texts, especially "modern" ones, he is too aware of the variety of human situations that cannot be subsumed under any text. However, in keeping with the referential conception of language informing all of the disputes he reviews in the *Provincial Letters,* his tendency is that of a probabiliorist or, as I put it, a least probabilist. As he says in a formulation famous from the fifth *Provincial Letter,* "I am not happy with the probable; I seek the sure." His use of the verb *seek* indicates his awareness that one cannot know the sure in matters of the kind under discussion. Nevertheless, this does not mean that one is without some guidelines, some framework. For him the Scriptures and the church fathers provide such a framework or, in current critical terms, a "seme" of ethical injunctions of which particular opinions must, as clearly as possible, be the "lexemes." In this, he resembles his Jansenist friend of the first two letters, who had asked of the Dominican whether his elucubrations on grace and human capacity in matters of faith and morals were consistent with faith and tradition (a resemblance seen more directly in the third letter as the reporter demonstrated the consonance of Arnauld's "words" with the "words" of the early fathers).

It is not the Scriptures or the early fathers whom the Jesuit cites here in his elucidation of the company's concept of "probable opinions." It is the members of a religious order little more than one hundred years old at the time. Its very modernity is sufficient to appall Pascal, with his respect for the origins of the Church in Christ and the early fathers more than a millenium earlier. As Pascal skillfully has his Jansenist friend bring out in the first part of the letter, the very newness of the

Jesuit order underlies their doctrine of favoring the probable opinion that most accommodates the worldly situation of the confessant who comes to a Jesuit for moral guidance. The design of the Jesuits is not to reform mores, but to gain ecclesiastical power over all of the faithful. Thus, not only does their doctrine of probabilism incorporate the most latitudinarian of opinions but also the most strict, with the former accommodating the most licentious of sinners and the latter responding to those seeking to live within "Christian severity."

The laxity of this morality, the crassness of the political character of the Jesuits, appalls the Jansenist and friend.

> That is how they have spread over the whole earth, thanks to the doctrine of probable opinions, which is the source and base of all this disorder. It is something you must learn from them themselves. For they hide it from no one, no more than what you have just heard, with this difference that they cover their human political prudence with the pretext of a divine and Christian prudence, as if faith and the tradition, which maintain it, were not always and everywhere one and invariable throughout time and in every place, as if it were the rule to bend oneself in order to accommodate the subject, which ought to be in conformity with the rule, and as if souls, in order to purify themselves of their stains, had only to corrupt the law of the Lord; whereas, instead, the *law of the Lord, which is without stain and all holy, is that which must convert souls,* and conform them to its salutary instructions.

However appalled he may be by the Jesuits, the Jansenist friend is also "deeply saddened by all these disorders." For his part, the author says (ironically, of course, and as a way of preserving his stance of neutrality), he is impressed with the "excellence of the politics" of the "good fathers." As in every instance of Pascal's use of the term "fathers" to designate the Jesuits, his text is replete with an ironic contrast between these new or good fathers and the early and *true* fathers of the Church, Augustine, Chrysostomos, and the rest.

In his "curiosity" and "esteem" of the good fathers, then, he takes his Jansenist friend's advice and seeks out "a good casuist" of the Society of Jesus. (That the society is "of Jesus" is an irony on which Pascal need not lean.) It is of more than passing interest that in letters 5, 7, and 10 unlike the first three letters, he does not have a Jansenist friend confront the most adamant adversaries of the Jansenists, the Jesuits themselves, as he had that friend confront the lackeys of the Jesuits, the Dominicans, who were adversaries as if in spite of themselves.

Such a direct confrontation is out of order, for esthetically speaking, in terms of Pascal's strategy the likelihood of such a confrontation at the time would be small. Again, the ethical aspect of the strategy would be vitiated by such a confrontation. It is crucial that a neutral observor mediate the confrontation, doing so not as intermediary or arbiter seeking compromise but as a man of the world concerned only with the truth and fact of a private dispute whose consequences have spilled over into the public realm.

Although the "good casuist" is a comic figure of the highest order, it would be to misunderstand Pascal's purpose to laugh at the Jesuit without listening to what he says. Claiming to have problems with respecting the ethical injunction to observe fasting, the reporter leads his Jesuit interlocutor into a spate of accommodating citations from a host of Jesuit authors. The effect is to relieve the practicing Christian from the necessity of fasting under any and all circumstances: here, a text dispensing one who cannot sleep unless he has eaten; there, a text dispensing the case (his own, as the reporter says) of someone who can go without breakfast but not without an evening meal, for, as the quotation from the text of the *Moral Theology* 24 of the Jesuit fathers puts it, "no one is obliged to change the order of his meals"; on through the *Treatise on Penance* of the "celebrated casuist Bazile Ponce, . . . cited by Father Bauny," which announces that one can even in good conscience seek an occasion directly and for its own sake to avoid an observance to fast (or any other observance!) "when the spiritual good of ourselves or of a neighbor so bids us." The confessor is obliged to grant absolution in this instance even as he is to those who remain in an occasion of sin.

From the *specific* and simple injunction to fast under certain situations Pascal has moved his good casuist to a general proposition of justifying not only the remission of all sin but the very encouragement to commit sin. "Really," says the reporter after this demonstration, "it seems to me that I am dreaming when I hear a religious speak in this fashion." But the casuist defends himself by saying that he speaks not from his own conscience, but from that of the Jesuits, Fathers Ponce and Bauny, whom one can follow "in safety, for they are skilled people." When the reporter replies that he thought it his duty "to take as a rule only Holy Scripture and the tradition of the Church," the casuist explodes: "O Good God! . . . you remind me of those Jansenists!" Here again, in the very sequence of these two remarks, is an instance of Pascal's strategy of separating the Jesuits not so much from the Jansenists as from the general belief of Christianity, of allying the Jansenists with Pascal rather than Pascal with the Jansenists.

Pascal, Jansenist, early fathers, and Scriptures line up against the casuist interlocutor and the Jesuit confrères whom he cites (296 of these drawn up by the casuist Diana as the good father reports, "of whom the oldest dates from eighty years ago").

Pascal himself draws the lines in a telling passage:

> That is, Father, upon your arrival on the scene there disappeared Saint Augustine, Saint Chrysostomos, Saint Ambrose, Saint Jerome, and the others in this matter of ethics. But at least let me know the names of those who have succeeded them. Who are they, these new authors? "They are people who are very skilled and well known," he said to me. "It is Villalobos, Conink, Lamas, Achokier, Dealkozer, Dellacruz, Veracruz, Ugolin, Tambourin, Fernandez, Martinez, Suarez, Henriquez, Vasquez, Lopez, Gomez, Sanchez, de Vechis, de Grassis, de Grassalis, de Pitigianis, de Graphaeis, Squilanti, Bizozeri, Barcola, de Bobadilla, Simancha, Perez de Lara, Aldretta, Lorca, de Scarcia, Quaranta, Scophra, Pedrezza, Cabrezza, Bisbe, Dias, de Clavasio, Villagut, Adam Mandem, Iribarne, Binsfeld, Volfangi à Vorberg, Vosthery, Strevesdorf." "O Father," I said to him all affright, "all those people there, are they Christians?" "What do you mean, Christians?" he replied. "Did I not tell you that they are the only ones through whom we govern Christianity today?"

The chauvinistic mockery of the reporter's reaction to this long list of foreign names has long been noted. Only "Tambourin" might have appealed to Pascal's gallic ear (and ironically at that, for a *tambourin* was a long narrow drum of Provence). Yet, the main point of his thrust is not whether all these people are French, but whether they are Christians. In the very cacophony of the sound of their names, it is as if they were people without names and thus, in view of Pascal's referential conception of language, not really people, "only wind" as his Jansenist friend had said of some of the words used by the Dominicans in an earlier letter. They may be the governors of the world for his Jesuit interlocutor, but for Pascal they are not Christians. The wind of their names is like the wind of their newness; they are people without the substance and solidity of those names that are truly Christian, the names of those early, ancient, and first governors of ethics whom they have succeeded: Augustine, Chrysostomos, Ambrose, Jerome, and

Christ himself as he is known through the Holy Scriptures, as the reporter brings out in calling attention to the Scriptures as well as the popes and the councils of the Church as obstacles to the Jesuits' plan to govern the faithful. Of course, the casuist pompously reassures him, he suspected that the reporter believed the Society of Jesus to be at odds with the Scriptures, so he promises to reassure him that such is not the case in a subsequent encounter, and thus we have the grounds of the subsequent letter.

Prior to that letter there occurred at Port Royal an event probably affecting the subsequent letters (although it will not be directly evoked until the sixteenth letter), the "Miracle of the Holy Thorne." The beneficiary of the miracle was Pascal's niece, Margot Périer, the daughter of his sister Gilberte. The child, living at Port Royal, had been afflicted with a lachrymal ulcer, which was cured on the twenty-fourth of March by the application of a relic of the crown of Christ recently presented to the convent's Paris house. The miracle, accepted as such by adversaries as well as partisans of Port Royal led to some relief for the Jansenists. More important for our purposes is the possible effect of the miracle on Pascal in his continuing dialogue with the Jesuits in the *Provincial Letters*. Some commentators have seen a close relation between the miracle and Pascal's cause of defending the Port Royalists. Stewart, for example, believes that "the effect on Pascal's mind was enormous . . . if confirmation were needed of the justice of the cause in which he was engaged, here it was ample."[4] Perhaps so, if one is to read "confirmation" in a strictly religious way, as in the sacrament. However, one should beware of reading in the term the notion of *convincing*.. In Pascal's theology, miracles do not convince and they are far from converting. As Pascal will maintain in his projected *Apology for the Christian Religion,* miracles may even *confound* belief. At most then the miracle of the thorn would confound the adversaries of the Jansenists, who did not, it should be noted, accept the cure as miraculous. Their very refusal to accept it would thus be, if anything for Pascal, an encouraging sign of the justice less of his defense of the Jansenists than of his attacks upon the Jesuits, who, with some exceptions, appeared to him to be without the faith that miracles only serve to confirm in those who have received it from God. In the granting of the grace to believe lies the real miracle for Pascal, one requiring no material sign as provocation to reception of grace by fallen man.

For those who do not share Pascal's Augustinian and Saint Cyranian view of charity (the obligation to love God more than one's fellow man), the seventh letter is most likely to reveal par-excellence the horrors (the term is frequent in the *Provincial Letters*) to which Jesuit doctrines lead. The letter concludes its general discussion of the Jesuit doctrine of "directing the intention" (of the individual conscience) in application to a number of specific cases dealing with the killing of one human being by another. The examples progress from killing in self-defense to the ultimate justification by the Jesuit of priests killing another human being without the justification of self-defense or accidental homicide—in sum, with the Jesuit's justification of ecclesiastical murder.

"Vengeance is mine, sayeth the Lord"—but not his alone, according to the Jesuits. In fact, the Jesuit interlocutor here cites the scriptural injunction "not to render evil for evil and to leave vengeance to God" as the springboard for elucidating the society's "marvelous principle," its "grand method" of "directing the intention" of the sinner: one absolves oneself from the potential guilt of a particular sin or crime by directing one's conscience to another intention of motive. He tells the reporter, "Just as I indicated in a previous conversation that servants may in clear conscience deliver certain annoying messages by diverting their intention to do harm thereby to the profit they will thus enjoy, so one may apply the same method, showing forth all its glory, in the matter of homicide." For example, on the matter of killing someone as a point of honor, the killer has only to direct his intention "from the desire for vengeance, which is criminal, and to carry it over to the desire to defend one's honor, which is permitted according to our fathers. And thus they accomplish their duties toward God and toward men. For they satisfy the world in permitting the action, and they satisfy the Gospel in purifying the intention. There is what the ancients did not know; there is what one owes to our fathers. Do you understand it now?" In answer to this patronizing question, the author succinctly indicates that the arrant materialism of these propositions has not escaped him: "Quite well, I said to him. You give to man the gross substance of things, and to God the spiritual movement of the intention." The Jesuits give nothing to God but empty words, an interior monologue that is but a blowing of wind.

It is like the wind of the numerous quotations from the members of the Society of Jesus into which the reporter now leads his Jesuit interlocutor. The latter proceeds from a text justifying killing for the point of honor to another text justifying the desire for the death of someone from whom one is to inherit goods of this world, to still another text more generally defending killing in a duel (the proscription of dueling had been one of the key policies of the state since the time of Richelieu, a policy badly implemented and not likely to be encouraged by Jesuit ethics), to a further text justifying the secret killing of a false calumniator. On the latter "species," as the reporter brings out, hardly anyone is safe from murder, since life is full of defamation and unflattering gestures. Acknowledging this, the Jesuit admits that the society does counsel against applying the doctrine of directing the intention with respect to killing in the case of "simple defamation." With some relief, the reporter notes that this must be because the society recognizes that "the law of God forbids killing." But no, says the Jesuit: the fathers "do not look upon it that way, for they do find it permitted in conscience, looking only at the truth in itself." Here again is one of those telegraphic juxtapositions by which Pascal illustrates the abyss between Jesuit notions of language and his own. For him language is referential and thus upon hearing of a signifier (the caution not to apply the doctrine of directing the intention to murder), he immediately leaps to the assumption of an antecedent signified, (in this case, the law of God). For the Jesuit, however, language tends toward a pure internality: signifier (the caution he notes) and signified are conjoined in a single, a simultaneous cross-referentiality. As he puts it, we look at the truth in itself, and the truth in question here is the permission to kill in conscience someone who has been guilty of no more than simple bad-mouthing. Nor does his explanation for this caution modify his linguistic philosophy: that if one were to kill all the bad-mouthers, one would soon depopulate the entire state. There is the sense of another reality here, a signified to which the signifier of the caution does seem to refer. However, the reality signified is not object-bound, the referent of the signifier but a condition upon it of which the Jesuit would gladly be rid. It is not an antecedent referent but a concomitant referent, a limiting case that is disturbing logically to his concept of language only so long as one pushes that concept to the limit. Prior to that limit, as the spate of citations from the fathers in support of one another makes clear, for these Jesuits there are no antecedent realities upon which words depend for their meaning. Words refer only to one another.

They do so, as Pascal brings out in his retort to the Jesuit at this point, for political rather than religious reasons: "What, Father, we have here then is only a defense of politics and not of religion?" Throughout the *Provincial Letters* thus far (as in those that are to follow), Pascal brings out that the Jesuits are, in effect, more concerned with politics than with religion.

The Jesuit conception of language as purely internal or self-referential is a tendency rather than a fixed position. Yet, paradoxically, aside from their own desire to "govern all of the faithful" (thereby manifesting that *libido dominandi* that the Pascal of the *Thoughts* would see as the very nature of man since the Fall), the Jesuits share a view of human nature not unlike that of Pascal: that it is corrupt, self-serving, self-loving, confused, devious, and God-bereft. In this light, the Jesuit conception of language may also be said to be referential, for its use of signifiers is designed to refer to the antecedent reality of a corrupt human nature. This is not to say that the Pascalian concept of referential language and (implicit) Jesuit concept of referential language are one and the same. In the Jesuit concept the referential axis is purely horizontal; in the Pascalian concept it is both horizontal and vertical, a triangulation of the Supreme Signified or the Antecedent Reality of God at the apex and the human signifiers of sense and word at the base. Graphically, the difference is as illustrated in the figure.

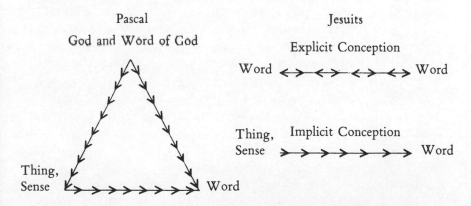

In the Pascalian triangle the arrows indicate the source and direction of referential validity, the ontological priority of the signified over the signifier. The *sense* points horizontally toward the *word*, such that both *sense* and *word*, in appropriate referential circumstances, receive significance from God and the Word of God. I use the term *sense* as well as *thing* in order to highlight the fact that for Pascal the word *sense* is richly bivalent in the relation between words and things. In fact, when *sense* is taken as the meaning of a word, the term is polyvalent (as for example, when he says that one knows God through the heart as well as and in fact better than through the mind). Moreover, the physical senses, especially of sight, are also signifiers, not only of the Godhead but also of certain social interactions (for example in the perceptions of the *esprit de finesse* as distinguished from the *esprit de géométrie*). The *sense* as well as the *word* that refers to it at the base of the triangular representation of Pascal's linguistics is, as I have noted, as corrupt as they are in the purely horizontal representation of their relationship for Jesuit linguistics in my illustration. However, it is the very presence of the transcendent Guarantor of Meaning at the apex of the Pascalian triangle that permits of any pure (uncorrupted) meaning. Similarly, it is the absence of this transcendence that leaves both *sense* and *word* corrupt and incapable of purity in the model of the *implied* Jesuit linguistics. Naturally, the representation of the Jesuit tendency toward an explicitly and exclusively self-referential notion of language (the one Pascal fears they really hold) is best represented, as I have indicated, by a horizontal line with the term *word* at either end, with meaning traveling (meaninglessly in Pascal's view) in either direction. As we shall see, beyond the first ten *Provincial Letters* and especially in the last two, Pascal will become increasingly and uneasily aware of the tendency not only of the Jesuits but of all men (including, ruefully for him, those laymen or members of the general public on which the strategy of the entire series is based) to regard words or, more generally, language as a purely internal phenomenon, a secondary modeling system without a primary model or figure guaranteeing meaning. This very perception of the skepticism of and toward language, this aporesis, in Louis Marin's terms, will dictate the paradoxical architecture of fragments of his projected *Apology for the Christian Religion* we now call the *Thoughts*.

It is to the most horrible instance of internality that the Jesuit interloctor ultimately comes in his continuing demonstration of the most horrible application of the doctrine of directing the intention in order to kill another human being: the justification of murder by a priest for simple bad-mouthing.

It is permitted [he quotes from the Jesuit Father L'Amy] to an ecclesiastic or to a religious to kill a calumniator, who threatens to publish

crimes scandalous to his community or to himself, when there is only
this one means to prevent him from doing so, as if he were ready to
spread these defamations were one not to kill him immediately. For in
this case, as it would be permitted to this religious to kill one who
wished to take his life, so is it permitted to him to kill him who would
deprive him of his honor or of that of the community, as it would be
to men of the world.[5]

The reporter is surprised at this opinion in view of the Church's long-
standing prohibition for ecclesiastics even to attend public executions.
This reminder does not phase the Jesuit. He adds still another opinion
by "Caramouël, our illustrious defender," that a priest can "not only
in certain situations kill a calumniator, but moreover that there are
some situations where he must do so: *etiam aliquando debet occidere.*"
The redundant Latin is another of Pascal's thrusts at the sheer irrele-
vancy of the Jesuit's language to any common, ordinary understanding
of what a priest's views on murder should be. His thrusts are not
merely implicit. The Jesuit gives, as an instance of these various "per-
missions" from the great Caramouël, whether Jesuits can kill Jansenists. Without saying whether they can or cannot in general, he answers that they need not do so because the Jansenists do them no harm
in calling them Pelagians and, in fact, only enhance the reputation of
the society by their attacks. Putting this answer in the mouth of his lo-
quacious Jesuit permits Pascal a multiple irony: the Jesuit accepts the
charge of Pelagian; he thereby gives some credence to Jansenist criticism of the Jesuits; he leaves the door open to the justified killing of
the Jansenists by priests (Jesuits) — and, clearly, of the killing of Jesuits
themselves.

That Jesuits might become victims of the Jansenists is implicit in a
concern that Pascal expresses for his own safety. Because, he reminds
the Jesuit, he writes of their discussions from time to time to a friend
"in the country," he fears that some "bizarre spirit" might think he is
calumniating the Jesuits and thus make an attempt on his life. The
Jesuit offers his guarantee that the reporter has nothing to fear, since,
after all, he is saying (and the reporter reporting, therefore) only what
the fathers have published, which is neither bad nor dangerous and
with the approval of their superiors. Amusing as this passage is for its
demonstration of the Jesuit's simplistic mind and as touching as it may
be in showing the Jesuit's concern for the reporter, it is even more interesting rhetorically. It suggests that the Jesuit is clearly an invention,

a composite of Jesuits to exposit Jesuit doctrines. The previous letters have had such notoriety by now, with the Jesuits beginning a continuous series of refutations of them beginning with the third, that it is hard to imagine any Jesuit serving as a key to this one. Furthermore, the passage raises the possibility that the reporter is concerned less about his personal safety than his moral integrity, for he drops a certain amount of his anonymity. Some commentators have seen him dropping that anonymity as early as the third letter, which had been signed with the initials "E. A. A. B. P. A. F. D. E. P.," which might be easily spelled out, as Stewart says, "Et ancien ami Blaise Pascal Auvergnat Fils de Etienne Pascal."[6] There is throughout the *Provincial Letters* a certain restiveness on the part of the writer about his use of pseudonymity. It can be detected in the use of the initials early on in the series or, here, in what might be called the narrative self-consciousness of the author. It is also detected in the tone of mounting indignation that informs many of his reactions to the Jesuit interlocutor's positions. At certain points, as he tells his correspondent in continuing preoccupation with the questions of his identity at the beginning of the eighth letter, he has to conceal his horror at hearing these positions precisely in order to allow the horror to emerge in its full force — that is, to maintain his initial strategy for the sake of fully exposing the Jesuits in all their abominations. This restiveness, this authorial self-consciousness, this slippage away from anonymity suggest that Pascal may have been disturbed by the contradiction between his recriminations of the Jesuits for their abuse of language and his own abuse of language in the use of a pseudonym. The invented self for the Pascal of the *Provincial Letters* may have been as hateful to him as the real self for the Pascal of the projected *Apology for the Christian Religion*.

The tenth letter of the series is, for Pascal, the occasion to demonstrate the final and most soul-searing of the horrors emanating from Jesuit ethics, the facile exemption of Christians from the obligation to love God. It is also the ultimate demonstration for him of the purely internal semiosis that underlies the entire parade of the Jesuits' moral abomination of the sacred Word of God.

This axiological emphasis on loving God more than self and neighbor is evident in the topical progression of the letters between the seventh and tenth: the eighth is the last in the Pascalian offensive to deal with public aspects of Jesuit ethics, as Pascal reveals their casuistical accommodations on material concerns centered around money in particular. As in the case of ecclesiastical murder, so here the nadir of Jesuit thinking on the matter is that priests as well as men of the world are authorized to profit usuriously. Pascal's proscription of usury, of a gain that is in excess of the signified debt that generates it, is of a piece with his proscription of the Jesuit use of words that are in excess of the signified, Christian severity that words should represent. Interest or surplus value is an empty signifier, a wind of sound that has no relation to the meaning the Jesuits (and the increasingly mercantilist world of seventeenth-century Europe) attach to it. This rhetorical and moral movement toward the consideration of the relations between words and words rather than between word and things is even more evident in the ninth *Provincial Letter,* with its consideration of the Jesuit notion of "easy devotion." The consideration becomes the occasion for the Jesuit to propound still another ingenious doctrine of the society, that of "mental restrictions" whereby the sinner can obey the "letter of the law" overtly and aloud while uttering a "saving" restriction under his breath that relieves him of the obligation and thus absolve himself of sinful actions, committed or contemplated. For example, as the Jesuit says, citing Father Filiutius: "Thus, after having said aloud: 'I swear that I did not do that', one adds in quiet 'today'; or, having said aloud: 'I swear', one says in quiet; 'that I say', and one continues aloud: 'that I did not do that.' " "This" I say aloud, "that" (its contrary or implied contrary) I say in quiet: word refers to word; empty sound refers to unheard sound; sense of sound refers to the non-sense of meaning. The abrogation in not only sensory (one does not hear it), it is also moral. Little wonder, then, that, as the interlocutors turn to the matter of the quality of sins, the Jesuit tends to assimilate capital or mortal sins into venial sins. In the violence that the Jesuits do to language all sense of nuance, of difference, of hierarchy is obliterated.

In the tenth *Provincial Letter* this violence reaches the ultimate horror, the dispensation by the Jesuit fathers from the injunction to love God. The Jesuit first cites a host of authorities who refine the injunction along a temporal axis: on the point of death, upon being baptized, on holy days, once a year, every three or four years, every five years, maybe never, as is clear in the last authority he cites, Filiutius, who "leaves it to the judgment of the sages." At first, the reporter lets pass "all this badinage, in which the spirit of man plays so insolently with the love of God." But the Jesuit, carried away into his purely verbal world of Jesuit quotations, goes on and on, culminating triumphantly with a quotation from "our Father Antoine Sirmond" in the latter's "admirable book, *The Defense of Virtue,* where he speaks French in France, as he tells his reader":

> God, in commanding us to love him, contents himself with our obedience to his other commandments. If God had said, "I shall condemn you, whatever obedience you show me, if in addition your heart is not given to me," in your opinion, would this motive have been proportionate to the end that God had to have and could have had in mind? It is thus said that we will love God in doing his will, as if we loved him from affection, as if the motive of charity brought us thereto. If that happen in reality, so much the better; if not, we shall nonetheless not fail to obey in all rigor the commandment to love him through the deeds [of obedience], so that (you can see the goodness of God) it is not so much commanded to us to love him as it is not to hate him. [Then, supporting this position with a number of other Jesuit references, he concludes with one which] will make you appreciate the value of this dispensation, by the price that he says it cost, which is the blood of Jesus Christ. This is the crown of this doctrine. You see therein, then, that the dispensation from this annoying obligation to love God is the privilege of the evangelical law, as distinguished from the Judaic law.

For the neutral reporter this language does not resemble the French in France that he, his correspondent, and all other Frenchmen speak in France. It is not even a language, for it violates the essential reference through language to something outside of language. It is a fiction that leads him to end the fiction of his own neutrality:

> O Father, there is no patience that you would not push to its breaking point, and one cannot listen [*ouïr*] without horror to the things that I have just heard [*entendues*]. It is not from me, he said. I well know that, Father. But you have no aversion to it and, far from detesting the authors of these maxims, you esteem them. Are you not afraid that your consent makes you an accomplice of their crime? And can you ignore that Saint Paul judges "worthy of death not only the authors of evil but also those who consent to it?"

Understanding (*entendues*) makes a mockery of listening (*ouïr*); meaning is violated by sound; common sense is voided by sensation. In Pascalian linguistics, sense vitiates sense by this Jesuit dispensation not only from the law of God but from the law of language. "One" (everyone, any speaker, all people) can only be horrified by this Jesuit usurpation of the law of God, this reversal of the meaning of God's entry into this world in the person of Jesus Christ: "It is the height of impiety. The price of the blood of Jesus Christ will have been to obtain for us the dispensation to love him! Before the Incarnation one was obliged to love God; but, since that time when 'God so loved the world that he gave to it his only Son,' the world redeemed by him will be discharged from loving Him. Strange theology of our times.' " As in earlier letters with their exposure of Dominican and Jesuit verbalism through analogies with concrete, familiar, and generally recognized situations and events (eating enough, health of the body for walking), so here Pascal brings the criss-crossing abstractions of the Jesuits (commandments, laws, formalities of paragraph citations) down to earth in the signal example of what is for many the abstraction of God himself: God coming down to earth as man, to suffer and die there for man. The Incarnation is the signifier of the signified love of God, and the signifiers that we use in speaking of that event and of its moral consequences must be in the relation of Divine Father to Divine Son, the relation of unalloyed love.

The tenth letter is also the occasion for Pascal to reprise the quarrel over contrition and attrition that had set Saint Cyran and Richelieu at odds with each other a generation earlier. One must be sorry for one's sins not because one fears the pains of hell or any other sensorial deprivation but solely because of having failed to love God, maintain the contritionists. In purely verbal fashion, the Jesuits would hold God to the explicit and strict formulating of such an injunction to love him. Thus their attritionist position with its accommodating secondary guarantee of absolution through the observance of the other commandments. (The rest of their accommodations obviously empty this observance of all applicability.) In keeping with what I have called the paradoxical, implied referential linguistics of the Jesuits, one might see in Jesuit attritionists a greater human sympathy than that manifested by contritionists like Saint Cyran and Pascal. Confronting the corruption of human nature, the Jesuits seem even more convinced of the hiddenness of God than the Jansenists, indeed, they seem to read it as a veritable absence if not the nonexistence of God. Thus their probabilism, their direction of intention, their mental restrictions are like Pirandellian lies: they make life possible. The Jesuits seem to look upon God as at most a lawgiving abstraction who at times speaks to man out of the blue, an unseen entity, a fiction permitting some measure of civil order in a humanistic and humanitarian framework that understands man's basic weakness. For Pascal, such an interpretation of the Jesuit position is not possible. The Jesuits empty experience of all meaning through their seemingly endless accommodations to human weakness (seemingly endless, for we remember the limit case to which their views on murder for defamation leads them). More important they have not understood the *linguistic and religious* meaning of the *sign* of Christ's entry into the world. Jesus Christ is not the abstract and unseen God of the Judaic law: he is the *In-carnation*, the Word made Flesh, the Unseen God Seen: a fiction become fact. The sensorial lesson of this *sign* is that which common sense would lead anyone to learn from the example of any person who lays down his life for a friend. Basically, for Pascal, then, the Jesuits are neither humanistic nor humanitarian; in fact, their very humanity is in question, for they do not seem to understand what even the simplest human being can understand.

Not surprisingly, at this juncture the reporter separates himself from the Jesuits, from the fiction, the created narrative of his and others' coming and goings to see and hear the Jesuits in a Horatian intention to instruct while amusing. Whatever the degree of a possible personal misgiving about the fictionality of his own person in this narrative, the tactical and strategic logic of the narrative dictates such a separation at this point. In *Provincial Letters* 4–10 he has led the Jesuits, like the Dominicans in *Letters* 1–3, with ever increasing pressure, from simple to most extreme horror of position. Narrative logic and theologic coincide: it is now appropriate, both esthetically and ethically, to leave the Jesuits hung up on the petard of their own wilfull and verbal alienation from the rest of the world.

Provincial Letters 11–16

In principle, Pascal might have maintained the offensive of the first ten letters as he kept the promise made to his correspondent at the end of the tenth letter to continue to write on the Jesuits, if necessary, not by reporting his personal exchanges with them but by consulting their books. The books he seems to have had in mind were the various publications he had already used in the first ten letters, texts not specifically related to the controversy provoked by his letters themselves. Such texts had been appearing from the third letter on, however, and had, typically, become increasingly *ad hominem* with respect to the author of the *Provincial Letters,* seeing in him at best a misquoter and, at worst, a liar and a scandal to the Church. From the eleventh letter on, then, Pascal finds himself not on the offensive but the defensive, justifying the exactitude of his quotations from the Jesuits and, more generally, the very spirit of the earlier letters.

Each of these letters is carefully argued according to a general three-stage plan of attack: first, a general discussion of the topic under review, usually in light of support drawn from the Scriptures and early fathers; second, a demonstration of Jesuit inconsistency with those supporting sources as well as, frequently, a demonstration of Jesuit inconsistency within the texts of the society itself; third, a conclusion drawing the implications of this confrontation of Jesuit with Church (as well as Jesuit with Jesuit) for religion and, with increasing emphasis as the letters progress, the state. Axiologically, the plan proceeds along the same lines as that of the earlier letters: Pascal does not concede any points to the Jesuits with respect to the validity of the Pascalian or Jansenist position in the specific issues under dispute, most of these a reprise of the subjects of the earlier letters. The Jesuits are shown to be at odds with the rest of Christianity. What was implicit in various earlier letters, that the Jesuits are separated in their outlandish language from humanity itself, is made quite explicit in the course of this series: "Where are we, my Fathers? Are these religious and priests who speak in this fashion? Are they Christians? Are they Turks? Are they men? Are they demons? And are these 'mysteries revealed by the Lamb to those of the society', or abominations suggested by the Dragon to those who follow his lead?" (*Provincial Letter* 14).

In reviewing these letters I shall consider only the eleventh in some detail because of its obvious relevancy to the rhetorical and strategic concerns central in an interpretation of the doctrinal issues of the *Provincial Letters* and in Pascal's psychological and intellectual posture in this connection. For the remaining letters (12–16) I shall trace these concerns more generally and examine some new concerns (for example, the relations between state and Church) that they raise.

The subject of the eleventh letter is raillery used in the exposition of religious matters. Pascal begins by protesting that the Jesuits have repeatedly charged that "I have turned holy things into mockery [raillerie]." He noted that the Jesuits are particularly susceptible in the matter with respect to his demonstration of their views, first, on usury as illustrated in the "Mohatra contract" propounded by the Jesuit Escobar, whereby "one buys goods dearly and on credit in order to resell them, at the same moment and to the same person, for liquid cash and at a cheaper price" (*Provincial Letter* 8), and, second, with respect to the story of Jean d'Alba, a domestic at the Jesuit College of Clermont in Paris who had stolen some precious tableware from the Jesuits and, when caught, had been prosecuted in law by the Jesuits and imprisoned in spite of his invocation of the Jesuit Bauny's judgment that domestics could be absolved from such crimes if they had stolen because their wages were not sufficient. Through their Father de Montrouge, the Jesuits denied this defense as "illicit, pernicious, and contrary to all laws—natural, divine, and human—and capable of overturning all families." In the view of Montrouge, the accused deserved to be "whipped before the door of the college at the hand of the public butcher, who, at the same time would burn the writings of those fathers treating of larceny, and they should be forbidden henceforth to teach such a doctrine, upon pain of death" (*Provincial Letter* 6). The demonstrations on Mohatra and Jean d'Alba had seemed sufficiently clear to the Pascal of the eighth and sixth letters, respectively, and they still seem so to the author of the eleventh letter. Citing these cases by name only, Pascal asks, "But is that what you call holy things?" He wonders whether the Jesuits think that the Mohatra contract is so "venerable" and the opinions of Father Bauny so "sacred" that they have the right to treat as impious anyone who makes fun of them: "What, my Fathers, the imaginations of your writers are to pass for truths of the faith, and one is to be unable to make fun of the passages of Escobar and of the so fantastic and so little Christian decisions of your other authors, except at the risk of being accused of laughing at religion?"

Imaginations, fantastic, so little Christian: so many synonyms for Pascal of Jesuit windiness of language. He will use others in the course of this letter: *extravagant, surprising disproportion, beyond measure (démésurée),* violent, stubborn, disordered. The synonymy of linguistic and moral disorder is architectonically integrated into an apology or defense of railery in the discussion of holy things that is the architecture of this logically composed letter.

  1. Citations from the Scriptures of God himself to Job and on Adam; of Jesus Christ on Nicodemus, and of the early fathers, especially Augustine, Chrysostomos, and Tertulian, indicate the highest warrent for the use of raillery.

2. Rules for the use of raillery:
   a. "The spirit of piety always brings one to speak with truth and sincerity, whereas envy and hate use lying and calumny."
   b. "to speak with discretion."
   c. "to use them [*railleries*] only against errors and not against holy things."
   d. [abridging the first three] "The spirit of charity brings us to have in the heart the desire for the salvation of those against whom one speaks and to address one's prayers to God at the same time that one addresses one's reproaches to men."
3. The demonstration that the Jesuits offend against each one of these rules.
4. The reply to another charge of the Jesuits that the author of the *Provincial Letters* unfairly makes reproaches to the Jesuits that have already been made.

The short fourth part of the letter (one page of thirteen) may seem to be on a subject different from raillery, but Pascal integrates it by noting that the Jesuits have done nothing to extirpate these opinions that have been condemned by others as well as himself. He is thus able to return to his main theme of laughing at the Jesuits: "Who could not but laugh in seeing the decision of," and there follows a spate of Jesuit decisions from Bauny, Cellot, Hurtado, and others, crowned by a return to Tertullian's authorization of mockery against the enemies of religion and concluding with a quotation from the Scriptures that "there is a time to laugh and a time to cry" and final citation of the Proverbs that Pascal hopes does not apply to the Jesuits: "there are people so unreasonable that one can do nothing with them, however one acts with them, whether one laughs or whether one becomes angry."

This argument in good form ends where it began, with the first of sacred sources, the Holy Bible, New and Old Testament. The linguistic triangle of the earlier letters, with its Transcendent Guarantor of Meaning, the Word of God, is still at work here as Pascal attacks the purely immanentist conception of language and ethics held by the Jesuits. Laughter is, however, not an end in itself for Pascal; it is a weapon. He does not separate the esthetic and the ethical. He is, in fact, suspicious of the notion of the esthetic as a realm unto itself. In demonstrating that the Jesuits offend against the first of the rules for the use of raillery, he scorns an ode written by the Jesuit Le Moyne,

"Eulogy of Modesty, wherein it is shown that all beautiful things are red or inclined to redden" (*rougir*). I shall quote only a few verses of this precious conceit: "The cherubim, those glorious / Composed of head and plume / Whom God with his spirit alights / And whom he illuminates with his eyes; / These shining winged faces / Are always red and burning, / Either with the fire of God or their own." And in a conclusion that infuriates Pascal, the poem makes a comparison to the woman for whom the poem was composed, called Delphine here, "But the redness bursts forth in you, / Delphine, with even more advantage, / When honor is upon your visage." Do these comparisons, Pascal asks the Jesuits, "appear to you to be very Christian in the mouth of someone who consecrates the adorable body of Jesus Christ?" He is, as he says, aware that Le Moyne writes only "to play the gallant and to amuse," but "that is just what one calls to laugh at holy things." Nor is Pascal's indignation merely circumstantial here, an exchange of blow for blow in a demonstration of Jesuit inconsistency. A larger issue, of principle, is at stake.

On the matter of poetry in general, Le Moyne has made a declaration that is no less censurable for Pascal than his verses themselves: "That the Sorbonne has no jurisdiction over Parnassus, and that the errors of that realm are subject neither to censure nor to the inquisition, as if one were forbidden to blaspheme or be impious only in prose." Like the Boileau of *On Poetic Art* Pascal proscribes as subjects of poetry "holy things." Moreover, in his reproaches to the verses of Le Moyne as in his subsequent reproach in this paragraph to the Jesuit Garasse's metaphor that "the human personality was grafted or, so to speak, saddled (*mis à cheval*) on the personality of the Word," one senses a sexophobic repugnance for the worldly concerns of so much poetry, whether its purported subject be of "holy" or "worldy" things. (In French, Le Moyne's word for *redden* is *rougir,* which also means "to blush".) Pascal stigmatizes Parnassian or, in more contemporary formulations, literarocentric conceptions of poetry and art as an autonomous and self-sufficient system of intra-acting signs, a "Referantial" rather than a "Referential" code, in the distinction of the philosopher Jacques Derrida.[7] Pascal's esthetic is thereby an antiesthetic. For him, the *esthetic* (the word is not his, of course, in this context) is manifest in the *sense,* in *sentiment* (these words *are* his: *sens, sentiment*), the nonverbal signifiers of meaning that are in an indissoluble referential relation to words (*mots, paroles*). As they are not for the Jesuits, who may be said, from Pascal's point of view, to write novels (*romans*), of which, he writes in a subsequent letter in replying to still another Jesuit charge, he has never read any. He may have written some poems, as we have seen, but it is crucial to recall the impulse that may have led to this uncharacteristic and philosophically aberrant behavior: it was out of rivalry with his sister. Poetry and novels are works of the imagination, the most suspect of faculties for Pascal (and one with whose allure he here and elsewhere finds the Jesuits far too taken). Better to write works of the *mind* (whose signifiers are words) and the *heart* (whose signifiers are the senses), for these are the faculties allowing for "truth and sincerity" to be seen and heard.

His preference for literality over literariness casts a paradoxically intrinsic and verbal light across the eleventh and the subsequent letters of this series, where Pascal defends himself as the author of the *Provincial Letters* as such. In defending "making fun" he does not have much fun, nor do his readers. The letters are relentlessly serious, often self-referential, and increasingly plaintive in tone. They are concerned less with what was said than with who said it. Pascal seems to have fallen into the Jesuit mode of language in spite of himself. The point of view and the tone are now univocal as he is the only character who speaks. His powerful mind forcefully builds the coherent logic of argument in each letter. He explicitly announces the development his argument is to take; he carefully links his transitions in an argumentative syntax of "thus" and "but" and "therefore"; he lines up texts. His personal sense of scandal now erupts in outbursts of sadness or indignation and extends itself in prophetic peroration recalling that of his Jansenist friend at the end of the second letter. All in the first person: the editorial "I" who is the author of the earlier letters is now one who "being alone as I am, without force and with no human support, against such a large body, and being sustained only by truth and sincerity, have exposed myself to losing all in exposing myself to being convicted of imposture." He still writes as if the simple "telling of the truth," of the way things are, will win over that general public, but it is as if he has forgotten the wisdom of that earlier strategy of making his points through the use of secondary characters as buffers. Now it is him against the Jesuits and thereby, by his own understanding of *their* strategy of saying anything and everything so long as one touches all possible points of view, he finds himself jumping to their tune in a purely internal quarrel of pedants who launch texts at one another.

The public has been shunted aside. One senses that Pascal may be beginning to understand his "natural" friend's caution to him at an earlier point that he "would not talk that way if he knew the world." He concludes the twelfth letter (a reprise of Jesuit views on almsgiving, simony, and bankruptcy) with the following remarks:

> You believe you have force and impunity [on your side]; but I believe I have truth and innocence [on mine]. It is a strange and long war, the one where violence tries to oppose truth. All the efforts of violence cannot weaken truth, and they serve only to raise it up even higher. All the lights of truth can do nothing to stop violence and only serve to goad it on. When force combats force, the stronger destroys the lesser: when one opposes discourse to discourse, those that are true and convincing confound and dissipate those that have only vanity and lying within them; but violence and truth can do nothing to each other. But do not claim therefrom that things are equal, for there is this extreme difference: that violence has but a limited term, by the order of God, who guides the effects to the glory of the truth that it attacks, whereas truth subsists eternally and finally triumphs over its enemies, because it is eternal and powerful, like God himself.

It is perhaps with this awareness of issues larger than the confrontation of text with text that Pascal sets the subject of the next two letters (13 and 14), a reprise of Jesuit positions on homicide, in a larger philosophical framework. He invokes the generality not in the person of members of the Academy or ladies of high society but of the public symbol of the generality, the state, and more especially of the king and his magistrates. Pascal does continue to confront text with text, especially, Jesuit text with Jesuit text to reveal the Society of Jesus' theological corpus to be a tissue of contradictions. However, he weaves these texts into a constant refrain of the dangers that Jesuit views on homicide imply for the state: "What, my Fathers, you will tell us that one has the right to kill for simple defamation in considering only the law of God, which forbids homicide? And, having violated the eternal law of God, you believe you can avoid the scandal you have caused, and persuade us of your respect before him, by adding that you forbid the practice for reasons of state and out of fear of the magistrates?" This is the tone of the imperiled citizen. However, Pascal does not rest his case there: "I do not reproach you for fearing the magistrates but to fear only the judges and not the Judge of Judges. That is what I blame, because it is to make God less the enemy of crimes than men. If you said that one can kill a defamer according to men, but not according to God, that would be less insupportable; but that what is too criminal to be suffered by men be innocent and just in the eyes of God, who is justice itself, what is it to do but to show everybody that, by this horrible reversal so contrary to the spirit of the saints, you are bold before God and timid before men." This is the tone of the scandalized believer.

Scandalized believer (the defender of the faith) and imperiled citizen (the public defender) are one in the Pascal of these letters. Both make their defense in horror of the abuse of language that is at the core of Jesuit ethics: "What horrible language that, in saying that some authors hold a damnable opinion, is at the same time a decision in favor of this damnable opinion and which authorizes in conscience all that only relates to it!" (*Provincial Letter* 13). Only sovereigns have the right to take a life, as Pascal brings out (*Letter* 14), citing now Saint Paul, because that right "descends from Heaven," now Saint Augustine, " '[that he] who without authority kills a criminal renders himself criminal, by this principal reason that he usurps an authority that God has not given him'; and judges, on the other hand, who have this authority, are nevertheless murderers if they condemn to death an innocent against the laws that they are obliged to follow." Therein, Pascal argues, lie the principles of public peace and security, respected by all legislators everywhere and at all times "holy and pagan," as he puts it. In citing both, Pascal is not falling into purely naturalistic reasoning. Natural law is assimilated into the supernatural law, the former but an instance of the latter in the theocratic tropism that informs his discourse. He invokes the combined forces of Church and state against the Jesuits, the conjoined interests of public safety and Christian morality, the twinned severity of, on the one hand, "civil and even pagan laws," and, on the other, "ecclesiastical laws." As to just which of these laws is grounding and primary, his final sentence in the fourteenth letter (apart from the final paragraph, which is appended as a note commenting on the Jesuit reaction to the last letter) leaves no doubt: "And, to conceive further horror of the crime of homicide, remember that the first crime of corrupted men was a murder of the first just man, that their greatest crime was the murder of the head of all the just, and that murder is the only crime that destroys all at once the state, the Church, nature, and piety."

The declarative mode of the first ten *Provincial Letters* has obviously yielded in the letters after the tenth to verbal modes suggesting discrepancies between appearance and reality, the imperative and the hortatory subjunctive. As Pascal sees it, Jesuits always write in a conditional mode, describing a world of "as if," but this is a mode that seems so to prevail (they go on and on, and the world apparently finds their verbal mode accommodating) that Pascal has to shift from the mode not of what *is* but of what *ought to be*. In the fifteenth and sixteenth letters, Pascal returns to a declarative mode but one that deals not with the surface of Jesuit language and of the language of the Port Royalists whom he defends but with the intention of these opposed speakers that he perceives in that surface: to calumny in the one case and to sincerity in the other. He will, in sum, take the Jesuits at their word that words mean nothing, showing in their many declarations on this question that, as far as they are concerned, all language is in the conditional mode: if language serves the aggrandizement of the society, it is to be considered "true;" if language does not serve that aggrandizement, it is to be considered false. For Pascal, the two hypotheses cancel each other, leaving Jesuit language a totally political epiphenomenon of true language. By this measure, as Pascal insistently brings out, the Jesuits can readily condemn as heretics not what people say against the Jesuits but the fact that they say it. Not only Arnauld's heresy, then, but all heresies so called by the Jesuits are personal.

Arnauld and, more particularly, the nuns at the convent of Port Royal are very much on his mind in these two letters, especially the sixteenth. That letter is very long, the longest thus far and will prove to be longest of the entire series, as he brings out in an oft-quoted postscript, that he did not have enough time to write a shorter letter. One wonders, however, if it was only the lack of time that prompted him to such length in this, the most personal and the most indignant of the letters. His attachments at Port Royal were both of the heart as a way of knowing God and of the heart as an affection we know to have been the closest of his life; the Jansenists whom he defends here had been his spiritual counselors just after his conversion and among the nuns whom he defends was to be counted his sister Jacqueline. These attachments do not consciously emerge in all their personal character. In this letter he takes great pains to portray his defense as transcending any attachment: "For, although I have never had any establishment with them, as you wish to have it believed without knowing who I am, I nevertheless know some of them and honor the virtue of all of them. But God has not included with this number alone all those whom he wishes to oppose your disorders." The justification borders on the specious, to be saved therefrom only by the strictest interpretation of the word *establishment*. He has not joined Port Royal by becoming a member of the community, like the solitaries, for example. The establishment that he has with his family, however, one of them very definitely established at Port Royal as a religious under its tutelage, is not to be gainsaid by this linguistic exactitude. It underlies the fervor of expression and the sharpness of argument that informs his writing here.

That argument is a defense of the Port Royal community against two charges that the Jesuits have leveled against them: first, that their views on the sacrament of the Eucharist are Calvinistic; and second, that the community has a long and continuing history of conspiracy against the Church. He begins the letter with a brief defense of a charge against Cornelius Jansen himself as an embezzler of ecclesiastical funds while Bishop of Ypres. In the context of the entire letter, however, the clarification of this charge can be seen as a part of the overall strategy of demonstrating the falsity of the Jesuits on the two main charges: first, the hypocrisy of the Jansenists with respect to their claim to be members of the Church in their doctrines (the charges on the Eucharist) and, second, their false acceptance of the Church's authority (the charge of conspiracy). As Pascal shows in both instances, it is the Jesuits who, in their calumny on these counts, are the hypocrites.

On the issue of the Eucharist, the Jesuit charge is tripartite: first, Arnauld and his coreligionists do not believe in the "real presence" of Jesus Christ in the Eucharist; second, Saint Cyran had taught, in the *Petrus Aurelius*, which the Jesuits attribute to him, that the character of the priesthood is effacable (in sinful priests, an issue linked to the question of the Eucharist with respect to the validity of that sacrament when consecrated by a priest in a state of sin); third, when Arnauld claims, in his book *On Frequent Communion*, that in the Eucharist Jesus Christ is veiled as he is not in heaven, the Jansenist author is heretical in the manner of Calvin. Pascal answers each charge in turn, with each answer anchored in the referential conception of language that has guided him throughout his exchanges with the adversaries of Port Royal, Jesuit and other. That conception is now broadened to stress to an unprecedented degree the conception of *sens* as a sign. He does, to be sure, confront word with word, in the parade of texts from Arnauld and Saint Cyran that he lines up as evidence of their belief in the transubstantiation of the bread and wine of the Eucharist into the Body and Blood of Christ; or again, in replying to the second charge, in the quotation he cites from the *Petrus Aurelius* (whether by Saint Cyran or not, he seems to be saying to the Jesuits) clearly stating " 'in the ordinary language of the Church, one can say that they [sinful priests] no longer are priests, although they always are so with respect to the character [of the priesthood].' " Thus, as if only in passing, Pascal also notes that the *Aurelius* had really upset the Jesuits because it had clearly demonstrated the heresy of their confrères in England on the political issue of episcopal authority. As for their illogical leap from the charge that Saint Cyran does not believe in the ineffacable character of the priesthood to the charge that he does not believe in the real presence of Christ in the Eucharist, Pascal sees the Jesuits guilty of "an arrant [*insigne*] extravagance and a large mortal sin against reason." He says that the Jesuits should not expect any further reply from him on this leap in their logic, for "if you do not have any common sense, I cannot give you any." The concern with verbal language that has referential validity is obviously still very much a part of Pascal's armament as he charges the Jesuits with being without reason and common sense. The intellectual faculty is clearly linked for him with the sense, or faculty, of being able to see what is written in noncontradictory language. As the French word that I have translated "arrant" shows, the Jesuits are without signs (*in-signe*), without a valid conception of signs.

Yet, for all this by now familiar emphasis on the signs of verbal language, the sixteenth letter makes an even greater emphasis on signs of conduct as a way of refuting Jesuit charges against Port Royal. He is concerned to defend the nuns of Port Royal against the Jesuit Meynier's charge that "their faith on the matter of the Eucharist is as suspect as that of M. Arnauld." Pascal does note that the nuns have testified verbally to their orthodoxy in the very names that they have given themselves ("Daughters of the Holy Sacrament") and to their Church ("Church of the Holy Sacrament"). However, he stresses the conduct that gives witness to their orthodoxy in the matter: "Why would they have obligated themselves, in a particular devotion, also approved by the pope, to have incessantly, night and day, some of their religious in the presence of the Sacred Host, to repair through their perpetual adoration of this sacrifice the impiety of the heresy that sought to abolish it?" Undoubtedly, some part of this perpetual adoration is conducted in prayer, aloud or silent, but it is to the very presence, the act of being there, that Pascal's text draws our attention. His summary question of the Jesuits in the passage makes this clear: "What is your response, my Fathers, to such evident witness, not only in words but in deeds [actions], and not of a few particular deeds, but of the whole train of a life entirely consecrated to the adoration of Jesus Christ in residence upon our altars?"

Pascal asks the Jesuits to "respond," in words, of course, for that is the only sign that they can give of their faith. As he says at a later point in this letter

> I am astonished therefore not that you impute to them [the Jansenists] crimes so great and so false, but that you impose upon them, with so little prudence, such hardly probable [si peu vraisemblables] crimes. For you dispose very well of sins as you wish, but do you think you can dispose in the same way of the credence [créance] of men? In truth, my Fathers, if the suspicion of Calvinism has to fall on them or on you, I would find you on bad terms [en mauvais termes]. Their discourses are as Catholic as yours, but their conduct confirms their faith, and yours belies it.

Discourse, conduct, faith: the Pascalian linguistic triangle demonstrates the orthodoxy of those at Port Royal, faithful in word and sense to the real presence of God in both the Eucharist and in his Word in the Scriptures as well as in the writings of the early (true!) "fathers" and in the councils of the Church. As for the Jesuits, theirs is a discourse that contradicts conduct that contradicts faith. The horizontal line of Jesuit linguistics demonstrates the hereticality of the Jesuits in their manipulations of the real presence of God in the Eucharist and of his words wherever they be found.

Pascal's demonstration of this vacuous Jesuit conception of language and, thus, of faith in the sixteenth letter brings full circle the general premise he posited at the outset of the fifteenth letter: "One can indeed say false things in believing them to be true, but the quality of liar includes the intention to lie. I shall show, therefore, my Fathers, that your intention is to lie and calumniate, and that it is with awareness and design that you impose on your enemies crimes of which you know them to be innocent, because you believe you can do it without falling from a state of grace." He detected this Jesuit intention in the host of citations from their fathers. The most striking was Caramouël's; "It is a constant that it is a probable opinion that there is no venial sin in calumniating in order to conserve one's honor. For it is sustained by more than twenty serious doctors, by Gaspard Hurtado and Dicastillus, Jesuits, and others; so that, if this doctrine were not probable, there would hardly be any which would be in all theology" (*Provincial Letter* 15). But, as the sixteenth letter brings out, it is not only their written words that show their intention to lie and calumniate, it is their conduct, for example, their absolution of and, indeed, authorization to licentious behavior not only by the world but by priests, like themselves, in such deeds as frequenting occasions of sin (like whorehouses) or tolerating that a priest in a state of sin consecrate in the mass the bread and wine transubstantiated into the Body and Blood of Christ.

The latter case is one in which we may find Pascal to be flirting with Protestant notions. Yet, it would be a mistake to view Pascal's position in this light. Like Saint Cyran he may be said to proceed in the matter with the most conservative interpretation of the Catholic concept of *ex opere operato* (from the act the validity of the act) as distinguished from the Protestant concept of *ex opere operantis* (the validity of the act depends on the validity of the actor). In his conservatism, Pascal puts himself (and the priest in question) on the hither side of the act, echoing Saint Cyran's famous dictum of "withholding oneself from the altar." A priest in a state of sin should withhold himself from saying mass just as any Catholic in a state of sin should withhold himself from receiving communion at mass:

> If you believe as well as they [Jansenists] that this bread is really changed into the Body of Jesus Christ, why do you not ask, as they do, that the heart of stone and ice of those whom you counsel to approach it be sincerely changed into a heart of flesh and love? If you believe that Jesus Christ is therein in a state of death in order to teach those who approach it to die to the world, to sin, and to themselves, why do you lead those to approach it in whom vices and criminal passions are still most alive?

Here one sees Pascalian linguistics applied to the deepest semantic structures of the self—before words and before deeds, so to speak. The sacrament as signifier can have meaning only if it refers to the signified of a pure heart. If Pascal defends Arnauld's views that communion could not be frequent (in *On Frequent Communion*), it is not because he is tainted with Calvinist denials of the validity of the sacrament of the Eucharist (or of sacramental religion as such). Rather, it is because he is aware of the frequency of the sinful state in which so many communicants do approach the altar.

When one couples this awareness with Pascal's frequent awareness throughout *Provincial Letters* 11–16 that the Jesuits do find so much support in the world, one senses that he is implicitly acknowledging the inefficacy of his initial strategy of appealing to the general public. He may from time to time write in that vein in these letters, for example, when he says at one point in the sixteenth letter that "one has only to publish this strange maxim, which exempts them for crime, to deprive you of all credence." Significantly however, it is not with such invocations that he concludes this longest, most personally fervent and most disputatious of the letters. It is, rather, with long citations from the prophets Isaiah and Ezekiel and shorter ones from M. de Genève (Francois de Sales, an ironic thrust at the Jesuits for their linking of the Jansenists with Calvinist Geneva) and from Saint Bernard. All bear on the chaotic effect of calumny on the soul in itself and in community with other souls. It is on high that the defender of the faith and the public defender here looks for the warrant to arrest the horrors of the Jesuits.

PART III

The
Advocate

· 8 ·

THE
FINAL
PROVINCIAL
LETTERS

IN THE LAST two complete *Provincial Letters,* the adversary becomes primarily an advocate, especially in the very last. Both deal with the question of fact and faith raised by the Jansenists in their earliest self-defense against the censured "Five Propositions," with the seventeenth letter concentrating on the matter of fact in the presumed hereticality of the Jansenists, the eighteenth on the faith of the Jansenists. In each letter Pascal abandons for the most part the exclamatory and hortatory mode of the most recent letters. He returns to the declarative and interrogative modes of the earliest letters (that interrogative, in its irony, was really a declarative), but in doing so he is more tentative and conciliatory. Similarly, he continues to assign to the Jesuits the conditional mode that has been theirs throughout all of the letters, but now it is designed not to hang the Jesuits on their own petard, but to get them off the hook. Although there are still some hard thrusts, these are friendlier duels, fought within the family rather than between families.

The least friendly thrusts are made at the outset of the seventeenth letter as Pascal defends himself against Father Annat's "audacity" in "treating me as a heretic." Significantly, as he had defended the nuns at Port Royal chiefly at the level of deeds rather than words alone, so he here defends himself on the same level: "I ask you what proofs you have. When have I been seen at Charenton [the seat of Protestant practice]? When have I missed mass and not observed the duties of Christians in their parishes? When have I committed any action linking me with heretics of any schism against the Church? Which council have I contradicted? Which papal constitution have I violated? You

213

must answer, Father, or . . . you understand what I mean." The familiar Jesuit attack of personal attack being this time leveled at Pascal himself, he responds with a flat profession of orthodoxy in the most declarative of terms: "It is therefore certain, Father, that I have said nothing to sustain these impious propositions, which I detest with all my heart. And, even if Port Royal held them I declare to you that you can conclude therefrom nothing against me, because, thanks to God, I am connected on this earth only with the Catholic Church, apostolic and Roman, in which I wish to live and die, and in communion with the pope, its sovereign head, beyond which I am fully persuaded that there is no salvation." Yet, however personal this self-defense and declaration of faith, it is uttered not out of that sense of personal beleagurment that informed his earlier description of himself as a man "alone . . . without force and without human support" (*Provincial Letter* 12). Rather, he speaks of his worldly status precisely out of disdain for the things of this world that his fidelity to the faith and the Church dictates: "All the credit that you have is useless in my case. I hope for nothing from the world: I fear nothing from it, I want nothing from it; I have no need, by the grace of God, of either the goods or the authority of anyone. Thus, Father, I escape your tentacles." The stance could be seen as Protestant as Pascal goes on to insist on his personal independence ("being free, with commitment, without relations") stating his resolve to continue his refutation of the Jesuits "inasmuch as I believe that God commits me to do so, without any human consideration being able to stop or slow down this pursuit."

The Protestantism, as in his views on the validity of the Eucharist, is only seeming. The issue is not one of faith at this point, but of fact. Not merely and not even primarily of *his* faith and the *fact* by which one may determine his orthodoxy, but of "other people whom you treat as heretics in order to include me in this accusation." That he is so "included" is the warrant he now takes to demonstrate, in three-quarters of this long letter, to show that the charge is as wrong about them as it is about him. He does so with the same logical coherence and clarity that has guided him in all the letters. Basically, this letter is constructed from this point on in the same way as the recent letters to the Jesuits, with an extended first part citing authorities on the validity of the position of those whom the Jesuits attack, a second part citing Jesuit positions in contradiction of this authorities, a conclusion setting these opposing references in their implications for the general public.

Dealing with the issue of whether, in fact, the "Jansenists" sub-scribe to the Five Propositions, Pascal, at the outset, insistently relies on the concept of language as referential. I put the name of the Jesuits' adversaries in quotation marks, because, as Pascal puts it to Father An-nat, "I ask in what does the heresy consist in those whom you call Jansenist." His basic reproach to the Jesuits' position in this con-troversy over "fact and principle" (*fait et droit*) is that they have used the word *Jansenist* to *label* a certain position by this name. But, Pascal argues, that position cannot be found word by word in the writings to which the Jesuit applies the label. "It is not that there could be no ap-pearance that you were telling the truth, for to say that words [*paroles*] are to be found 'word for word' [*mot à mot*] in an author, that is something that no one could mistake." He is thus not "astonished" that so many people in France and in Rome have believed "in effect" that the words were to be found in Jansen. On the other, he is "hardly surprised" (*si peu surpris*) to find that this "very point of fact" was "false" and that "one has defied you to cite the pages of Jansen where you have found these propositions 'word for word.' " *Astonished, sur-prised*: this familiar semantic refrain of the earlier letters is used again as a tactical ground of appeal to the general public along the lines of or-dinary language and common sense. To be astonished or surprised is to be struck dumb, to be rendered incapable of making any sense whether of the senses or of the mind that controls the use of words. In the nar-rowed and personalized exchange of this letter, however, the appeal to the general public has been severely circumscribed if not compromised. "I am not astonished," Pascal begins this two-sentence development, and his "one has defied" in the second sentence has the air not of a generalized *everybody* but of an editorial *we* assimilated into the first person pronoun of that first sentence. The exclamatory countercharges of earlier letters (*impostors, horrible,* and so on) may be missing from Pascal's discourse here, but the tone is hardly less accommodating.

It becomes more so as Pascal moves the argument to the question of the different ways in which a meaning may be read in "Jansenist" or any other text (the ways of reading meaning, not meaning itself, which will be the subject, rather, of the next letter). Pascal cites a number of disputes within the Church throughout its history showing the effects of reading meaning in different and opposing ways, begin-ning with Saint Basil and Saint Athanasius on the orthodoxy of the views on the Arian heresy held by Saint Denis of Alexandria and carry-

ing on to the very dispute at issue here with the condemnation by the
present pope of Jansenist writings. In all his examples, Pascal is concerned with showing that, as in the quarrel between Basil and Athanasius,

> if you and they [the "Jansenists"] agree on the meaning of Jansen, and
> they were in accord with you that he holds, for example, "that one
> cannot resist grace," those who would refuse to condemn them would
> be heretical. But when you argue about his meaning, and they believe
> that, according to his doctrine, "one can resist grace," you have no
> cause to treat them as heretics, whatever heresy you attribute to them
> yourself, since they condemn the meaning that you suppose therein,
> and you would not dare condemn the meaning that they suppose
> therein.

Meaning (*sens*) here takes on the same logical status as *word* (*mot*) in
Pascal's argument: it is the *fact* of two opposing interpretations with
which he is concerned.

Nevertheless, it is significant that, in this regression to the disputa-
bility of the *things* that *words* designate, he is moving away from the
denotative literality of the referential conception of language that had
informed his earlier letters. He moves toward a connotative conception of referentiality that allows for shading and nuance. The shift provides a ground of reconciliation not only between him and Father Annat but between the Jansenists and the Church, especially the pope,
with whom they have been put at odds by the Jesuit's purely verbal
imputation of heresy. Pascal maintains that the *fact* of "*meaning* to be
heretical" is not to be found in their writings; their doctrine itself
shows that it "is in conformity with the natural meaning of this proposition." Thus, given this ancient and continuing evidence of the possibility of different interpretations of texts, Pascal justifies the refusal
of the Jansenists to sign a declaration positing that the Five Propositions are to be found in Jansen. To do so would be to subscribe not
only to the fact of the literal expression of heresy by Jansen but to the
meaning, the intention of heresy, that the Jesuits interpret therein. In
the face of the Jesuit insistence that they sign and subscribe to such
facts of language and meaning, Pascal can, as in earlier letters, find the
Jesuits' motives to be merely political: "But all that is conducted in
mystery. All of your steps are political."

However more flexible his conception of language here, Pascal is less accommodating than he is in the following letter of the series, the eighteenth. The last of the complete letters is second in length only to the sixteenth and, like that letter in relation to the preceding one, its timing in relation to the seventeenth suggests something about Pascal's spirit on the subjects he treats in these key Letters. The sixteenth and longest was sent in the shortest time between itself and the preceding letter, a period of nine days. The average time between successive letters is about three weeks, with the shortest being six days (if we are not to count as Pascal's the "Reply of the Friend," which followed only three days after the second) and the longest being the sixty days between the seventeenth and the eighteenth. The sixteenth letter was that in which Pascal came to the fervid defense of the members of the Port Royal community, especially of the nuns, who included his sister. In its passion and length it may be considered the most passionately antagonistic toward the Jesuits. On the other hand, the eighteenth, almost as long as the sixteenth, is written after the longest period of time between any of the letters and is in a far greater spirit of accommodation than any. It is the most conciliatory and the most advocative of the letters.

Even this letter is not without some of the hard blows that we have seen him strike in the last bout with Father Annat. Because the letter is designed to reconcile Jansenist and Jesuit in the matter of *faith,* such blows are struck only rarely, in the clinches, as it were—for example when Pascal says, "Let everyone learn then by your own declaration that this truth of efficacious grace, necessary in all pious actions, which is so dear to the Church and which is the price of the Blood of its Savior, is so constantly Catholic that there is not a Catholic, including the Jesuits themselves, who do not recognize it as orthodox." If Pascal is literally Catholic in his declaration of faith in the seventeenth letter, he is here metaphysically and psychologically Catholic in his elucidation of the orthodoxy of Jansenist views on the relation between God's grace and man's freedom. Catholicism is the reconciliation of antinomies, the assimilation of seemingly antithetical beliefs and stances into a unitary, unifying, and universal belief and stance.

The shift in spirit is signaled by an even more flexible and subtle conception of the referential character of language than that of the seventeenth letter. It is appropriately so, for we deal not with the fact of words to be found or not found in this or that text nor with the fact of various and possibly contradicting meanings to be found in such texts. We deal with meaning itself, with, in terms of the dispute, faith. Pascal quickly dismisses those earlier grounds of argument in the first three pages of this twenty-page letter in order to turn to those texts that will show Jansenist and Jesuit to be in Catholic agreement on the issue of efficacious grace.

Not surprisingly, those common texts are to be found in the early Church fathers, particularly Saint Augustine, and they separate both Jesuit and Jansenist from Calvinist:

> I declare to you, then, Father, that you have nothing more to reproach in your adversaries, because they most assuredly detest what you detest. I am astonished only to see that you do not know it and that you have so little knowledge of their sentiments on this subject, which they have so often declared in their works. I assure myself that, if you were better informed, you would regret not having instructed yourself, in a spirit of peace, on a doctrine so pure and so Christian, which passion makes you combat without knowing it. You would see, Father, that not only do they hold that one effectively resists these feeble graces that are called excitatory and inefficacious in not performing the good that they inspire in us, but they are just as firm in maintaining against Calvin the power that the will has to resist even efficacious and victorious grace as they are to defend against Molina the power of this grace on the will, as jealous of the first of these truths as they are of the other. They know only too well that man, by his own nature, always has the power to sin and to resist grace and that, since his corruption, he bears an unfortunate fundament of concupiscence that infinitely augments in him this power; yet that nevertheless, when it please God in His mercy to touch him, He makes him do what He wishes and in the manner that He wishes, without this infallibility of God's operation destroying in any way the natural liberty of man, by the secret and admirable manners in which God effects [opère] this change, that Saint Augustine has so excellently explained, and which dissipate all the imaginary contradictions that the enemies of efficacious grace configure for themselves [se figurent] between the sovereign power of grace over free will [le libre arbitre] and the power that this free will has to resist grace. For, according to this great saint, whom the popes and the Church have given as the rule in this matter, God changes the heart of man by a celestial sweetness that He therein infuses [répand] which, overcoming the delectation of the flesh, makes man, sensing [sentant] on the one hand his mortality and nothingness, and discovering [découvrant] on the other the grandeur and eternity of God, conceive [conçoit] disgust [dégoût] for the delights of sin, which

separates him from the incorruptible good; and, finding the greatest
joy in the God who charms him, he bears himself infallibly and of himself thereto, by a movement that is fully free, fully voluntary, fully loving, such that it would be a pain and a torment to move away therefrom. It is not that he cannot always move away therefrom and that he
might so move away effectively if he wished, but how would he wish
it, since the will never bears itself except to that which most pleases it,
and nothing pleases it so much then as this unique good, which includes within itself all other goods? *Quod enim amplius nos delicate,
secundum id operemur necesse est* [Of necessity are we moved to that
which most pleases us], as Saint Augustine says.

Psychologically, linguistically, and doctrinally this is an extraordinary
text when placed in the context of *Provincial Letters* 1–16. It is obviously of a piece with the spirit of accommodation that began in letter
17, a spirit far from the antagonistic irony, indignation, and invective
of the prior letters. Linguistically and doctrinally it is of equal import.
In terms of Pascal's conception of language it continues and makes
even more marked the shift from literality and denotativeness evident
in the seventeenth letter. This shift is inseparable, by the very referentiality of Pascal's conception of language, from the doctrinal position it
posits. I shall, therefore, discuss both linguistics and doctrines in their
inescapable Pascalian involvement with each other.

The effect of the denotative, literal notion of referential language
informing letter 1–16 is separatist. The common reader is radically
separated from expert reader or, in thelogical terms, one set of believers from the others. As Pascal saw the manner, this meant aberrant
Jesuit readers, or users of language, from normal readers or users of
language. This linguistic separation implied, except in rare moments
of nonironic charitableness on his part in those letters, that the Jesuits
were not even *believers* ("Are they Christians? Are they men?" and so
on). Doctrinally, the effect of this notion of language was to depict the
Church in the most conservative orthodoxy, to make a strict reading
of its constitutions, so to speak. In such a reading, the notions of
pleasure, of delectation, of charm were hardly invoked or, when they
were, only in a vein of irony and dubiety. Thus, in the eighth letter,
having heard one of the Jesuit's expositions justifying usury, "O
Father! I said to him, these are really powerful words! I protest to you
that, if I did not know that they come from a good source, I would
take them for some of these enchanted words that have the power to

break a charm. Undoubtedly they have some occult virtue to chase away usury that I do not understand." In such a use of language, words or other ways of signifying (from this striking passage from letter 18) functioned in a linear, denotative, concise, and exclusive referentiality. God's words and God's ways function here in a spatial, connotative, expansive, and inclusive referentiality. Note that it is still a referentiality. In terms of the linguistic triangle I used to represent the earlier denotative conception, however, there is now an effect of the Supreme Signified not only along the legs of the triangle but along the entire base.

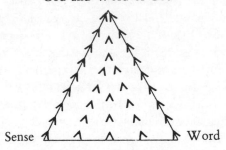

God and Word of God

Sense   Word

In terms of the specific issue being discussed by Pascal, the relation between God's role and man's role in the working of grace, this relation may be expressed not as a triangle but as a vertical line with all human signifiers (words and deeds) at the base and God's action at the top.

Divine Action

Human Action

In both representations the direction of the arrows now expresses a different relation from that of the linguistic triangle as applied to *Provincial Letters* 1–16. There, in insisting on the way the relation between man and God is, Pascal looked at the relation between human action and divine action as one that was to be initiated by man in light of the clear meaning of God's word in Scripture and early fathers: man must always base his words and his deeds on the word of God; meaning comes from God. Here, he speaks from a view of the relation in which the upward directions of the action by man expresses the magnetic attraction of the Supreme Signified; meaning comes back to God—especially the meaning of life itself. The relation is not mechanical as in letters 1–16; it is electronic. Man is attracted not in terms of the metonymic restrictive and reductive notion of referentiality, the reality principle of language informing the earlier letters. Rather, he is pulled in terms of a metaphoric and illimited (*secrettes et admirables*) notion of referentiality, in the name of a pleasure principle.

It is in the name of this pleasure principle that Pascal would formulate the projected *Apology for the Christian Religion* contained in the *Thoughts*. The inclusion in that work of various fragments obviously bearing on the *Provincial Letters* gives evidence of the contemporaneity of the projected *Apology* with the *Provincial Letters* (at some point well into the latter, probably). The very passage under discussion here echoes the motif of pleasures in the famous fragment on the wager, for example. Significantly, however, Pascal does not characterize here, as he does in the fragment on the wager, the relation between the pleasure one finds in God and the pleasures of this world in an adversative fashion. In the wager, the pleasures of this world are described as foul (*empestés*); here the "delectation of the flesh" is expressed as a force that must be "overcome," a magnetism that is countered by the greater magnetism of delectation in God. (Some of the tone of the fragment with respect to pleasure informs the later phrase on man conceiving "disgust for the delights of sin," but all sins are not of the flesh, it should be noted.) Moreover, the pleasure principle is operative at both ends of the relation, in the divine as well as the human. The "celestial sweetness," means by which God "effects this change," indicates that God's will, like man's, carries itself toward that which most pleases it.

Of necessity, for, in Catholic orthodoxy, man is made in the image of God. It is to this orthodoxy that Pascal fully returns, in this passage as in the eighteenth letter as a whole, moving away from his pessimistic emphases and views of the Jesuits and, increasingly as Letters 1–16 progressed, of man in general. Though it is of man *after* the Fall that Pascal is writing here, there is something, if not prelapsarian, then surely eschatologically optimistic about this passage, even as there was something postlapsarian and eschatologically pessimistic about the earlier letters. In his use of the word *man* to designate humanity in this passage there is an inclusiveness that gets away from the restrictive term for the human of the earlier letters dealing with the operations of efficacious grace: the just. The concentration on that term in the earlier letters indicates that the real argument between Pascal and the Jesuits was not on the operation of grace, even if we are to grant that Pascal's notion of that operation had always been that which he elucidates here. Rather, the argument was about whether that operation was effective for all men. His explicit denial of believing in predestination in the seventeenth letter is here corroborated by the implicit inclusiveness of the use of the word *man* in the eighteenth letter. In the literal-minded linguistic conceptions of the first sixteen letters, he lends himself, however much in spite of himself, to a verbal justification of predestinarianism that is gainsaid by the more probing, flexible linguistic and doctrinal positions of the eighteenth letter.

The letter shows him reconciling not only Jesuit and Jansenist but Jansenist and "new Thomist" as well, in a passage that, very likely, finds the associative warrant for such an accommodation in the citation of the scriptural injunction to " 'convert yourself to God . . . and to make yourself a new heart and a new spirit: I will give you a new spirit and I shall create in you a new heart.' " The letter incorporates into the body of the faithful if not Molina himself, at least his defenders: "so that one sees today, by a kind of prodigy, the defenders of efficacious grace and the defenders of Molina, so admirable is the conduct of God to have all things concur in the glory of his truth." Of course, such a concurrence is conditional on the good will of the Jesuits: "You say that you understand the error of Calvin, they reply that they condemn it; and thus, if you do not wish to have to do with the syllables, but with the thing that they signify, you should be satisfied." This is as it should be, Pascal implicitly argues, going over the head of the Jesuits in an appeal to the head of the Church on this earth, the pope. In the elaborate demonstration that occupies so much of this last letter, he shows that many a pope has been wrong on matters of fact. Pascal does not leave his appeal at this purely rhetorical level. He is at great pains to note that popes, more than anyone else, are subject to such errors of fact because they are assaulted on all sides by demands for attention on doctrinal disputes. Such demands oblige them to rely more on hearsay then on direct knowledge of the actual terms of the disputes they are asked to adjudicate. Pascal's appeal to the pope is at once personal and impersonal: personally, it is abhorrent to him to be at odds with the "holy father," as abhorrent as it would be for him to be at odds with his earthly father or his Father in Heaven. Impersonally, he appeals to the pope in the name of those other sons and daughters of the Church who are unjustly cast from the house of the holy father through his practical inability to know their loyalty to and love of him consistently expressed in their words and deeds.

This "impersonal" concern for the members of the Port Royal community perhaps even more than the doctrinal expansiveness of this letter best demonstrates the spirit of inclusiveness and charitableness informing this letter. "For finally," he writes in concluding, "to take things at their worst, even if it were true that Jansen had held these propositions, what misfortune would come from some people doubting it, provided that they themselves detest them, as they do publicly? Is it not enough that the propositions be condemned by everyone without exception, in the very sense that you have explained that you wish them to be condemned? Will they be more censured when it will be said that Jansen held them?" In this closing appeal in the last of the complete and published *Provincial Letters* Pascal concedes what he had made the very issue at dispute from the outset: that the Jansenists did subscribe to the Five Propositions. The text does not specify, but, in the context, we may assume that he meant in both fact and faith. However, they had since publicly detested both fact and (heretical) faith. Clearly, Pascal does not believe his supposition to have any validity in reality. He posits it in a gesture of reconciliation. It is not in the name of the denotative and humanly alienating Saint Cyranian conception of charity that he makes this concession. It is rather in the more usual connotation, the more accommodating and, it could be said, Jesuit sense of charity toward one's fellows that he makes the concession. At the end of the tenth letter the "neutral" reporter explosively dropped his neutrality in exclaiming that there was "no patience that Jesuit excesses would not push to an end." Here the author concludes with astonishment at the patience of the members of the

Port Royal community. This time, however, the astonishment is not at an abuse of language. Rather, it is a figure of a charity toward those victims and their calumniators, toward all of one's fellows that has its source in divine charity.

This charitable concern is resounded in the one-page fragment that would have been the nineteenth in the series. We may speculate that Pascal did not continue the letter because of the formal opposition of the authority figures he most respected on earth, the pope and the king. As Stewart notes, the hostility of both toward the Jansenists and, through decrees from Rome, toward the *Provincial Letters* themselves, was widely reflected in France itself. This is ironical, given Pascal's appeal to the generality, first on narrow linguistic grounds and, in the last two letters, on more inclusive linguistic grounds. As a defender of the faith, he may also have perceived that the strategy of the *Provincial Letters,* particularly of the first sixteen, was, if not mistaken, inappropriate.

9

THE
LETTERS
TO THE
ROANNEZ

THE ADVOCATE of the final *Provincial Letters* had begun to appear in another series of letters written between September 1656 and December of the same year to Charlotte de Roannez, the sister of Pascal's patron, the Duc de Roannez, if not through her to both.[1] To be sure, the concerns of the ongoing struggles with the Jesuits (from the eleventh through the sixteenth *Provincial Letter* of December 4) are reflected in this personal correspondence. Like the *Provincial Letters,* each of these nine, much shorter, personal letters tends to turn around a particular topic: the abominations within the "houses of holiness themselves" (the first letter); separation from worldly attachments, especially personal ones (the second); the difference between God's will and the sinful will of man (the third); God's hiddenness (the fourth); the "new language" of the faithful and "grace" as the "measure of the glory that God prepares in the next . . . for his elect" (the fifth); the Church and Pascal's personal "communion" with it (the sixth); disdain of the honors of this world (the seventh); human inability to live in the present (the eighth); counsels of courage to the beleagured and the weak (the ninth). As even this schematic summary indicates, the topics are treated more personally, as in the sixth letter, on Pascal's communion with the Church. In texture and tone these letters are also in sharp contrast to the *Provincial Letters* contemporaneous with them: relaxed where they are tense, comforting where they are scolding, sensitive where they are stern. The first sentence of the very first informs all nine letters (even those where a certain theological punctilio—the second, fourth, and fifth—is apparent): "Your letter has given me an extreme joy."

Pascal shares his joy with "friends in Christ." Whatever the relations between Blaise Pascal and Charlotte de Roannez may have been (Bishop believes he hoped to marry her),[2] the intensely personal character of these letters is that of a man writing to a woman who, like himself, advocates Jesus Christ. Sadness more than indignation runs through the passages that echo the "abominations" within the "house of holiness itself," the abominations that Pascal excoriates so indignantly in the *Provincial Letters* of this same period. The personal fear of losing Christ and his Church rather than the Jesuits' public scandal of denying them runs through all of these letters:

> The body is no more alive without the head [a reference to the pope] than the head without the body. Whoever separates himself from one or the other is no longer of the body, and no longer belongs to Jesus Christ. I do not know if there are any persons in the Church more attached to this unity of body than are those whom you call ours. We know that all virtues, martyrdom, austerities, and all good works are useless outside of the church and outside of communion with head of the Church, which is the pope.
>
> I shall never separate myself from his communion, at least I pray God for the grace [not] to do so; without which I would be lost forever.   (Sixth letter, November 1656)

The tone of these letters is in such sharp contrast with that of *Provincial Letters* 11–16 that we might wonder if Pascal is not, at best, schizoid and, at worst, two-faced. On the latter count, the difference in tone may be related to that social and rhetorical skill that his sister Gilberte reports (and that he more theoretically brings out in his treatise on "The Art of Persuasion"): an ability to adjust his discourse to the disposition of his interlocutor(s). Given the Jesuits' disposition to bad faith, they deserve the scolding he shows them in the fall of 1656; given the Roannez' disposition to good faith, they merit the comfort he shows them in the same period. All sincere believers (including himself) deserve the consolation that the theological and personal advocacy of the letters to Charlotte provide. That consolation is in and of Jesus Christ. The very writing of these letters, the "extreme joy" of receiving hers (the first letter) and of the "joy of finding God" (seventh letter), recalls the "joy in Christ" that he had known in the *Memorial.* It also adumbrates the "joy in and of Christ" that is the central motif of the *Apology for the Christian Religion* he began, according to Sellier, to contemplate in 1656. In this connection, the letters to

Charlotte seem to me to be a catalyst of the shift from the adversary spirit of the first sixteen *Provincial Letters* to the advocacy of the last two as well as of the projected *Apology*. The Augustinian motif of God's "attractive delectation" is sounded as early as the second letter (September 24) in even more personal terms than in the eighteenth *Provincial Letter*: "It is very sure that one never detaches oneself without pain. One does not feel one's bond [*lien*] when one follows voluntarily the one who draws [*entraîne*], as Saint Augustine says. But when one begins to resist and to walk away [*en s'éloignant*], one truly suffers; the bond stretches and endures all the violence; and this bond is our body, which does not break until death." Charlotte de Roannez is (possibly both she and her brother are), in a Thomistic sense, the occasion of this deeply personal and humanly touching expression of a doctrinal premise Pascal has pronounced before; she is (they are), in a sense that Pascal will magnificently develop in the projected *Apology*, a figure of this expression.

The subject and terms of the fifth letter to this intercessionary figure (November 5, 1656) are especially important in this respect. Implicitly (if not explicitly, as I have suggested) all of the letters may be written to both Charlotte and her brother, but in the fifth he explicitly indicates this plurality: "I do not know why you complain that I have written nothing for you: I do not separate the two of you, and I think incessantly of one and the other." He goes on to record his delight with the "zeal" of his correspondent for "it is altogether new to me; it is the *new langauge* that the *new heart* ordinarily produces. Jesus Christ has given in the Gospel this *mark* to recognize those who have faith, that they shall speak a *new language* (Mc. 15:17) and in effect the renewal of *thoughts* and *desires* causes that of the *discourse*" (my italics here and in the subsequent quotations from the letter). Further on in the same letter, developing the significance of a "miracle," he writes: "It is certain that the graces that God makes in this life are the *measure* of the glory that he prepares in the other" and "I enter in a veneration that overwhelms me with respect toward those whom he *seems to have chosen for his elect*" and, finally, speaking of those who make up the "*unfortunate (malheureux) number of the judged*," "the fright [*effroi*] that I would have to see them in this eternal state of *misery*, after imagining them with so much *reason* in the other state, makes me turn the *mind* (*esprit*) from this idea, and come back to God to pray Him not to *abandon* the weak creatures he has acquired unto himself." The plurality of his concern (both Roannez); graces as a measure or figure of celestial glory; the nuanced awareness that God's act of "election" must be only "seeming"; the perspectives of a "new language" with such terms as *heart, mark, unfortunate, fright, misery, reason, turning (away) of mind, abandon*—these are the linguistic and doctrinal motifs of the projected *Apology*.

That work, as we shall see, is different in spirit and form from the first sixteen *Provincial Letters* and in form if not in spirit from the final two. Formally, all of the *Provincial Letters* may be said to constitute Pascal's finished apology. (The lady of high society of the *Reply* had already given some warrant for the notion of at least the first letter as "an excellent defense" [*apologie*].) I say *finished* in the sense of a coherent, carefully constructed, rather comprehensive work of a kind that the projected apology within the fragments of the *Thoughts* is not. I say apology with respect to the *Provincial Letters* in the sense of a defensive work that apologizes for the positions it evinces. While finishing this "apologetic" *Apology* and while writing to the Roannez, Pascal seems to have arrived at the idea for a nondefensive and non-apologetic apology, an exposition of the "Truths of the Christian Religion" (an alternative title for the project, according to some scholars). By the insights he had gained into the nature of language (of the Jesuits and of all human beings) in the debates with his year-long adversaries of 1656, the projected *Apology* had to be paradoxical, elusive, elliptical, figural, and fragmentary or informal (without form).

10

THE
THOUGHTS

THE BEST-KNOWN presentation of Pascal's *Thoughts* is the edition prepared by the great scholar and historian of philosophy, Léon Brunschvicg (the basis for W. F. Trotter's English translation in the Modern Library edition). It is an arrangement (of the nearly one thousand fragments) emerging from various structures of nineteenth-century thought: philosophies of becoming; liberal-bourgeois undermining of the Ancien Regime with its grandees and Jesuits who seemed to be Pascal's particular targets; Romantic conceptions of a "poetic" Pascal furiously dashing off inspired insights into man's psychological, social, and religious situation; realistic and naturalistic rebellions against classical preoccupations with the impersonality of the author and the perfection of the work of art. However much these structures of thought may have been at odds with each other in other settings, they have conflated to produce the Brunschvicg edition with its image of a secular if not skeptical Pascal, a gloomy, quasi-Hobbesian figure dubious about the validity of his own effort to reconstruct a Christian humanism from the shards of stained glass that are the fragments of his projected *Apology for the Christian Religion*.

True, the Brunschvicg edition does retain Pascal's bipartite plan, as announced in one of the fragments, for a first part on man's misery without God and a second on man's felicity in God. The edition dilutes this fundamental and informing intention in the very order of the fragments though. It is no accident that the first fragment is the reflection on "The Difference between the Mathematical and the Intuitive Mind" (*esprit de géométrie, esprit de finesse*) and that the first subsection in which this reflection occurs deals with various secular reflections on man: his language, his poetry, his passions. This "introduction" to the "The Misery of Man without God" casts Pascal very much in the mold of Montaigne culling quotations and insights from the ancients (Cicero, Martial, Epictetus, and others) and moderns (Montaigne himself, for example) with no apparent philosophical or theological base of his own. The second subsection itself reads very much like a *Treatise on the Passions* in the mold of Descartes' own work of the same name. In a fragment of this section we do find Pascal's celebrated dismissal of Descartes for having been "quite willing to dispense with God" (Br 77), but this fragment does no more than note Descartes' mechanistic deism: God as the First Mover for whom, beyond the first move, no others were required. With the other fragments on Descartes (Br 76, 78–79), the fragment considering theology as a "science" (Br 115) and the 119 other fragments, this early subsection shows us a brilliant psychologist cum sociologist cum philosopher, but hardly an apologist for the Christian religion.

The looseness of the Brunschvicg edition with its inevitable secularism has not satisfied other editors, particularly those of a theological bent. Thus, Jacques Chevalier's 1950 edition (Bibliothèque de la Pléiade) has restored a clear Catholic focus in its arrangement of the fragments. The very first fragment in Chevalier's edition provides the basis for a personal relation between "thoughts on religion" and "thought on other subjects":

> *Order.* Men despise religion. They hate it and are afraid it may be true. The cure for this is first to show that religion is not contrary to reason, but worthy of reverence and respect.
>
> Next make it attractive, make good men wish it were true, and then show that it is.
>
> Worthy of reverence because it really understands human nature.
>
> Attractive because it promises true good.   (Ch 1)

Chevalier presents this introduction as part of a brief general preface subordinating a number of fragments dealing with Pascal's *ordre,* his plan, for the projected *Apology* and then organizes the remaining 800-plus fragments of his edition under the two large parts announced by Pascal, on man "without God" and man "in God." Moreover, through the various religious and philosophical rubrics he has created for relatively short sets of fragments within the overall three-part organization, Chevalier focuses his reader's attention even further on an all-encompassing religious and, more pertinently, proselytizing purpose. Doctrinally speaking, the effect is to present a Pascal who is orthodox, if rather conservative, in his Roman Catholicism. The potentially scandalous implications of Pascal's famous fragment on the wager, for example, are skillfully edulcorated by Chevalier's placement of it only after a humbling of man's pride that borders on a humiliation of man, leaving him desperately flailing about for a lifebuoy, salvation by any means.

Chevalier smooths out Pascal's *Thoughts* in one direction as much as Brunschvicg in another, the one orthodox and rigorous, the other liberal and casual. Each claims to its own universality: Chevalier's catholicism of man's fate *through* all time and beyond, Brunschvicg's liberalism of man's fate *in* time. These universal poles enable us to situate both editorial and interpretive scholarship on Pascal. The Christian rigor of orthodox editions has not appealed to many modern interpreters. The Brunschvicg edition has thus been the most widely used by both amateurs and scholars of whatever religious or philosophical persuasion, for it allows at once for as strict or as loose a construction of Pascal's thought as one wishes.

Yet it seems to me that to continue to use Brunschvicg for any purpose is to cut ourselves off unnecessarily from that access to Pascal's thought that is one of the most important gains of modern editorial scholarship: the restitution of the text of the *Thoughts* as Pascal left it to us. In a paradox that has at last ceased to amaze specialists, if not others, this means not in the autograph manuscript of the so-called *Original Collection* (*Le Recueil original*, the actual fragments handwritten by Pascal or, in some instances, by his secretary and assembled by his nephew, Etienne Périer) but rather in the two copies that had been made of these autographs "as they were," in the words of Etienne, "and in the same state of confusion in which they had been found." That there are *two* copies has, of course, further complicated the interpretation of Pascal's projected *Apology*: are we to respect the *First Copy* (manuscript 9203 at the Bibliothèque Nationale) validated by Louis Lafuma in his edition of 1951 as the original, which, as is clear, served as the basis for the edition of 1670 by Port Royal; or are we to respect the *Second Copy* (manuscript 12449 at the Bibliothèque Nationale) validated by Philippe Sellier in 1976 as the expression of the original copy of the fragments made by Etienne just after his uncle's death. In each case, Etienne's contention (in his preface to the edition of 1670) would *seem* to apply: "The first thing we did was to copy them [the writings] as they were, and in the same state of confusion in which they had been found."

Lafuma's validation of this state of confusion reproduces the two large collections into which Pascal had himself divided these writings: a first part of twenty-seven folders (*liasses*), in which the contents are classified and in a certain order within each separately titled folder; a second part of thirty-four folders, in which the contents are not classified nor the folders titled. Sellier, on the other hand, notes the intrinsic integrity of the *Second Copy*: unlike the *First Copy*, its notes are not in the handwriting of the various collaborators (Arnauld, Nicole, Etienne, and others) who prepared the edition of 1670, but exclusively in that of Etienne. Sellier also stresses the closeness of Etienne to his mother, Pascal's sister Gilberte, who regarded her brother's literary heritage as sacred, and he notes as well the existence of a table of contents (which must, he concludes, have come from Pascal's papers) containing not twenty-seven but twenty-eight titles. The additional one, "Nature Is Corrupt" (*La Nature est corrompue*), obviously indicates, the editor maintains, the incorporation of certain fragments found in Lafuma's unclassified folders within the so-called classified folders. Finally, Sellier traces the evolution of Pascal's project for an *Apology for the Christian Religion*: its first premises are to be found in the fragments on miracles (mid- and late 1656); thus, the *Apology* takes the form of the first twenty-seven folders through 1658, when Pascal's bad health prevented him from continuing the project, but between 1659 and his death (1662) he was able to return to it in the form of a more enriched reflection on the same motifs that take the form of the fragments constituting Lafuma's series of unclassified papers. In sum, for Sellier, the *Second Copy* gives a far more integral and comprehensive original than Lafuma's.[1]

Internally, presented as a nearly finished *Apology*, it enlarges the image of the fervent Christian apologist that emerges from Lafuma's Pascal of the classified papers, both of these obviously differing from the pessimistic, skeptical humanist emerging from Brunschvicg's edition. Within this perpsective Sellier's edition also differs in thrust and emphasis from Lafuma's own "integral edition" (Delmas 1952), in which that editor, still relying exclusively on the *First Copy*, conjectures his own integration of the unclassified fragments into a finished

Apology. In this connection Sellier's conjectures seem to me more solidly based on both external and internal evidence of the complete fragments. They thus provide a more reliable presentation of Pascal's *Apology for the Christian Religion* as he projected it over the period between some point during the writing of the *Provincial Letters* to the end of his life.

The Sellier edition distributes the fragments (814 in all, with certain differently numbered fragments of other editions subsumed into his own numbering) into five different categories dated as carefully as possible on the basis of external and internal evidence

A. The project of 1658, consisting of twenty-eight folders (*liasses*) rigorously apologetic in character.

B. Notebooks (*dossiers*) of the preparatory phase (summer 1656–May 1658, consisting of seven folders of notes toward project A.

C. Folders (*liasses*)of 1659.1662, consisting of six groupings of "mingled [*mêlées*] thoughts," two groupings on "*géométrie / finesse*" and one on authority.

D. The developments of 1659–1662, consisting of seventeen "folders" largely on the "relation between Jewish history ("State of the Jews," "Prophecies," and so on) and Christian history, but also on rhetorical and organizational aspects of the projected *Apology*: "Discourse on the Machine," "Letter for Leading One to Seek God," "Discourse on Corruption."

E. Fragments not registered on the *Second Copy,* conisting of seventy-five fragments found in other editorial presentations since their discovery, many of them bearing on the *Provincial Letters* (including, in fact, the fragment of the nineteenth letter) and other polemical writings such as Pascal's collaboration on the *Writings by the Curates of Paris*) as well as the *Memorial*; and *The Mystery of Jesus.*

Through incisive and often brilliant editorial, historical, and doctrinal grounds Sellier justifies the authenticity of this arrangement as the expression of Pascal's intention for the general lines if not, in fact, approximate expression of his projected *Apology.* All the more rightly so, it seems to me, in that the arrangement expresses the development of Pascal's thought and spirit that I have traced since his "second conversion" and especially in the *Provincial Letters*: from an adversarial to an advocate position, from an exclusionary, argumentative, and denotational conception of language and doctrine to an inclusive, sympathetic, and connotational conception of both.

The first two sets of folders that Sellier presents (A, the project of 1658, and B, notebooks of the preparatory phase), in particular, constitute an apology that is neither defensive nor offensive. In terms of Pascal's overall plan of showing, first, man's misery without God and, then, man's felicity in God, it moves from a sympathetic astonishment at man's failure to take account of the grounds of the misery of *separation* from God to the felicity of *union* with God and of *membership* thereby with others who have been miserable: "to be insensitive so as to scorn interesting things and to become insensitive to the point that interests us the most" is the first fragment of the Sellier edition (S 2, with S 1 being the "Table of Titles" that, as Sellier argues, though not in Pascal's hand, is undoubtedly his, given the scrupulosity of the copier in transcribing what he found). "Members—Begin with that—In order to regulate the love one owes oneself, it is necessary to imagine a body full of thinking members, for we are members of all, and to see how each member ought to love himself," Pascal writes in S 401. This is not the last of the 414 fragments making up the "Project of 1658" but it informs the felicity of "knowing God" that is the thrust of fragments 402–414. The longest of these (S 404) is an extension of the topic of membership: "To be a member," it begins, "is to have life, being, and movement only by the spirit of the body and for the body. The separated member no longer seeing the body to which it belongs no longer has but a being that is perishing and dying." One moves from being "insensitive" to God in these fragments to, in the title of the last fragment (S 414), "The Knowledge [*Connaissance*] of God."

One moves from insensitivity to knowledge. The language recalls the strategy of focusing on language that lay at the heart of the apology implicit in the *Provincial Letters*. As an apology, the major mode of defense in letters 1–16 was adversative, putatively impersonal in the neutrality of the reporter and overtly personal as Pascal defended those personally close to him like his sister, who had become the objects of Jesuit derision. In a large way, the apology of the project of 1658 corresponds in its first part, the "Misery of Man without God" (folders 1–11, fragments S 1–S 179, pp. 31–102) to *Provincial Letters* 1–16, even as its second part, "Man's Felicity in God" (folders 11–28, fragments S 180–S 414, pp. 103–201) corresponds to *Provincial Letters* 17 and 18.

Yet, the quantitative distributions are indicative of a pronounced shift in attitude. The major portion of the *Provincial Letters* had been doctrinally adversative and linguistically literal-minded; the major portion of the Project of 1658 is doctrinally advocative and linguistically figural. However, the very doctrinal and linguistic conceptions to which Pascal had come in the last two letters (17 and 18) indicate that this "large" resemblance between the two apologies is misleading. In the first part of the Project of 1658 there is much of the assaultive formulation of the first sixteen *Provincial Letters*, for example, in the long fragment attacking imagination, which seems but one of the subjects on which Pascal keeps his promise of S 163 in folder 8: "If he boosts himself, I reduce him / If he reduces himself, I boost him / And always contradict him / Until he understands / That he is an incomprehensible monster." However, this assault on man, led by the nose in his unwitting reliance on imagination rather than reason or in his contradictory self-exaltation and self-deflation, is rendered here not in mocking or indignant reaction to his adversary's abusive separation of meaning from word. Rather, Pascal writes in a regretful and sympathetic awareness of man's willful inattention, his willful aversion to relate not only meaning to word but meaning to conduct.

The sign system from which Pascal proceeds in the Project of 1658 (and in the supportive notes of Sellier's grouping of the fragment in B, C, and D) is broadly semantic, elaborating the emphasis on nonverbal and paraverbal signs that informs the seventeenth and eighteenth *Provincial Letters*. The emphasis there (on the pious acts of devotion of the members of Port Royal, on the magnetic pull of God's grace, on the perpetuity and thus the authenticity of all those who share community in God) becomes the strategic and persuasive base from which Pascal addresses his proselytizing project of apologizing for the Christian religion. He no longer argues from fact as he claimed to in letters 1–16 or even from the fact of possibly different interpretations of fact (letter 17); he now argues from faith.

Pascal's reliance on faith dictates the arrangement or ordering of the folders of the Project of 1658. The point to which he regrets seeing so many insensitive in the first fragment is the truth of the Christian religion, as is clear in the subject of the thirty-six fragments making up the first folder and the ten fragments making up the second folder, labeled "Order." He begins in the Christian framework of the felicity in God to which some (including himself) have come before turning to the *problems* of those who have not come thereto. It is a Christian framework, for it is Jesus Christ who will "answer" these problems, as many fragments in these two "framing" folders explicitly indicate (3, 7, 35, 36, 40) and as the other fragments associatively or implicitly indicate. Jesus Christ (as in other evocations of him throughout the fragments in A, B, C, D of Sellier's presentation) is not the Speaker of Laws that he was so often in the *Provincial Letters*. It is not the *word* that he represents (or re-presents; presenting it once again in the name of his Father); it is the very *event* of his coming that is the crucial sign for Pascal here. This order is, historically, the paradoxical disorder of Christ's intrusion into the human condition as a God who is also man.

The fragmentary elucidation of the significance of signs (Christ's coming, the perpetuity in the terms of many a fragment, man's perception of unhappiness emerging from his confrontation with the contradictory; postulates of reasoning or behavior, and so on) was likely to characterize not only the individual stylistic expression of the projected *Apology* but its structural organization as well. The first two folders in Sellier's presentation of the "Project of 1658" contain frequent notations on letters on various subjects (S 27, 38, 39, 41, 45). Two of these notations ("Letter to bring one to the search for God," S 38, and "Letter that underscores the utility of proofs by the machine," S 41) do emerge as coherent "epistles" in Sellier's section D in fragments designated as such (S 681 and S 680, respectively). As Sellier has suggested, Pascal may well have had in mind a finished apology in the form of a series of letters along the lines of the serial presentation of the *Provincial Letters*. However, it seems important to stress that such a seriality would not have proceeded according to the incremental logic of accumulative effect (of horror in 1–10 and to a lesser extent along the same line in 11–16) in the *Provincial Letters*. Rather, as W. G. Moore has said of the "dramaturgical logic" of Molière's *The Misanthrope*, the "logic" would have been "suffusive."[2] The author illustrates from different angles or spotlights the main point posited in each of the two parts of the apology: first, man in his misery without God and, second, man in his felicity in God.

Pascal's own sport metaphor illuminates the strategy of projected *Apology*:

> Let no one say that I have said nothing new. The disposition of subjects is new. When one plays [a game like tennis], it is with one ball that one and the other play, but one places it better.

I would prefer to be told that I used old words. And as if the same
thoughts did not form another body of discourse by a different disposition, so the same words form other thoughts by their different disposition.   (S 575)

Here is an openness toward the new that the Pascal of the *Provincial
Letters* had so proscribed. This openness does not extend to new
words, however. The words upon which he insists are still the old
ones drawn from the Scriptures and the early fathers. The words as
such are not the main thing: the ball is still "one," it is with an "old"
ball in the game of eternity that he and his adversary play. It is the *placing* of the ball that counts in the civilized and unbloody game to which
he compares his enterprise here. Pascal varies (and dazzles) his opponent with a seemingly infinite array of returns and reactions to the opponent's vanity, his reliance on Descartes and philosophers in general,
his need for diversion. Pascal is neither so aggressive nor so confused as
his opponent: he serves without "fault" and without fear of being able
to return the opponent's return of his own initially straightforward
placement of the ball in the opponent's center court. he shows us an
opponent with some sense of worthiness (the fragments on gambling
in the Project of 1658, buttressed in the famous elucidation of the
wager in the "Discourse on the Machine" [S 680]), but Pascal culminates with a series of placements unreturnable for their power, the
spin of paradox on the ball, and their variety, unreturnable certainly
by an opponent whose repertory of return is now exhausted (the fragments on "Knowledge of God").

On the court of eternity where Pascal conducts the tennis lesson of
his *Apology for the Christian Religion,* he seeks not to win *against* but to
win *over* his opponent, "over" to a different disposition or style. He
does not seek to dominate his opponent as he had in *Provincial Letters*
1–16, but to attract him to a style with a greater possibility of his winning the match. Winning is a possibility only, since the outcome depends not upon the style itself (and, surely, Pascal's theology tells him,
not upon the teacher); it depends on God's gift of grace to the player
for him to adopt this more effective disposition. This is a gift the opponent is capable of receiving so long as he is willing to play for keeps.
All and any opponents are capable. To be sure, Pascal does not avoid
the issue of whether the match has been set against the opponent
from the outset. The doctrine of predestination, the election of some

and not others, with which Pascal had flirted in various earlier writings (especially, the first three *Provincial Letters*), seems an unbeatable serve against which only the most foolish opponent would match himself. However, the concept of the elect is used sparingly in the *Thoughts,* particularly in the Project of 1658 as presented in the Sellier edition (S 11 and S 268), and the context neither explicitly not implicitly permits of a predestinarian interpretation: "And yet to affirm the hope of his elect in all time, he makes them see the image thereof [of his coming], without ever allowing them without assurances of his power and his will for their salvation" (S 11); "There is enough clarity to illuminate the elect and enough obscurity to humiliate them. There is enough obscurity to blind the reproved and enough clarity to condemn them and render them inexcusable" (S 268). The concept of election operates not a priori, but ex postfacto — after the life of those who are elected as well as of those who have been reproved at the end of time. Both lives are the ground from which their final and eternal state will be decided by God.

The life each lives will have been of the choosing of each. It is not a choice, of course, in the Pelagian sense that Pascal so exacerbatedly attributed to the Jesuits in the first sixteen *Provinical Letters,* but, rather, according to the pleasure principle that constituted his explanation of the "cooperative" relation between divine will and human will in the eighteenth *Provincial Letter.* "Second Part: That man without faith cannot know the true good, nor justice . . . All men seek to be happy. That is without exception, whatever means they employ." (S 181) Significantly, this evocation of the pleasure principle is the premise from which Pascal will argue the second major part of his apology. The premise is one to which Pascal has clung at least since his second conversion, as we see in several fragments of section E (the fragments not registered on the Second Copy, but all dating from at least the earliest *Provincial Letters,* several dealing directly with the Jesuits): in S 648 (on the distinctions between *géométrie* and *finesse* and on authority, but also obviously extensions and deepenings of the rhetorical and doctrinal concerns of the projected *Apology*); and in S 681 (section D in Sellier) whose significance, by title and content ("Letter to bring one to seek God"), to the Project of 1658 I have already noted. Thus:

> We suffer only in proportion to that vice, which is natural to us,
> [which] resists supernatural grace; our heart feels itself torn between

these contrary efforts. But it would be very unjust to impute this violence to God, who draws us, instead of attributing it to the world, which holds us back. It is like a child whom a mother wrests from the arms of robbers: he must love, in the pain that he is suffering, the loving and legitimate violence of her who procures his freedom, and only detest the imperious and tyrannical violence of those who hold him back unjustly   (S 753)

Whence comes it then that it is glorious to reason to succumb under the impact of pain, and that it is shameful to it to succumb under the impact of pleasure? It is that it is not pain that tempts and draws us. It is ourselves who voluntarily choose it and wish to have it dominate us, so that we are master of the thing; and in that, it is man who succumbs to himself. But in pleasure, it is man who succumbs to pleasure. Now, there is only mastery and empire who makes for glory, and servitude that makes for shame.   (S 648)

This neglect in a matter where it is a question of themselves, of their eternity, of their all, irritates me more than it softens me. It astonishes and frightens me: it is a monster for me. I do not say that out of the pious zeal of spiritual devotion. I mean, on the contrary, that one should have this feeling out of an interest that is purely human and out of an interest of self-love. To see that it is necessary to see only what the least enlightened people see.

One need not have the most elevated soul to understand that there is not here true and solid saisfaction, that all our pleasures are but vanity, that our hardships [maux] are infinite, and that, finally, death, which threatens us at every moment, must infallibly place us, in a few years, in the horrible necessity of being eternally either nullified or unhappy. (S 681)

And later in the same fragment: "Men love naturally only what can be useful to them"   (S 681).

Pascal's insistence on a pleasure principle inherent in human nature ("out of an interest that is purely human and of an interest of self-love," S 681) may seem hardly Christian and more an anticipation of that moral sense that Gary Wills has posited, in his book on Thomas Jefferson's philosophical roots (*The Inventing of America*), by the Scottish philosophers of the late seventeenth and early eighteenth centuries.[3] Yet, for all the similarity, it should be noted that Pascal's moral sense is not only self-directed (in Hutcheson and others who influenced Jefferson, it is "other-directed," seeking good for the oppressed and the suffering); it is also misdirected, for the object to

which, as Pascal sees it, man directs his search for pleasure is inadequate and, ultimately, illusory in both time and quality. To the extent
that we may include S 681 within the *Apology* (as warranted by its
promised inclusion in the notation of the subject in S 38 and again S 45
of the "Project"), we understand that the naturalistic base of his concern here is to be subsumed and subordinated to the thrust of the entire first major part of the *Apology*. There, the use of "reason" and
"nature" is to demonstrate that there is no natural or rational grounds
on which to deny faith as the pleasure toward which man succumbs.

The proof does not come from an unaccustomed (and difficult) turning of the head of the kind that Pascal posits as a way of understanding
the principles of geometry (S 670). It is not a manner of turning the
head in order to succumb to the magnetic pull of God's grace. It is
more a matter of lowering one's head, of subjecting reason once it has
demonstrated in and of itself its final inadequacy to deal with the ends
of pleasure it so foolishly assigns to itself. The supreme faculty on
which the Pascal of the Project of 1658 and its related and increasingly
more sophisticated notes depend is the heart. It "has reasons that
reason does not know" (S 680, a formulation summarizing the extended "Discourse on the Machine" in Sellier's edition). In the
Apology, the heart is at once an instrument of knowledge and an order
of knowledge, a marked difference from its agency in the first sixteen
Provincial Letters. There it tended to be presented as the order of charity
in the Saint Cyranian restrictiveness that we have noted: the love that
was God as an order and the instrument that was man's obligation to
that order, however difficult the obligation be in view of man's separation from God and his confusion and resentment toward God's seeming injustice. In the *Apology,* it is the instrument through which man
relates to his world in all his thinking and doing, and it is the order
from which he has strayed in the very misuse of heart as instrument.
Yet, as the operations of the heart as order delineated in the *Apology*
indicate, the heart operates there as well as an instrument.

The polyvalence of the heart as order and instrument in all of man's
relations, immanent and transcendent, is a crucial instance of the shift
toward the connotational and inclusive that marks the linguistic and
doctrinal stance of the *Apology* in relation to the *Provincial Letters. Instinct, reason, sentiment, will, concupiscence,* are all so many manifestations
of the operations of the *heart* as an instrument. The ideal state can be

grasped in those two major formulations that Pascal gives of the distinctions between the orders:

> The infinite distance from bodies to minds figures the distance infinitely more infinite of minds to charity, for it is supernatural.
>
> All the brilliance of grandeur has no luster for those who are in the researches of the mind.
>
> The grandeur of people of mind is invisible to kings, to the rich, to captains, to all these people of the flesh.
>
> The grandeur of wisdom, which is nothing if not of God, is invisible to the carnal and to people of the mind. They are three different orders. In kind.   (S 339)

> *Concupiscence of the flesh, concupiscence of the eyes, pride,* and so on.
> There are three orders of things: flesh, mind, will.
> The carnal are the rich, Kings: they have as [their] object the body.
> The curious and scientists: they have as [their] object the mind.
> The wise: they have as [their] object justice.
> God must reign over all and relate all to himself.
> In the things of the flesh there reigns appropriately concupiscence.
> In mental things [*les spirituels*], curiosity appropriately.
> In wisdom, pride appropriately.
> It is not that one cannot be glorious for goods [of the world] or for learning [*connaissances*], but it is not the place for pride. For in granting to a man that he is a scientist, one cannot cease from convincing him that he is wrong to be prideful [*superbe*].
> The appropriate place for pride is wisdom. For one cannot accord to a man that he has made himself wise and that he is wrong to be glorious. That is a matter of justice.
> Also God alone gives wisdom. And that is why "he who glorifies himself glorifies himself in the Lord alone"   (2 Corinthians 10:17). (S 761)

This is the way things ought to be. However, after the Fall, "Nature is corrupted" (fragments 35, 40, and elsewhere) and a disastrous synonymy characterizes man's operations in all three orders: "All of our reasoning reduces itself to a surrender to feeling" (S 455); "The casuists submit the decision to the corrupted reason and the choice to the corrupted will, so that all that is corrupted in the nature of man has a part in his behavior" (S 498); and "Will is thus depraved. If the members of natural and civil communities tend toward the good of the body, communities themselves ought to tend toward another more general body of which they are members. One should tend toward the general. We are born therefore unjust and depraved" (S 680). Pascal's views on the corruption of nature in the Project of 1658 and on the depravity and corruption of will in other fragments reflect the more formal rhetorical concern with the epistemological and psychological grounds from which one should seek to persuade others in Pascal's treatise entitled "On the Art of Persuasion"[4]

> No one is unaware that there are two entries by which opinions are received in the soul, which are its two principal powers, the understanding [entendement] and the will. The most natural is that of the understanding, for one should never consent but to demonstrated truths, but the most ordinary, although against nature, is that of the will; for all that there are of men are almost always carried off to believe not by proof, but by pleasing [l'agrement].
>
> This way is lowly, unworthy, and strange: thus everyone disavows it. Each professes to believe and even to love only that which he knows merits it.
>
> I am not speaking of divine truths, which I would be far from putting under the art of persuasion, for they are infinitely beyond nature: God alone can put them in the soul and in the way that pleases him.
>
> I know that he wished that they enter from the heart into the mind, and not from the mind into the heart, in order to humiliate this prideful [superbe] power of reasoning, which claims to have to be the judge of the things that the will chooses, and in order to cure this infirm will, which has totally corrupted itself by its filthy [sales] attachments.

The coupling of these Pascalian premises on the art of persuasion with the preceding reflctions on the spirit of geometry suggests a dating not of 1657–58 (Lafuma) but of 1659–1662, when, in Sellier's arrangement of the fragments, Pascal extensively develops the distinctions between the geometric spirit and the spirit of finesse (S 670, 671, 690). However, whether of the preparatory phase for the Project of 1658 or of the developments of 1659–62, it is clear that Pascal's purpose in projecting an *Apology for the Christian Religion*" is not to convert but to divert, not to prove but to disprove, not to demonstrate but to remonstrate. Conversion, proof, and demonstration in the things of the heart are to be left where they "appropriately" belong: to God.

The epistemological difference with Descartes could not be more striking. I have already noted the psychological differences between Descartes and Pascal. In calling attention to the epistemological differences between the two, I do not mean to locate these differences in the overthrow of the father-figure by the younger epistemologist. Such psychological imperatives have, as I indicated in my review of the texts of Pascal's conversion, been themselves overthrown. Rather, the issue is fully philosophical. The thrust of the first part of this treatise, the section on the spirit of geometry, is Pascal's implied rejection of the central concerns of Descartes in such works as *Rules for the Direction of the Mind* (originally in Latin, 1628, later in French: *Règles pour la direction de l'esprit*) and *The Discourse on Method* (*Le Discours de la méthode*, 1637). In particular, the Descartes of *Rules for ...* is particularly concerned to ground ideas in a chain of reasoning in which the reasoner retains, clear to his mind, every step of the process of reasoning. To such an intellectual ambition Pascal implicitly replies in his treatise on geometry. Although he acknowledges that man is "in a natural and immutable impuissance to treat of whatever science in a fully accomplished order," it does not follow that one must abandon any idea of order, for:

> There is one, and it is that of geometry, which is, in truth, inferior in that it is less convincing, but not in that it is less certain. It does not define all and it does not prove all, and it is in that that it yields; but it does suppose only clear and constant things by natural light, and that is why it is perfectly truthful, nature supporting it for want of discourse. This order, the most perfect among men, consists not in defining everything nor in demonstrating everything, nor even in defining nothing or demonstrating nothing, but in holding to this middle of not defining things clear to and understood by all men, and defining all the others; and in not defining all the things known by men, and in proving all the others. Against this order sin equally those who undertake to define and to prove everything and those who neglect to do so in things that are not self-evident.

Not only in the order of the heart but in the order of the mind as well, Pascal finds that Descartes' philosophy is not worth an hour of one's time (S 118). The older philosopher lacks faith in the existence of a "primary model" on which discourse, whether scientific or other, is to be based. Not surprisingly, certain of his adepts, if not he himself, come to regard the secondary modeling system of language to be the only model—indeed, to the point that the notion of model itself becomes meaningless, because language becomes a purely intrareferential system that generates a plurality and, potentially, an infinity of models. I say "if not he himself," because in the *Discourse on Method*

(Part IV), seemingly aware of this aporesis as he wonders whether his clear and distinct ideas have come to him in sleep (dream) rather than in waking (reality), Descartes can have recourse only to a God-Guarantor. Pascal does not regress so immediately to this epistemological mediator; for him the God-Guarantor has provided in and through nature itself such mediation. That this mediation has been corrupted or diverted only makes the task of the apologist for the Christian religion more difficult, but not impossible. In the face of the postlapsarian diversion of nature, the apologist must meet diversion with diversion, use the very instability of language to restore man to that stability it originally signified.

The apologist can only divert man from man's own diversions from the order of the heart; the apologist can only disprove man's "prideful power of reasoning"; the apologist can only remonstrate man for the "filthy attachments" of his "infirm . . . depraved . . . corrupted will." He can only show, not to say "show up," the automatic, mechanical, habitual, customary, and postlapsarian natural operations of the three great rivers of fire:

> "All that is of the world is concupiscence of the flesh or concupiscence of the eyes or pride of life." *Libido sentiendi, libido sciendi, libido dominandi.* Unhappy [*malheureuse*] the world [*la terre*] of malediction that these three rivers of fire enflame rather than water. Happy those who, being on these three rivers, not plunged therein, not dragged along, but immobilely firm on these rivers, not standing, but seated, in a low and secure seat, from which they do not arise before the light, but after having rested themselves there in peace, tender the hand to the one who must raise them up in order to hold them upright and firm in the porches of the Holy Jerusalem, where pride can no longer combat and beat them down! And yet who cry, not for seeing the sinking of all these perishable things that these torrents carry along, but in the memory of their dear fatherland [*patrie*], of the Heavenly Jerusalem, which they remember uncreasingly in the longness of their exile.

This magnificent passage, with its Augustinian gloss on the text from Saint John (I: 2, 16) at its beginning coupled with Pascal's view of the corrupted will, shows that, in his fallen state, man has calqued onto the ideal linguistic triangle his own corrupted version of it.

The lines of force, as in the ideal and more sophisticated graph of the triangle I have derived from the eighteenth *Provincial Letter,* move upward from the orders of flesh and mind, magnetically and inevitably

libido dominandi (Will)

libido sentiendi   *libido sciendi*
(Flesh)   (Mind)

drawn by the force of the will to dominate that is a corruption of both God's will to love and be loved and man's will to love and be loved. Man seeks to dominate his fellow man in the acts of the flesh (ambition, sexual desire, avarice, dress, material possessions, among them) and in the acts of the mind (the researches of the spirit).

The author of the projected *Apology* is not unaware of his own submission to this corrupted magnetic pull: "Vanity is so anchored in the heart of man that a soldier, a churl, a cook, a porter boasts and wants to have his admirers, and philosophers themselves want to have them, and those who write against [*them*: philosophers? *it*: vanity?] want to have the glory of having written well, and those who read them want the glory of having read them, and I who write this perhaps have this desire [*envie*], and perhaps those who will read it . . ." (S 520). Given the generality, the universality and the absoluteness of Pascal's premise, his use of "perhaps" with respect to his own motivation may be read as still another sign of his effort to escape from his deconstruction of all discourse, including his own even as he writes of deconstruction. However, as in his reliance in purely intellectual operations on first sentiments (as opposed to Descartes' vain pursuit of first principles), so here, in the context of the projected *Apology,* his use of "perhaps" is anchored in the personal conviction of the good faith of his enterprise. It proceeds from a faith in God for which he is thankful to God:

> I love poverty, because he loved it. I love goods [of this world], because they provide means of helping the unfortunate [*misérables*]. I keep faith [*fidélité*] with everybody. I do not return evil to those who

do it unto me, but I wish them a condition like mine, where one does not receive evil nor good from men. I strive to be just, truthful, sincere, and faithful to all men. And I have a kindness of heart [*tendresse de coeur*] for those to whom God has united me more closely. And though I be alone, or seen by men, I have in all my actions the sight of God, who must judge them and to whom I have consecrated all of them.

    These are my sentiments.   (S 759)

This moving text is placed by Sellier in the "Fragments Not Registered" on the *Second Copy*, on which he bases his edition. Its chronological relation to the Project of 1658 and the related fragments of the registered fragments of the period 1656–1662 (sections A through D in Sellier) cannot be firmly established. Its spirit may be said to confirm the sympathetic and communitarian thrust of all those fragments, however. Sellier notes that at the beginning of this fragment there is a sentence that has been struck out: "I love all men as my brothers, because they have all been redeemed."5 It is possible that a theological punctilio may have impelled Pascal to strike out this sentence, for it presumes to know what only God can know: who has been saved. However, the pronominal aspect of many fragments that are part of or related to the Project of 1658 clearly show that Pascal is no longer writing in the exclusionary and theologically punctilious vein of the first sixteen *Provincial Letters*: "we . . . our . . . us." Again, in many other fragments, he speaks of "Man . . . all . . . one . . ." in a nonrestrictive syntax. Thus:

> Then *one shall no longer teach his neighbor, saying* 'Here is the Lord,' FOR GOD SHALL MAKE HIMSELF FELT BY ALL. YOUR SONS SHALL PROPHESY. I shall put My spirit and my fear IN YOUR HEART.
>
>   All that is the same thing.
>
>   To prophesy, it is to speak of God not by proofs from without but by sentiment that is interior and IMMEDIATE.   (S 360)

The interior and immediate sentiment is made known by God to all. If all do not act on this sentiment, the fault is not with God but with those among the all who do not act on it.

    The *all* are made up, necessarily and logically for Pascal, of three kinds: "There are only three kinds of people: those who serve God having found him, others who work at [*s'emploient*] at seeking him not having found him, others who live without seeking him nor having found him. The first are reasonable and happy, the last are foolish [*fous*] and unhappy, those in the middle are unhappy and reasonable" (S 192). The motif of the reasonableness that the first and the second kinds of people share is paradoxically reformulated in S 681, the "Letter to bring one to seek God":

Nothing is more cowardly than to play the hero [*faire le brave*] against God. Let them leave these impieties to those who are ill-born enough to be truly capable of it; let them be at least honest men [*honnêtes hommes*], if they cannot be Christians! And let them finally acknowledge that there are only two kinds of people that one can call reasonable: either those who served God with all their heart because they know Him, or those who seek him with all their heart because they do not know him.

In the context of the *Apology* the expression "with all their heart" is more than a synonym for "earnestly" or "sincerely." It is an instance of the epistemological axis around which the suffusive spokes of the wheel of the *Apology* are organized; it is the instrument by which they will know the order in which all meaning is to be found, the order of charity, of the heart, of the uncorrupted will, of the "state of nature" before nature was corrupted and thus became itself a custom: "I very much fear that this nature be itself but a first custom, as custom is a second nature" (S 159). In perhaps his greatest paradox Pascal finds warrant for urging man to prepare his soul for the possible entry of faith (*possible*: the decision is God's) by obliterating the distinction between nature or instinct and custom or habit:

You want to go to faith and you do not know the route? You want to cure yourself of infidelity and you ask for the remedies? Learn from those who have been bound [*liés*] like you and who bet now on their good [*bien*]: they are people who know this route that you want to follow and [have been] cured of a malady [*mal*] of which you wish to be cured. Follow the way by which they have begun; it is in doing all as if they believed, in taking holy water, in having masses said, and so on. *Naturally* even that will make you believe and will *bestify* you [my emphasis] (S 680)

The passage comes from the famous exposition of the wager, an exposition presented as a fragment under that rubric by some editors and commentators but which, as Sellier stresses in a note,[6] is a part of the

"Discourse on the Machine," that is, on the use of custom or habit as a way of bringing man to the threshold of belief. Before that threshold, as Pascal points out in the "Discourse," man behaves *automatically and naturally,* whatever the objects of his will. He wagers on all objects that he chooses for the realization of the pleasure principle that guides the operation of his nature, whether before or after the Fall. As Pascal tells this bettor in spite of himself the only difference (the crucial one, of course), is in the character, quality, and durability of the objects you have heretofore proposed yourself and those I here propose to you.

I: Pascal is an authority in the matter, but it is not the authoritative Pascal, adversary of Dominican and Jesuit of the first sixteen *Provincial Letters*. That Pascal tended to pit word against word rather than heart against heart, writing with increasing indignation at the sight and sound of a human nature that ought not to behave as if "all surrenders to sentiment." The authority who "reasons" with the bettor in spite of himself in the *Apology* is not the adversary of the bettor; he is his advocate, one whose authority is not doctrinal or bookish or verbal but personal: "If this discourse please you and seem strong to you, know that it is made by a man who has put himself on his knees beforehand and afterward, in order to pray this Infinite and Indivisible Being, to whom he submits all that is his, to submit to himself yours as well, for your own good for his glory, and that force thus accord with this lowliness" (S 680). The apologist does not convert; he testifies to the limited utility or exemplary futility of reason as such.

He also testifies to the utility of self-stultification as a preliminary condition of the only way by which man can acquire faith:

> There are three means of believing: reason, custom, inspiration. The Christian religion, which alone is right [*raison:* the play of terms also allows the translation 'has reason'], does not admit for its true children those who believe without inspiration. It is not that it excludes reason and custom; on the contrary; but it is necessary to open one's mind to proofs, to confirm oneself thereto by custom, but offer oneself by humiliations to the inspirations, which alone can have the true and salutary effect. *Ne evacuetur crux Christii* ['the virtue of the Cross is not to be voided'] (1 *Corinthians*, 1:17. (S 655)

It is out of this personal inspiration that the apologist appeals to the bettor to "humiliate" and "submit" his reason, to "bestify himself." Not inappropriately, the pseudonym Pascal gives himself in this fragment is Salomon de Tultie, he who is wise (Solomon) out of stupidity (from the Latin, *stultus*). The power of the order of mind, including his own, is as nothing compared to the simplicity of the order of faith.

It is to the possible reception of this faith that he constructs his *Apology* for "reasonable and unhappy" readers, "those in the middle" as he puts it in S 192. The characterization, coupled with the communal first person plurality in which he describes man's universal condition, suggests that these are the largest number. There may be few who are both reasonable and happy because they have found God, but this is not because of some predestinarian premise underlying Pascal's theology. Rather, it follows logically from the historical situation of man before and in history; of man on earth or in nature after his fall from paradise. By the same token, given man's inherent and necessary natural disposition to seek pleasure, it is reasonable to presume that most men are capable of being shown or reminded of their misery and of the unreasonableness of the customary ways in which they seek to relieve that misery. The characterization of those who have not found and yet do not seek as "foolish and miserable" is of a piece with this axiological and epistemological premise. They are foolish in the etymological sense of the term *fous*: they are in folly, they are unreasonable, they are madmen. The generality is not made up of madmen, not even if justice depends on force (S 135 and others); not even if the reasonable forms of social interaction men have come up with are, historically, under the aegis of "this beautiful reason that has corrupted all" (S 94). This is the best justice we can have "after the Fall." It is thus neither unreasonable nor cruel of him to "revile those [atheists] who parade it [*invectiver contre ceux qui en font vanité*]" (S 188). Invective against mad and miserable atheists is as warranted by God and man as was mockery and raillery against the contumelious and calumniating Jesuits (eleventh *Provincial Letter*).

Yet invective is not the informing spirit of the Project of 1658 nor of the clearly related fragments (Sellier sections B–D). There is some invective, stinging traces of the adversary spirit of the first sixteen *Provincial Letters* in several fragments obviously related to the Jesuits not registered on the *Second Copy* (Sellier, section E). But in the *Apology* (Sellier sections A through D) it is not for the Jesuits as such that Pascal writes. He writes for the sincere seekers. It is a long-standing assumption of Pascal commentary to assume that these are the libertines, the free thinkers, the atheists who had been the object of theological hostility throughout the century, the most notorious being the poet Théophile de Viau (1590–1626?), the defendant against charges of atheism in one of the most famous trials of the century (1623–1625). Interestingly, his principal prosecutor was the Jesuit Garasse, one of Pascal's specific targets in the *Provincial Letters* but also a theologian, who, like Pascal, sensed the indissoluble link between spiritual libertinism (*libertinage d'esprit*) and libertinism in mores (*libertinage de moeurs*), between atheism and debauchery.[7] However, it is striking to note that in the complete text of the *Thoughts* (Sellier edition) the term *libertinism* occurs only in the section of unregistered fragments (nor are there other substantive or adjectival instances) and that, like the majority of the final fragments therein, it is related to the *Provincial Letters:*

> One does not live a long time in open impiety, nor naturally in great austerity.
> An accommodating religion is appropriate for enduring.
> One seeks them by libertinism.   (portion of S 789)

From the content of other entries included under this fragment — Kings, Pope, *Third Request* (a text by a Jesuit, Hospinianus, authorizing the killing of kings and princes whom the pope or the Jesuits consider heretical) — we might place this fragment as early as the seventh letter, on homicide, or as late as the seventeenth and eighteenth, with their preoccupations with papal and royal opposition to the *Provincial Letters* themselves. This "Jesuit" context suggests the possibility that the "them" to whom Pascal alludes in the last sentence are those people who are referred to in the first sentence: (*everybody,* as the pronoun "one" indicates!) and it is a "libertine," "accommodating" religion that one provides for them. In this reading, the derisive overtones of *libertinism* are most marked. On the other hand, *them* may refer to the religions that would be appropriate to those people. In this sense the overtones of *libertinism* are derisive, but the derision is directed not only at the Jesuits who provide such a religion but to the manner in which people seek such a religion. Both readings, however, but especially the second, permit a reading of the text in the following sense in the context of Pascal's projected *Apology*: there is nothing wrong with seeking an accommodating religion, but one must find one that is truly responsive to the conditions posited in describing the two ways in which one lives (neither a long time in great impiety nor a long time in great austerity). The Christian religion is accommodating or responsive to these conditions in that it is the only religion that describes them accurately, providing, first, the explanation of one's inability to live in great impiety in demonstrating the corruption of nature that drives one to a spiritually *and* naturally exhausting, unendurable, and thus unenduring "impiety"; and, second, a remedy for this unendurable and unenduring impiety that posits a relief that cannot be of enduring austerity because the endurance in austerity depends not on man but on God, on the constancy of his granting of grace to live in austerity and piety. In this sense, if it is to combat libertinism that Pascal projected his great *Apology*, that libertinism is not the philosophy of particular thinkers (the so-called libertines of the period); it is to combat the libertinism of the human condition inherent therein since the Fall of man from the state of grace. In this light, it may be said that Pascal is not writing for or against the formal set of libertine thinkers of the time, those who proclaim their atheism and debauchery. It is against those alone, as we have seen, that he will inveigh, those alone whom he will revile.

But his spirit is not of the inveigher, the reviler; it is that of the illuminator and the consoler. He will even "begin by crying for [*plaindre*] the unbelieving [*incrédules*]. They are unhappy enough in their condition. It would be necessary to offend [*injurier*] them only in the case where it would be of use. But that [their condition] does them harm" (S 194). Should the unbelieving boast of their unhappy condition, they become mad, as we have seen, and thus deserve the little attention they do in fact receive in the *Apology*, for one cannot have a *reasonable* discussion with a madman. Better to reason with that majority who are libertine by corrupted nature, by custom, by flaccid accommodation, by that *sentiment* to which rationality (rather than reasonableness) cedes all. These people will be able to see that, in its reliance on languages, rationality fails to see that "languages are ciphers [*chiffres*], where it is not letters that are changed into letters, but words into words. So that an unknown language is indecipherable" (S 465); that "those who make antitheses in forcing words are like those who make false windows for the sake of symmetry. Their rule is not to speak justly, but to make just figures" (S 466); that "morality and language are particular sciences, but universal" (S 598); that "the last end is what gives names to things" (S 738). Now, Pascal is not concerned with proving that the last end is real, that God does exist. The *Apol-*

ogy is not written to answer atheists, to combat their denial of God's existence nor those who "blaspheme the Christian religion . . . in imagining that it consists simply in the adoration of a God considered great, powerful, and eternal: which is properly deism, almost as distant from Christian religion as atheism, which is altogether its opposite" (S 690). The *Apology* is for the *Christian religion*; it is written to underscore the consolation of Christ's coming.

For the Pascal of the first sixteen *Provincial Letters*, "in the beginning was the Word." The literal-minded, denotative opposition of the "Word of God" to the "words" of the Dominicans and especially the Jesuits showed us an apologist more concerned with God's justice than with God's mercy. The frequent invocation of the New Testament did indicate Pascal's essentially Christocentric religious outlook. Christ was "present" for Pascal there in a largely verbal way, even as he was absent from the verbality of Pascal's adversaries. And yet, Christ's mediation of man and God was largely mediated by recourse to the early doctors, of the "old" doctrine as greater warrant for Christian conduct than the new of Jesuit doctrine. Further, in his verbal sparring with the new Jesuit *fathers* through citation of the old Church fathers, both psychologically and doctrinally Pascal emerged as more Father-centered and deicentric than filicentric and Christocentric. The Christian *view*, in the most sense-oriented meaning of that word, was thus blocked: the rulings of Christ as authoritatively derived by the fathers of the Church obscured the rule of Christ by his sheer presence on this earth.

The presence of Christ in the *Apology* is quantitatively and qualitatively overwhelming. As we have seen from the texts on his conversion, the meaning of that presence in Pascal's own life cannot be underestimated. It had annulled the egocentric, arrogant, adversarial stance in which he had related to family, world, and, in reprise of the stance even after the conversion, to his coreligionists and their adversaries. The meaning of that presence in the *Apology* is as signal: Christ is invoked as the occasion for the release of self from self; He annuls the logocentric, facilely accommodating, political, and naturalistic "theology" of all who would provide answers to the sincere seekers who are Pascal's intended readers.

Nature is corrupt
Without Jesus Christ man must be in vice and misery.

With Jesus Christ man is exempt from vice and misery.
In him is all our virtue and all our felicity.
Outside of him there is only vice, misery, error, shadow,
death, despair.   (S 35)

This fragment from the Preamble folder, a table of contents, looks forward to numerous fragments in the Project of 1658 of which I give two of the most moving and doctrinally important:

God through Jesus Christ

We know God only through Jesus Christ. Without this mediator all communication with God is lost [ôtée], through this mediator we know God. All those who have claimed to know God and to prove it without Jesus Christ had but impotent proofs. But to prove Jesus Christ we have the prophecies, which are solid and palpable proofs. And these prophecies having been accomplished and proved true by events mark the certitude of these truths and thereby the truth of the divinity of Jesus Christ. In him and through him we therefore know God. Outside of that and without the Scriptures, without original sin, without a necessary mediator, promised and come, one cannot prove God absolutely nor teach either good doctrine or good morality. But through Jesus Christ and in Jesus Christ one proves God and one teaches morality and doctrine. Jesus Christ is therefore the true God of men.

But we know at the same time our misery, for this God is nothing if not the Repairer of Our Misery. Thus we can know God only in knowing our iniquities. Also, those who have known God without knowing their misery have not glorified him, but have glorified themselves. "Those who had not known him through wisdom, it pleased God to save by the madness of his predication" (I Corinthians I: 21.) (S 221)

I admit that one of these Christians who believe without proof will perhaps not have something to convince an infidel who will say as much of his [God]. But those who know the proofs of religion will prove without difficulty that this believer is truly inspired of God, although he cannot prove it himself.

For God having said through his prophets, who are undoubtedly prophets, that in the reign of Jesus Christ he would spread his spirit over the nations and that the sons, the daughters, and the children of the Church would prophesy, it is without a doubt that the spirit of God is upon those and that it is not upon the others.   (S 414)

The knowledge of God is, for the Pascal of the *Apology*, not only the knowledge of his existence; pagans and Jews, as so many fragments both in the Project of 1658 and the related dossiers attest, "know" God in that sense. It is to *know* him as a God of love, to *love* him as a God of love.

Such knowledge can come only through figures. The broadened and enriched relation between signifiers and signified that I have traced in discussing the eighteenth *Provincial Letter* finds it most complete application in the *Apology* in all those figures that signify Jesus Christ: perceptions of time and event that signify the figure of Jesus Christ. Words and propositions as such do not figure in this figuration—the Prophecies and the Miracles on whose significance Pascal insists throughout show that—but prophecies and figures "prove" through marking rather than convincing, for it is by "sentiment that is interior and immediate" that one is able to "discern" the figural truth of prophecy and miracle (and to distinguish between true and false among them). Through the *un-mediated* awareness of our own misery we find the ground for God's granting, should he so choose, the grace that will enable us to receive the *mediation* of Jesus Christ, consoler of our misery.

We are in a discourse of paradox and metaphor. I am not concerned to justify the theology of the discourse. I am concerned to note the psychological and spiritual import of this discourse in Pascal's development as a writer and thinker. As with many great writers, particularly, it seems to me, those of the classical period in France (Corneille, Racine, and others), we tend to extend to the writer's entire canon the stamp of his greatest work, that which has been consecrated historically as most representative of his genius. Thus, the Racine of *Phaedra* (1677) is said to be found (or, in a familiar teleology of literary scholarship, to be anticipated with more or, usually, less perfection) in the plays prior to it (or, later, departed or degraded therefrom, as the teleology would have it). Again, Corneille, the author of some thirty-three plays over a career of nearly fifty years, is said to be best exemplified in the four plays written in the second decade of his career (*The Cid, Horace, Polyeucte, Cinna*). The readings of the canons of Racine and Corneille in their entirety seem to me to belie such simplistic (often ideologically convenient) critical reductions, as does the reading of the Pascal canon.

To read Pascal backward from (or forward with respect to the few texts beyond) the *Thoughts* as a unitary writer epitomized in that great work is to miss the richness of the canon, to belie the complexity of both the psychology of the writer and the psychology that the writer proposes in his view of man. As I have indicated in my linking of Pascal's linguistics, theology, and personal development, I use the term psychology in its etymological sense, the study of the soul, a sense in which it seems to me the linking of language to meaning and forms of meaning is inescapable. With respect to what I have called Pascalian linguistics, the forms of language move increasingly through his canon from a word- and / object-bound conception toward paraphrastic, paraverbal, and parasyntactic conception of figures. This is the lesson of the psychology cum linguistics cum doctrine of his advocacy in certain texts dealing with his conversion of 1654, the last two *Provincial Letters* and the projected *Apology*.

Nevertheless, Pascal's linguistics is, throughout the canon, consistently extralinguistic in its referentiality: signifiers are designators of things outside of language. The capacity to read, to understand, and to act upon words and sentences, as Pascal sees it in those texts I have called adversarial, is the essence of the human; the capacity to read, to understand, and to act upon figures, in those texts I have called advocative, is also the essence of the human. To separate the two, to characterize Pascal as a great psychologist chiefly on the basis of his accurate reading of the contradictoriness of human behavior or to praise this Pascalian insight as kindred to the genius of one of the mentors on whom he obviously draws, Montaigne, in the *Thoughts* themselves by emhasizing those fragments that deal in a horizontal or immanentist perspective—this is, at worst, to secularize Pascal and, at best, to attribute to him a kind of humanism through stained glass windows. Moreover, his deliberate ferocity and injury toward man in so many of those fragments in which he bares man's contradictoriness ("What a chimera is man, what a novelty, what a monster, what a chaos, what a subject of contradiction" [S 164]) seems to make of him in such an emphasis a very grumpy humanist indeed, particularly when compared with a Montaigne who can smile rather than grimace at the same phenomenon. In such an emphasis even the religious Pascal seems presumptuous and arrogant, smugly cut off in his own sure seat on the rushing waters of the rivers of fire from those who plunge to the bottom.

Such emphasis betrays the *thought* of Pascal in the *Thoughts*. It is to see the trees, or more precisely certain of the trees, without seeing the forest.[8] Still more precisely, with respect to the reading of the *Thoughts* it is to see or enter one of the Pascalian forests and not the others. Thus, the prizing in literary history of those *Provincial Letters* that openly attack the Jesuits (first through irony, then through frontal assault) over those that seek a reconciliation is, methodologically, similar to the emphasis on the secular fragments of the *Thoughts*. Yet, underlying the openly adversarial *Provincial Letters* is a less sophisticated version of the psychology in and of language that underlies the *Thoughts*. This consonance seems to me to dictate that the *Thoughts* in their *entirety* should be entitled if not *An Apology for the Christian Religion, A Project for an Apology for the Christian Religion.*

The apologist of all of the fragments does not proceed from that truly smug emphasis of secular humanism that seizes on Pascal's own famous thought that "all our dignity consists then in thought" and that we must therefore "work at thinking well" (S 232). Nor does Pascal's thought join that of the secular humanist's that gainsays the feebleness of the thinking reed to insist on the thinking itself (S 231). Pascal returns again and again to this dignity of thought to stress its feebleness rather than its grandeur or dignity:

> Thought.
> All the dignity of man is in thought. But what is this thought. How silly [*sotte*] it is!
> Thought is thus a thing admirable and incomparable in its nature. It was necessary that it have strange faults to be despicable [*méprisable*]. But it has such that nothing is more ridiculous. How great it is by its nature, how lowly by its faults.
> The slippage [*écoulement*].
> It is a horrible thing to feel slipping away all that one possesses.
> (S 626)

He is aware of this slippage in his own thought even as he writes: "In writing my thought, it escapes me sometimes, but that makes me remember my weakness, which I forget at every hour, which instructs me as much as my forgotten thought, for I hold only to knowing my nothingness" (S 540). The slippage is a figure of his and man's relative nothingness.

Like the other figures on which he bases his *Apology* it is a process, an event, a paraverbal, and parasyntactic phenomenon. In verbal language, in words, it is often expressed through metaphor ("thinking reed . . . rivers of fire . . . sewer of incertitude and error"). Pascal is a poet in the *Apology,* depending on the connotations rather than the denotations of words in order to describe the human condition in its immanent and its transcendent relations. The metaphors, like the words on which he insisted in his adversarial texts, do not separate the esthetic from the ethical (the reproach he addressed to the Jesuit Le Moyne in the eleventh *Provincial Letter*). The language of poetry, like the language of other discourses, must of necessity figure realities antecedent to that language. This referential esthetics informs his theory of signs as applied to other arts: "What vanity painting, which draws admiration for the resemblance of things that one does not admire in the original" (S 74). Pascal seeks in all signs an authentic, an honest resemblance. It is this perspective that informs his fragment disdainful of poets: "Poet and not an honest man [*honnête homme*]" (S 503 and, in the same formulation, S 613). Sellier notes that after fragment 503 the autograph copy of the *Thoughts* contains a sentence that Pascal has struck out: "After my eighth [*Provincial Letter*], I believed I had sufficiently answered."[9] The linkage between the *Provincial Letters* and these "Dossiers of the Preparatory Phase: Summer 1656 – May 1658" suggests the continuity of Pascal's strictures against poetry in both the letters and the projected *Apology*. However, the strictures consistently express an opposition to the view of poetry as autonomous realm of discourse, an intrinsic and self-referential system of figures. Two closely related fragments from the same preparatory dossiers underscore this interpretation: "Eloquence / One must have the agreeable and the real, but it is necessary that this agreeable itself be taken from the true" (S 547) and "Sayer of fine [*bons*] words, bad character" (S 549]. For Pascal, the *honnête homme* is not that sociable creature conceived by his friend Méré who, precisely to get along in society, uses manners or, in a Pascalian sense, figures that may be empty of his true sentiments. Pascal's views of the *honnête homme* recall (with even greater moral astringency than the author's) those of Nicolas Faret's treatise of 1630, *The Honest Man or the Art of Pleasing at the Court.* This mimesis of truth-telling is the very ground, the only ground on which the projected reader of his *Apology* can understand the figures of Jesus Christ who will extend to the reader the consolation out of which Pascal himself writes.

Jesus Christ can be for that reader what he has been for Pascal himself: the consoler who wrests him from his hateful self. In the total context of the *Apology*, as in the total context of Pascal's canon thus far, "the self is hateful" not in being a self. Pascal's pleasure principle denies the reading of this famous formulation in these narrow terms. It is rather self-regard that is excoriated in this and related fragments. Indeed, in order to surmount self-regard "it is necessary to know [*connaître*] oneself. Even when that would not serve to find the true, it serves at least to regulate [*régler*] one's life. And there is nothing more just." (S 106) What one will know without finding the true is the misery of those purely human values that our corrupted reason and corrupted will would have us prize most: ambition, priority, sensual pleasure, material possessions, social and political prestige, professional success. These are all figures of our self-regard whose emptiness we can recognize in simply considering how the most successful of us, kings and captains of the earth, constantly reach beyond these figures to that ultimate figure of our misery: diversion. The self-regarding scientist who had insisted on the priority of his physical and mathematical researchers, the self-regarding brother of Jacqueline Pascal who had resented and attempted to forestall her entry into the religious life; the self-regarding convert, in fact, who had sought to direct his spiritual directors in matters of faith; the self-regarding son who seems to have resented his father's love for the wife who was the son's mother; the son who may have been jealous of and angry at the sister who had "caused" the beloved mother's death—this Blaise Pascal had come to know his own "secret malice" (*The Mystery of Jesus*) of self-regard and thus been prepared to receive the consolation of that Son who is one with the Father. In both of them one at last finds that "rule" by which one can distinguish one's "fantasy" from one's "sentiment" (S 455)— the rule of God's "good and just will" (S 769).

It is in his typicality, his unexceptionality, his common humanity that the apologist builds for other men his *Apology* around this rule. "I is another" for Pascal here as for Rimbaud but not an "authorial" invention who, in the language of contemporary criticism, "deconstructs" himself in the very act of writing or for purposes of allowing his work of art to be free of psychologistic intepretation. Rather, in the language of the Scriptures that are his constant reference, the "I" of the *Apology* is "another" because he is no longer "the old Adam." This "I" is a new Adam, an Adam renewed in and through Jesus Christ, as "real" referentially as the "old Adam," more "real"—that is: true—than the old Adam because he no longer lives in the illusions of the corrupted reason and the corrupted will (or hopes to do so long as God's grace is, by God's will, in him). This transformation makes it possible for this "another I" to identify himself with those others for whom he writes, to make, as we have seen in so many fragments, the "I" a "we." This plural prevails by far in the first person pronouns of the *Apology* and even the first person singular pronouns are figures of that plurality. It is this sense of community that underlies Pascal's clear-*headed* and *heart*felt respect for and reproach to Montaigne: "What is good about Montaigne can be acquired only with difficulty. What he has that is bad, I mean beyond mores, could be corrected in a moment, if one had warned him that he made too much of little things [*faisait trop d'histoires*] and that he spoke too much of himself" (S 534). Through Jesus Christ Pascal gets beyond Montaigne and beyond his own "hateful self-regard."

The ascendancy of the Son in the theology of the projected *Apology* is not without some paradoxical political as well as theological and psychological interest. For all the sweetness of the Son of God who here succeeds the Father while assimilating the God figure dominating the implied apology of the *Provincial Letters,* the displacement of Father by Son is quite real. The God of the *Apology* projected in the *Thoughts* is less hidden than some of its most famous fragments might suggest and, in the person of Jesus Christ, he is anything but forbidding. That person enters individual lives with a directness, with an autonomy in relation to God the Father verging on independence from the patricentric ground of being to whom the Pascal of the *Provincial Letters* appealed in his call to order in the name of God, the early Church fathers and a Christ figure who was more stern than loving. This suggests, politically, that the conservative rule of the fathers has yielded to a liberal rule of the sons. In this connection, the theocratic thrust of the *Provincial Letters* (the appeal from on high by Louis de Montalte to the king on high and, ultimately as I have suggested, to God the Father) is considerably abated in the projected *Apology.*[10] To be sure, the disdain of the order of the flesh, that of the great captains of the earth, is crucial to the suffusive concept of the three orders. For Pascal himself, the order of the flesh is the most susceptible of giving the *libido dominandi* its freest reign, so, as the various fragments on justice indicate, it is best to leave things as they are, civil war being the greatest public evil. Pascal preaches not a reactionary politics but, it would seem, a nonpolitics, a retreat to the altar. Nevertheless, it is a retreat *to* and not, as in the Saint Cyranian tendencies of Pascal's policies on the Eucharist before the *Apology, from* the altar. Communion with Jesus

Christ, with the son of man who is the Son of God, provides a psychological ground for human action that bears not only on the spiritual but the public weal of those who prepare themselves for the ascendancy of the Son. Reform of self and society is validated. We can thus perhaps see some coherent explanation of Pascal's acclaimed acts of private (Christian) charity as well as of his continuing concern with the public project of the "five-penny bus" until very near the end of his life and long after he had turned away from his distinguished activity in science and mathematics. However much the latter concern may have begun in an adversarial preoccupation with self-regard and personal ascendancy, for the author of the projected *Apology* the concern has become advocatively selfless, communitarian, and nonsectarian. He is even less of Port Royal than in the *Provincial Letters*; if he is of any party, it is of the party of the son of man. Yet, the Pascal of this key work is leery of parties, for, as the partisanship of both Jansenists and Jesuits shows, parties too readily lend themselves to exclusionary codes of membership and accountability. The composition in fragments of the *Apology* suggests that the inclusionary theology of Pascal's advocacy is, as for Proudhon's politics, *an-archic*: that theology governs man best that governs him least. Without being antiecclesiastical, the *Apology* loosens the catechetical, institutional, and rule-bound theology of the *Provincial Letters* and institutes only the rule of love and hope. The Father-centered apology of the letters preached a theology of faith, a faith that can but does not always come from God; the Son-centered *Apology* we know as the *Thoughts* preaches a theology of hope, the hope that can and does come for all through Jesus Christ. Voltaire, that relentless enemy of Christianity who excoriated Pascal as an enemy of humanity, might well have more closely heeded Pascal's liberal emphasis on Jesus Christ as both Son and man.

IN THE FRAGMENTS of his *Apology for the Christian Religion* Pascal fragments the tense coherence of the formalized defensive apology of that religion he had assayed in so many earlier texts. The apology of those texts reflects etymologically the secondary genitive sense of Greek *apo* derived over time from a connection with Latin *ab* ('from, off') leading to the bivalence of, for example, English *from* meaning either 'away from' or 'coming from, of, belonging to' as in words for many chemical compounds. Thus, the *Provincial Letters* insisted on the catechetically, apodictically close relations of word and thing, of signifier and signified. The *Apology* we call the *Thoughts* also uses words, of course, going through words to asseverate the faith of the Christian religion. However, alerted through the experience of the *Provincial Letters* to the hold of catachretical Jesuit discourse on the readers of any apology, in the texture of the writing of the projected *Apology* Pascal uses language in the original etymological sense (*apo* = sundered + *logos* = word); he assails apodixis, writes aporetically, to use Marin's term. There is, indeed, at this close level what Sellier has called "an esthetic of the fragment."[11] This loosening effect, this fragmentation at the microcosmic level of the text is compensated by a skillfully orchestrated effect at the macrocosmic or structural level with its progression from the aporesis of "Man's Misery without God" toward the apodixis of "Man's Felicity in God."

In Derridian terms, the textual aporesis / skepticism toward language "figures" an absence, to be sure. But it is the absence not of the psychologistic subject-author of the text, Blaise Pascal, but of the object-reader of the text, the unhappy and reasonable seeker in his centerless suffering without God. The apodixis of structure cannot signify the presence of the center that will console the sufferer, Jesus Christ who is Son of God and who will return the sufferer to the bosom of God the Father; Pascal still subscribes, however less obtrusively in this text, to the theology of efficacious grace precluding such assurances by any but God himself. Nevertheless, the structure can figure the possibility of assurance as it apodictically orchestrates its theme of alienation and longing toward the magnificent crescendo of faith in and through the person of Jesus Christ. The contextual orchestration itself has seemed to some readers to be but a model of the textual antimimesis, but this is so because such readers seek a transitive and linear profession of faith, a grammar of belief in which subject (God) governs verb (saves) governs object (you). The argument of the *Apology* does not proceed with such *géométrie*. Rather, it proceeds with *finesse,* in a radial and suffusive fashion. The combination of aporetic esthetic of the fragment and apodictic esthetic of the structure thus produces a paradoxical architecture very different from that of the earlier defensive Pascalian apologies. Indeed, it produces an *anarch*itecture, the appropriate compositional figure of the lesson it seeks to *re*-present.

This anarchitecture is the figure of the suffusive vision of the human condition. In the last stages of the *Provincial Letters,* Pascal had become painfully aware of not only Jesuit but others' skeptical, nominalistic

conception of language, the view of language as an endlessly manipulable model whose very aporesis figured not the hiddenness of God but
the absence of God. His own coreligionists at Port Royal had
themselves developed a linguistics, in part appropriated from his own,
in which the supreme figure of the Incarnation, of the Man-God/God-
Man Jesus Christ bid to be configured through grammatical preoccupations as a subject rather than an object of discourse.[12] He believed
that the object was God, the Son of man who is at one with the
Father. To enact this conviction to which he had come after his own
now rigidly dependent, now rebelliously skeptical relation to the
Father, he knew he would have to *deconstruct from within* the decon-
structive (and destructive) linguistics of advocates as well as adversaries
of God's Word and Figure. Hence the fragmentary, assaultive, and
relatively aporetic style, and tone of the *Thoughts*. In modern terms,
this masterpiece might thus appear not as an intertext of the Pascalian
canon but as a contratext, especially to the other masterpiece of the
canon, the *Provincial Letters*. Yet, each masterpiece proceeds from an
unshakable awareness of the existence of a Supreme Signified whose
presence can be realized through the signifiers of language — apodictically or literally in the *Provincial Letters,* aporetically or "processionally"
in the *Thoughts*. Each is complete and completed; the letters in a beautiful order, the *Thoughts* in what his contemporary, Boileau, considered a hallmark of the work of art: a "beautiful disorder" (*beau désor-
dre*), an order proportionate and appropriate to the human condition.

CONCLUSION:
ADVERSARY
AND
ADVOCATE
IN THE
FINAL WRITINGS

IT IS ALSO proportionate and appropriate to the more sophisticated psychology of human nature at which Pascal arrives in his advocative writings that, in the few texts he wrote from 1659 until his death on August 19, 1662, that do not figure in the *Apology*, he reverts from an advocative to an adversarial posture.

The Prayer to Ask God for the Good Use of Sickness[1] (probably late 1659 in the view of Lafuma; November 1659 for Sellier) is consonant in tone and premise with the advocative hatred of self-regard and the dependence on Jesus Christ as man's Savior from that self-regard found in the *Apology*: "Oh God, who leaves sinners hardened in the delicious and criminal use of the world . . . make me consider this sickness like a kind of death, separating me from the world, denuded of all the objects of my attachments, alone in your presence, to implore from your mercy the conversion of my heart." Echoing the *Apology*, the *Prayer* records that all figures—the illness that eventually led to his death, but including those of the world and those of the tradition of faith itself (Scriptures, sacraments, and others)—can be *discerned* in their true meaning only "if you accompany all these things through the altogether extraordinary assistance of your grace." In the very act of making this prayer he sees God's will at work rather than his own: "I render thanks to you, then, my God, for the good movements you give me, and for that one even that you give me to render you thanks." The supplicant is aware that he had misconstrued the meaning of the figure of health itself: "Yes, Lord, I confess that I have esteemed health a good, not because it is an easy means to serve you usefully, to spend more care and watch in your service, and for help to my neighbor; but because thanks to it I could abandon myself with less reserve to the abundance of the delights of life and better enjoy its deadly pleasures. Grant me the grace, Lord, to reform my corrupted reason." That the "Lord" to whom he prays is at once God the Father and God the Son emerges in such appeals as "Remove from me, Lord, the sadness that the love of myself could give me for my own suffering and the things of the world that do not succeed to the satisfaction of the inclinations of my heart, which does not look to your glory; but put in me a sadness conforming to yours." Still more explicitly in an evocation of the person of Christ, the *Prayer* concludes:

> Enter into my heart and into my soul, to bring therein my suffering, and to continue the duration in me of what remains to you to suffer in your passion, which you accomplish in your members right up to the perfect consummation of your body; so that being full of you it no longer be I who live and suffer, but you who live and suffer in me, O my Savior; and that thus, having some small part of your sufferings, you fill me entirely with the glory that they have acquired for you, in which you live with the Father and the Holy Spirit, through the centuries. So be it.

Doctrinally, the theology of grace is perhaps even more insistent here than in the *Apology*. Personally, Pascal may have been prompted to this insistence by an awareness that in spite of the conciliatory doctrinal stance he adopted in the last two *Provincial Letters* and even in preparing an advocative *Apology for the Christian Religion* since 1656, he had in the intervening years little "esteemed his health" in the combative and, theologically, presumptuous continuation of his arguments with the Jesuits in the assistance he gave to the Curates of Paris in their adversarial *Writings* (February–July 1658) on the theological positions of the Jesuits, not to speak of his use of that poor health for a return to such worldly pursuits as mathematical researches on the cycloid and the roulette. In terms of the pseudonym he used in the matter of the roulette, M. Dettonville, the Pascal of the *Prayer* may have felt that he had too readily used whatever health he had to acquit himself of such "debts in town" (*dette en ville*).

The spirit of abjuration of such worldly commitments in the *Prayer* is resounded in the letter cited earlier of August 1660 to his fellow mathematician Fermat: "renouncing geometry in its own sphere," but also announcing that "there is now this also in my case: that I am pursuing studies so distant from that frame of mind that I hardly remember what there is to it." Pascal does not specify to Fermat what these studies are, but the characterization of them as distant from geometry and its like echoes the attitude toward geometry we find in the *Apology,* on which we know him to have been at work for several years.

But not uninterruptedly before nor after the letter to Fermat. He will use his ever-declining health, for example, to work on the plan for an intraurban, public passenger transportation system for Paris (which was, in fact, inaugurated with Pascal present in March of 1662, six months before his death).

More significantly for our purposes here, he does not abjure the combative and adversative tendency of his spirit. He reverts to it in the *Writing on Signing of the Formulary* (probably of October 1661 according to some editors) and, to the extent that we can consider the document as Pascal's, in *Three Discourses on the Condition of the Great* (probably in the last third of 1660 according to Lafuma, sometime within that year according to Chevalier). Because of its probable anteriority and, in full awareness of its possibly tentative status as a text by Pascal, I shall comment on the *Three Discourses* first.[2]

Certainly, the political, philosophical, and theological premises of the *Three Discourses* are Pascalian. The first of these discourses, all presumably written for the son of the Duke of Luynes, begins with a situational metaphor or figure, in which the author invites his pupil to imagine a man who survives a shipwreck to find himself on an unknown island where, because of his resemblance to the disappeared king of that island, the inhabitants take him for and treat him with all the respect they have for the king, a situation the shipwrecked stranger decides to accept. He does so with a double awareness: "the one whereby he acted as king, the other by which he recognized his true status, and that it was only chance which had put him in the place he was." A fragment (S 527) of the *Apology* comes to mind: "The most important thing in the world is the choice of one's métier: chance disposes of it." Similarly, the insistence on the establishment of kings as "not a title of nature, but a human establishment" that is nonetheless under the aegis of "some excellence above" kings and nobles echoes many a fragment of the *Apology* on the paradoxically just injustice of force in the corrupted state of nature. Again, in the *Second Discourse,* the author warns the pupil that his "grandeurs of establishment" do not oblige the author to fail "to have for you the inner scorn that your baseness of mind would merit"—echoes of the famous fragment on the three orders in the *Apology* as well as of the much earlier *Letter to Christina, Queen of Sweden*. Finally, in a refrain of the famous fragment on the three orders, the *Third Discourse* succinctly moves from a consideration of "concupiscence" (as the force of both the king's power and his subjects' fealty) to conclude that "it is necessary to scorn concupiscence and its realm and aspire to this realm of charity where all the subjects breathe only of charity and desire only the good of charity."

The tone of this essayistic and nonfragmentary illustration of the concept of the three orders is haughty and preachy. If these *Discourses* are by Pascal or even if they are close to the tone and form of the conversations between Pascal and his pupil (reported by another hand), they show us a Pascal who has reverted to the adversative spirit of texts like the first sixteen *Provincial Letters*. To be sure, all three *Discourses* are overt reminders to "the great" that they, like all men, are "dispossessed kings" (S 148 and others in the *Apology*). However, the *Discourses* do not have the saving grace, linguistically, doctrinally, and psychologically, of the consoling figure of Jesus Christ. The charity to whose order the author compels his pupil here is more reminiscent of that Saint Cyranian love of God that creature owes God than of that love that God, in the person of Jesus Christ, showed toward man in the *Apology*. The "order of charity" in the *Discourses* is one ruled by God the Father; it is an order of justice rather than of love.

The Writing on the Signing of the Formulary[3] is definitely by Pascal, the last text we have from his pen, probably dating from the mid-fall of 1661. In writing it Pascal intervenes once again in the debate on subscription by the members of the Port Royal community that in doctrine [*droit*] the Five Propositions drawn by the Sorbonne from Jansen's *Augustinius* are in fact [*fait*] the doctrine of Jansen and thus heretical and to be condemned. To obtain this formal subscription by Port Royal to this interpretation, a formulary text had been drawn up in the beginning of 1661 to which, by order of the Assembly of the Clergy on February 1, confirmed by the Council of the State on April 14, all interested parties were to affix their signature. On June 8, the vicars general proposed a modification of this formulary that would have permitted signing with some reservations, but the king's council annulled the modification on July 14. The debate between hard-liners and moderates among the adversaries of Port Royal continued through

CONCLUSION   267

the summer and the early fall, but on October 31, 1661, no doubt
under the influence of the earlier papal condemnation of the compromise by the vicars general, the latter issued a new mandate that the
formulary to be signed would be one without any distinction between
fact and *doctrine*.

Reenter Pascal, a Pascal who had lost his beloved younger sister: on
October 4, 1661, Sister Jacqueline Pascal of the convent at Port Royal
died. Did the death of Jacqueline, like the miracle of the Holy Thorn
that had involved his niece at an earlier stage of the controversy, strike
Pascal as still another miraculous mark of the rightness of the need to
oppose the signature? Had God withdrawn his sister from the temptation to sin in signing the formulary? Or had that death released him
from the anxiety of his own possible surrender to temptation to the sin
of approving her possible signature out of a concern for her own
spiritual and material well-being at Port Royal? Again, had her death
released him from the anxiety of a renewed falling out with his sister
at the sight of her possible acceptance to sign and his own adamant opposition to signing as brought out in his *Writing on the Signing of the
Formulary*?

Whatever the personal influence on his decision to enter the fray, he
does so in the logically careful, word-bound, patricentric, literal-
minded, and disputatious manner of his discourse as reported in his
youthful debates with Saint Ange and to be read in his textual bouts
with the Jesuits in the first sixteen *Provincial Letters*:

> The whole question today being on these words, *I condemn the five pro-
> positions in the sense of Jansen,* or *the doctrine of Jansen on the five proposi-
> tions,* it is of extreme importance to see in what manner one subscribes
> to them.
>
> It is necessary first of all to know [*savoir*] that in the truth of things
> there is no difference between condemning the doctrine of Jansen on
> the five propositions and condeming efficacious grace, Saint Augus-
> tine, Saint Paul.

Pascal argues on a point of faith (the consonance of Jansen and the
early fathers) as preemptively as he claims that "the pope and the
bishops" argue preemptively on a point of fact (that, in Pope Alex-
ander VII's declaration, " 'to be in the true faith, it is necessary to say
that the words of sense [*mots de sens*] of Jansen work only [*ne font que*]
to express the heretical sense of the propositions,' and thus it is a fact
[*fait*] that carries off a doctrine" [*droit*]). For Pascal, of course, his equa-

tion of Jansen with the early fathers in the matter of doctrine is a matter of fact. Moreover, as Pascal points out, the words *fait* and *droit* are not to be found "in the mandate nor in the [papal] constitutions nor in the formulary, but only in certain writings which have no necessary relation to the signature." Hard fact meets hard fact within a framework of discussion in which, *in fact,* the argument about *fait et droit* is without verbal relevance. The occasion was appropriate, one might think, knowing the seventeenth and eighteenth *Provincial Letters* and/or the *Apology,* for Pascal to appeal to the polyvalent notion of *sentiment,* especially to its conciliatory and salvatory reference to Jesus Christ.

He does use the term, but it is not in that reference:

> For that, my sentiment is that, as the sense of Jansen has been expressed in the mandate, in the bulls and in the formula, one must necessarily exclude it formally by one's signature, without which one does not satisfy one's duty. For to claim that it suffices to say that one believes only what is of the faith, in order to claim to have indicated [*marqué*] enough thereby that one does not condemn the sense of Jansen, by this sole reason that one imagines that there is in that a fact that is separated from doctrine [*droit*], this is a pure illusion: one can give many proofs thereof.

Sentiment is a matter of that way of knowing designated by *savior,* the French verb for knowing with which Pascal began his resolution of the dispute at the outset of this text ("It is necessary first of all to know"). The way of knowing designated by the French verb *connaître,* a knowing that is metaphoric and figural, a knowing that is linked more with the *esprit de finesse* than with the *esprit de géométrie,* a knowing not things or facts but places and people, a knowing Jesus Christ that runs through the *Apology* and culminates in the Project of 1658 in the fragment entitled "Connaissance de Dieu"—this way of knowing is missing from the final text of Pascal, the one in which he deals with the most convincing evidence of the bad faith of his adversaries.

He falls back on the order of mind, using his own powerful mind in forceful logic, subtle analysis, and punctilious precision. He closes his discourse,

> From which I conclude that those who sign the formulary purely without restriction sign the condemnation of Jansen, Saint Augustine, and efficacious grace.
> I conclude in the second place that he who excludes [*excepte*] the

doctrine of Jansen in formal terms saves from condemnation both Jansen and efficacious grace.

I conclude in the third place that those who sign in speaking only of the faith, not formally excluding the doctrine of Jansen, take a middle road [*voie moyenne*], which is abominable before God, despicable before men, and entirely useless to those that one wants to condemn [*perdre*] personally.

Q.E.D., one is tempted to write at the end of this demonstration. However, the passion is too apparent for such a geometric commentary. Rather, this is the tone of the Jansenist friend at the end of the second *Provincial Letter* and of the reporter who at last drops his neutrality in hearing the horrors of the Jesuit at the end of the tenth letter. This is an adversary Pascal who seeks to advocate true faith not in apposition with the Son of God who had come to reconcile in himself man in dispute with himself and his fellow men, but in apposition with the old fathers, Augustine and Paul, and with the only new father of doctrine he seems to find on their road [*voie*], Jansen. All are fathers in apposition with the God Pascal invokes in the last sentence we know him to have *written:* God the Father.

In the silence that followed this final adversarial thrust, did the advocate reemerge? If we are to accept the testimony (it is much controverted) of Father Beurrier, Pascal's confessor at his deathbed, the dying Pascal regretted his spirit of adversity, his disputation within the Church. It is not controverted that the last words he uttered were "May God never abandon me!" These are appropriate last words for the adversary who, in his most disputatious and inhumane moments, had never lost hope that God would save him. They are also appropriate for the advocate who, in his most conciliatory and humane moments, had never presumed to regard that salvation or, indeed, the hope for salvation as a thing of his own mind and heart.

NOTES

In the notes I have given only the title of the work and appropriate page number(s). Full bibliographical information is found in the bibliography.

INTRODUCTION

1. "Lettre à Fermat," *L'Oeuvre de Pascal,* ed. Chevalier, 299–300. This edition is cited hereafter as Chevalier.
2. "Préface sur le traité du vide," *Ouevres complètes,* ed. Mesnard, II, 778–779. This edition is cited hereafter as Mesnard, with the volume and pages.
3. "La Vie de Pascal (la deuxième version)," Mesnard, I, 617. Except as otherwise noted, hereafter references to and quotations from Gilberte's biography of her brother are based on the second version as authenticated by Mesnard (I, 603–642).
4. "Lettre dédicatoire à Monseigneur le Chancelier," Mesnard, II, 332–334.
5. *Language and Responsibility,* 43.
6. *La Critique du discours: sur la "Logique de Port Royal" et les "Pensées" de Pascal,* 140.

I. ADVERSARIAL BELIEVER, ADVERSARIAL MAN OF SCIENCE

1. My review of the encounter with the abbé de Saint Ange and attendant quotations from the relevant text are based on the editor's history of the event in Mesnard, II, 362–420.
2. Mesnard, II, 498–501. Subsequent references to this work are from this edition.
3. Mesnard, II, 513–518.

4. Mesnard, II, 509–510.

5. Mesnard, II, 556–576. Subsequent references to this work are from this edition.

6. "Lettre d'Etienne Pascal au Père Noël," Mesnard, II, 584–602. Subsequent references to this work are from this edition.

7. Mesnard, II, 542.

8. "Extraits de la correspondance de Descartes avec Carcavy," Mesnard, II, 716–719. Subsequent references to this work are from this edition.

9. Mesnard, II, 804–813. Subsequent references to this work are from this edition.

10. Mesnard, II, 814–816.

11. Mesnard, II, 817–818. Subsequent references to this work are from this edition.

2. THE ADVERSARIAL BELIEVER AND HIS FAMILY

1. Mesnard, II, 552–555.

2. *Pascal and Theology*, 195–201.

3. The dating of the *Writings on Grace* still remains problematic. The habits of Pascal's mind might well suggest that Miel is right in making the *Second Writing* the first to be written. Its matter-of-fact tone may mean that it is written not so much for another who is not so sophisticated but for Pascal himself, whose sophistication had been put into doubt by Rebours. He would, therefore, first justify himself by outlining the problem in all its simplicity as if to make sure that he had a clear hold on the essential matters in dispute: the positions of the disputants whose works, on both sides, he had assured Rebours he knew. Troubled and confused by the encounter, he would not have wanted to begin with polemic. But, then, confident of his ground, he would have returned to his habit of self-assertion and self-defense and composed the *First Writing* specifically with Rebours in mind and perhaps in view as a prospective reader. On the other hand, his pride having been wounded by Rebours, he may well have written the *First Writing* precisely to "show" Rebours. Then, consistent with Gilberte's observation on the readiness with which he corrected the faults of vivacity and impatience, he would have written the more matter-of-fact *Second Writing*, in which he retracted the egomanic motive of the *First Writing*. Of course, the simplicity of the *Second Writing* may also have represented a defensive reply to Rebours. He would make this simple exposition of the points in dispute precisely to show that he "knew what he was talking about," unaided by the scholarly supports that, in part, Rebours—like de Sacy later—would find "too much with Pascal." Whether dictated by repentance or pride, then, the very simplicity of the *Second Writing* would argue for its composition after

the *First.* Finally, whatever the order of composition, I would suggest that, if subsequent to the encounter with Rebours, their tone suggests that it is more likely that they were written sometime between April and November of 1648. As we shall see, in April of that year Pascal would write to Gilberte on a religious note suggesting that he is still somewhat troubled by the encounter and that it is the awareness of a faith beyond reason that preoccupies him. But by November he would write a letter to Gilberte, in which the aggressive tone and peremptory treatment of grace and prayer accord with the defensive, rationalistic, and egocentric thrust of the *First* and *Second Writings on Grace.*

4. *First Writing,* Chevalier, 724. The full text is found on pp. 722–729 and subsequent reference and quotation is therefrom.

5. *Second Writing,* Chevalier, 731. The full text is found on pp. 729–736 and subsequent reference and quotation is therefrom.

6. Mesnard, II, 553–555.

7. Mesnard, II, 580. The text of the letter, from which I quote here, is found on pp. 581–583.

8. Mesnard, II, 694–698.

9. Mesnard, II, 704–706.

10. Mesnard, II, 701–703.

11. Mesnard, II, 845–863. Subsequent references to this letter are from this edition.

12. Mesnard, II, 748.

13. Arthur R. Jensen, "How Much Can We Boost IQ and Scholastic Achievement?"

14. "Mémoire sur sa famille," Mesnard, I, 1077–1089, and "Mémoire sur Pascal et sa famille," Mesnard, I, 1090–1105.

15. Mesnard, II, 571–602.

16. Mesnard, II, 920–926.

17. *Pascal: The Life of Genius,* 142–156.

18. Mesnard, II, 863–868.

19. Mesnard, I, 652–671.

20. Mesnard, II, 909–916.

21. Mesnard, II, 916–917.

22. Mesnard, II, 954–998.

23. Mesnard, II, 886–867.

3. THE ADVERSARIAL BELIEVER AND THE WORLD

1. Bishop, 150.

2. Mesnard, II, 934–935.

3. Mesnard, II, 1101.

4. "Celeberrime Matheseos Academiae Parisiensi," Mesnard, II, 1034–1035.

5. Mesnard, II, 1010–1011.

4. THE CONVERT

1. "Mémoire sur Pascal et sa famille," Mesnard, I, 1090–1105.
2. Recorded in Sellier's footnote 13 on p. 433.
3. Mesnard, II, 1146.
4. Mesnard, II, 1158.

5. THE CONVERT'S AGONY

1. Chevalier and Lafuma place this text at the end of 1653. However, Mesnard, who proceeds chronologically, does not yet include it in the first two volumes of his edition. The second volume contains documents only as late as October 1654. Editorial circumspection and the intrinsic character of the work lead me to place it later than do Chevalier and Lafuma. References and quotation are from Lafuma, *Pascal: Oeuvres complètes*, 290–291.
2. Sigmund Freud, *Beyond the Pleasure Principle*, passim.
3. Marcuse, 234–237.
4. Miel, 122.
5. I use the text as given by Lafuma (L 919, 553 and 791 in *Pascal: Oeuvres complètes*, 619–621). Sellier, following the *Second Copy*, separates the text into two fragments (S 749 and S 751) at the twenty-first passage in my description here and continuing beyond the fortieth passage. Sellier's editorial scrupulosity need not prevent us from seeing the thematic continuity of the two fragments.
6. *Dictionnaire de la langue française*, III, 789.
7. *Demian*, trans. Roloff and Lebeck, 68–69 and 118, respectively.
8. Lafuma indicates that this passage is found on the verso of the copy he uses. In Sellier's edition, this passage is found after what I have numbered as the fortieth passage here.
9. *Pascal: Oeuvres complètes*, Lafuma, 297–310.

6. THE CONVERT AS PRIVATE ADVERSARY

1. Chevalier, 343–358.
2. Chevalier, 339–343.
3. The full title as given by Chevalier is "Fragments of a Letter on the Possibility of the Commandments, the Seeming Contradictions of Saint Augustine, the Theory of the Double Abandonment of the Just, and Proximate Power" (p. 736).

7 · THE CONVERT AS PUBLIC ADVERSARY

1. I have used the edition prepared by H. F. Stewart, *Les Lettres provinciales de Blaise Pascal.*

2. Stewart p. 256, note to p. 20.

3. Cited by Sellier, p. 293, n. 38.

4. Stewart, p. 270, note to *Letter* 6.

5. Need one stress Pascal's ironic use of the Jesuit named L'Amy (The Friend) in this context—the name of a French translation of an Italian "Francesco Amico" (1578–1651), as Stewart indicates on p. 279 in a note to his p. 79?

6. Stewart, p. 259, note to p. 29. Translated, Stewart's decodification is "And old friend, Blaise Pascal, of Auvergne, son of Etienne Pascal."

7. *La Dissémination,* passim.

9 · THE LETTERS TO THE ROANNEZ

1. I have used Chevalier 282–296 for the text.

2. *Pascal: The Life of Genius,* 144.

10 · THE THOUGHTS

1. Sellier is surprised at Lafuma's validation of Copy 1 especially in view of the fact that Lafuma writes that Copy 2 is "the manuscript that conserved the order that existed at the beginning [*origine*]," Sellier, p. 10, n. 2.

2. *Moliere: A New Criticism,* 78–79.

3. Wills, passim.

4. This treatise follows a text, of about equal length, on "The Geometric Spirit." Both texts appear under the title, *Reflexions on Geometry in General* in *Pascal: Oeuvres complètes,* Lafuma, 348–359.

5. Sellier, p. 455, n. 63.

6. Sellier, p. 353, n. 2.

7. See Garasse's "La Doctrine Curieuse," in Frédéric Lachèvre, *Le Procès du Poete Théophile de Viau,* I, 152 and 287.

8. Hugh M. Davidson sees the tree—indeed, the "treeness"—of the *Thoughts* in his *Origins of Certainty: Means and Meanings in Pascal's "Pensées."* Davidson also sees the *Thoughts* as a key to much of Pascal's thought—its *genus*—in the rest of the Pascalian canon. Although I find much to agree with in Davidson's view of the thought of the *Thoughts,* I obviously find it but one *phase* of Pascal's thought in the whole of his canon.

9. Sellier, p. 272, n. 13.

10. Pascal's use of acronyms as pseudonyms bears on the question of his

own as well as others' concern with self. The order in which he adopts them reflects the progressive abandonment of the self-regard that the famous fragment on the *moi* characterizes as "hateful": the most personal (apart from the barely pseudonymous initials at the end of the third *Provincial Letter*) is Louis de Montalte with its references to his scientific achievements, polemical stance, and, possibly, to his maternal origins; Amos de Dettonville (with the *on* within the name permitting the acronym through a deviation, as I have suggested, of *en* = in) still shows self-regard for the order of mind, but as in the spirit of a "final payment"; Salomon de Tultie is a self-criticism, a Socratic thrust at the self as being wise only in knowing that it does not know in relation to the highest of orders, charity. As I have indicated in interpreting the "I" of the *Apology,* this does not mean that Pascal has no sense of self in that work. In fact, the Davidson–Dubé *Concordance* records 580 uses of "I" (*je* and *j'*), 261 of "me" (*me* and *m'*), 99 of *moi* (English: Now "I," now "me," again "myself" as well as "the self"). However, the first person has been subsumed into Jesus Christ (335 uses in various formulations in French and Latin—*J.-C., Jésus, Christ, Jesus-Christ, Jesu, Jesum, Jesus, J.*) and God (*Dieu*—687 uses), with the use of God theologically and psychologically inseparable from the ascendancy of Jesus Christ. Indeed, as I trust my interpretation permits at this point, the once self-regarding "I" has been subsumed into Jesus Christ / God not only in the suprapersonal fashion of which I spoke in the Introduction but in an interpersonal fashion as well, through the brotherhood of all human beings ("us" or "we"—*nous,* 893 uses) in and through Jesus Christ.

   11. Sellier, p. 37, n. 11.

   12. In *La Critique du discours,* Marin also stresses the importance of Jesus Christ in the discourse of the *Thoughts*:

> Jesus Christ, paradigm and singular being, person outside of and within man, present in his common humanity and in this very presence, absent like the Other, the All Other, who is without common measure: aporetic model of the ordinary discourse in which truth lies: "Sane the opinions of the people"—"Truth is indeed in their opinions but not where they imagine . . . " Discourse does not translate it, does not transmit it, or, more exactly, it has from all time communicated the meaning, but without difference, neutrally: neither in figures that discourse gives of it and which constitute it in its texture nor outside of these figures, since ordinary discourse is this interminable figuration of meaning, meaning that always *remains* there, but whose manifestation by which it communicates itself is always already an absence: indifference. (pp. 416–417)

Marin obviously understands the stylistic strategy (and thus the lectoral effect) of *The Thoughts* as what I would call a "process." However, for Marin the process is obviously interminable and thus, a view that would have scandalized Pascal not only as a believer but also as a writer, the organizing *figure* of Jesus Christ becomes not a consoling presence but a frustrating absence, simply a name that "would be the zero degree of proper names, the first and the last figure, original and founding, but a figure" (p. 140 — see my earlier citation of this passage from Marin, on p. 14).

By the very stress on the figural, exemplary, and aporetic import of Jesus Christ, Marin fails to communicate the subjective import of the reality of signified that both the name *within* and the relatively aporetic structure of the *Thoughts* (or, more appropriately here, *The Apology for the Christian Religion*) designate as both prior to and compensatory of verbal mimesis. However skeptical Pascal be in his *Apology*, he attains to this skepticism, as I have indicated, after a long period in which he himself is apodictic — and, as we have seen, at times apoplectic — before the too easy catachresis of others: Saint Ange in the mid-1640s, the Jesuits in the mid 1650s. Again, Marin misunderstands the architectural import of the seeming disorganization of the *Apology*. He assimilates that work and its fragmentariness into the fragmentariness (due to successive editorial modification over twenty years or so) of the *Logique de Port Royal* and thus arrives at a conception of the structure of the *Apology* as endlessly manipulable. As Hugh Davidson has emphasized, however, the organization of the assembled fragments was established by Pascal himself (*The Origins of Certainty*, pp. 143–144, fn. 2), a fact that is in dispute among most responsible modern editors only with respect to which copy of that establishment is to be respected. Intrinsically, as I have brought out, the ordering of the fragments in the Sellier edition shows a careful orchestration in a crescendo of increasing specificity and emphasis on the life and the meaning of the life of that Jesus Christ whose name figures so prominently throughout the text.

CONCLUSION

1. *Pascal: Oeuvres complètes*, Lafuma, 366–368.
2. Ibid., 366–368.
3. Ibid., 368–369.

BIBLIOGRAPHY

EDITIONS OF PASCAL

Blaise Pascal: Pensées sur la religion et sur quelqeues autres sujets, 2nd ed. Avant propos et notes de Louis Lafuma. Paris: Delmas, 1952.

Blaise Pascal: Pensées sur la religion et sur quelques autres sujets, 3 vols. Introduction de Louis Lafuma. Paris: Editions du Luxembourg, 1951.

Les Lettres provinciales de Blaise Pascal, ed. H. F. Stewart. Manchester at the University Press and London: Longmans, Green., 1920.

L'Oeuvre de Pascal, ed. Jacques Chevalier. Bibliothèque de la Pléiade. Paris: Gallimard, 1950.

Oeuvres complètes de Blaise Pascal, avec tous les documents biographiques et critiques, les oeuvres d'Etienne, de Gilberte et de Jacqueline Pascal et celles de Marguerite Périer, la correspondence de Pascal et des Périer, ed. Jean Mesnard. Paris: Desclée de Brouwer. Vol. I, 1964; Vol. II, 1970.

Oeuvres de Blaise Pascal, 2nd ed. 10 vol. ed Léon Brunschvicg. Paris: Librairie Hachette, 1923.

Pascal: Oeuvres complètes, Préface d'Henri Gouhier; Présentation et notes de Louis Lafuma. Paris: Seuil, 1963.

Pascal: *Pensées—Nouvelle Edition établie pour la première fois d'après la copie de référence de Gilberte Pascal,* ed. Philippe Sellier. Paris: Mercure de France, 1976.

OTHER WORKS

Agee, James, and Walker Evans. *Let Us Now Praise Famous Men.* Boston: Houghton-Mifflin, 1941.

Baudouin, Charles. *Blaise Pascal ou l'ordre du coeur.* Paris: Plon, 1962.

Bishop, Morris. *Pascal, The Life of Genius.* New York: Reynal and Hitchcock, 1936.

278

Chomsky, Noam. *Language and Responsibility—Based on Conversations with Mitsou Ronat,* trans. from the French by John Viertel. New York: Pantheon Books, 1979.

Davidson, Hugh M., and Pierre H. Dubé. *A Concordance to Pascal's "Pensées."* Ithaca, New York: Cornell University Press, 1975.

Davidson, Hugh M. *The Origins of Certainty—Means and Meanings in Pascal's "Pensées."* Chicago: The University of Chicago Press, 1979.

Descartes, René. *Oeuvres et lettres,* ed. André Bridoux. Bibliothèque de La Pléiade. Paris: Gallimard, 1966.

Derrida, Jacques. *La Dissémination.* Paris: Seuil, 1972.

Freud, Sigmund. *Beyond the Pleasure Principle: A Study of the Death Instinct in Human Behavior,* trans. by James Strachey, with an introduction and notes prepared for this edition by Gregory Zilborg, M.D. New York: Bantan Books, 1959.

Hesse, Herman. *Demian,* trans. by M. Roloff and M. Lebeck. New York: Bantam Books, 1965.

Jensen, Arthur R. "How Much Can We Boost IQ and Scholastic Achievement?" *Harvard Educational Review* 39, no. 1 (1969): 1–123.

Lachèvre, Frédéric. *Le Libertinage devant le parlement de Paris: Le Procès du poète Théophile de Viau* (11 juillet 1623–1er septembre 1625), 2 vols. Paris: H. Champion, 1909.

Marcuse, Herbert. *Eros and Civilization.* Boston: Beacon Press, 1955.

Marin, Louis. *La Critique du discours: sur la "Logique de Port Royal" et les "Pensées" de Pascal.* Paris: Les Editions de Minuit, 1975.

Mesnard, Jean. *Pascal.* 4th ed. Paris: Hatier, 1962.

Miel, Jan. *Pascal and Theology.* Baltimore: The Johns Hopkins Press, 1969.

Moore, W. G. *Molière: A New Criticism.* Oxford: Clarendon Press, 1949.

Sellier, Philippe. *Pascal et Saint Augustin.* Paris: Armand Colin, 1970.

Wills, Gary. *Inventing America: Jefferson's Declaration of Independence.* Garden City, New York: Doubleday, 1978.

INDEX

linguistic analysis of, 196, 236, 262.
See also Jesus Christ
Innocent X (pope), 165

Jansen, Cornelius, 26, 79, 266–268;
  Augustinius, 27, 165–166, 266
Jansenism, 6, 83–84; and Affaire Saint
  Ange, 27–28; and human reason, 52;
  Jesuit attack on, 165–166, 178–180,
  205–207, 266–268. *See also* Port
  Royal, Saint Cyran
Jensen, Arthur, 84
Jesuits, 13, 44, 207–208, 217–218, 222;
  and Affaire Saint Ange, 25, 27–28; attack on Jansenism by, 165–166, 178–180,
  205–207; political ambitions of, 179–180,
  183, 189, 216; Pascal's attack on, 180–
  196; as semioticians, 181–182, 192–193;
  and probabilism, 181–183; and direction
  of intention, 187–188, 190–191; and
  "mental restrictions," 193; and love of
  God, 192–196; and contrition, 195; attack on Pascal by, 213–214
Jesus Christ, 57–59, 132, 252–254; humanity of, 26; as mediator, 71, 82–83, 253;
  death of, 79–83; incarnation of, 130–
  131, 142; androgyny of, 133; as consoler, 252, 257. *See also* Father-son
  relationship
Judaism, 105

Knowledge, types of, 268

Lafuma, Louis, 231–232
Language, 145, 251. *See also* Linguistics
Le Maistre, Isaac-Louis, *see* De Sacy,
  Isaac
Le Moyne, Father, 169–170, 199–200
*Letters Written to a Provincial by One of
  His Friends,* see *Provincial Letters*
Liancourt, Duc de, 166
Libertinism, 250–251
Libido: sentiendi, sciendi, and *dominandi,*
  132, 244–245
Linguistics, 9–10, 12–14; Cartesian, 10,
  13, 243–244; of Etienne Pascal, 36–40; in
  Third Writing on Grace, 160; Pascal's
  interest in, 162; and the *Provincial
  Letters,* 166–176, 182, 189–190, 194–195,
  203–209, 215–216; of Jesuits, 188–190,

193, 195, 203, 204, 206–207; in relation
  to God, 189–190, 220–221; and reading
  of meaning, 215–216; denotative and
  connotative, 219–221, 240, 255–257; in
  Thoughts, 235–237, 251, 255, 260–262;
  and orders of heart and mind, 240; and
  aporesis and apodixis, 260–262

Magni, 43–44
Man: Augustinian, 58, 59; criminality of,
  70, 73; tripartite division of, 60–61,
  246–247, 251–252; two states of, 124,
  130, 162. *See also* Self
Marcuse, Herbert, 9, 126
Marin, Louis, 12–15, 276–277n12
Materialism, 187, 192
Mathieu, Félix, 40–41
Médaille, Father, 42–47, 65
Membership, religious, 234
Memorial, 118–123, 129, 130
Méré, Chevalier de, 8, 108, 110
Mesnard, Jean, 79; on Noël controversy,
  33, 34, 39; on experiments with
  vacuum, 40–41, 42, 44; on *Writings
  on Grace,* 54; on Jacqueline Pascal, 68,
  69, 78, 91, 95; on Pascal's worldly
  period, 108, 112
Miel, Jan, 53–56, 60, 127, 157–160, 162
Mind, order of: and order of the heart, 20,
  28, 36, 45, 52, 86–87, 120; and order of
  the flesh, 36, 86, 88–89; in *Provincial
  Letters,* 164; in *Thoughts,* 240–242,
  248–249. *See also* Orders, three; Reason
Miracle of the Holy Thorne, 186
Miton, Damien, 8, 108
Mohatra contract, 197–198
Molina, Louis, 54, 218, 227
Molinism, 54, 55, 60–64, 127; on
  predestination, 57, 218, 227
Monarchy, Pascal's attitude toward, 104,
  107, 265
Montaigne, Michel de: compared to Pascal,
  7, 20, 230, 255; and *Conversation with M.
  de Sacy,* 146, 147, 150–154
Montalte, Louis de (pseudonym of Pascal),
  275–276n10
Montrouge, Father de, 198
Moore, W. G., 236
Mother-figure of the Church, 63–64,
  132–133, 138, 155–157